P9-EJI-219

THE DAILY STUDY BIBLE

(OLD TESTAMENT)

General Editor: John C.L. Gibson

PROVERBS

PROVERBS

KENNETH T. AITKEN

WESTMINSTER JOHN KNOX PRESS
LOUISVILLE, KENTUCKY

Copyright © 1986 Kenneth T. Aitken

All rights reserved—no part of this book may be reproduced in any form without permission in writing from the publisher, except by a reviewer who wishes to quote brief passages in connection with a review in magazine or newspaper.

Scripture quotations from the Revised Standard Version of the Bible are copyrighted 1946, 1952, © 1971, 1973 by the Division of Christian Education of the National Council of the Churches of Christ in the U.S.A., and are used by permission of the National Council of Churches, New York, and William Collins Sons & Co., Ltd., Glasgow.

Published by
The Saint Andrew Press
Edinburgh, Scotland
and
Westminster John Knox Press
Louisville, Kentucky

PRINTED IN THE UNITED STATES OF AMERICA

8 10 12 14 13 11 9

Library of Congress Cataloging-in-Publication Data

Aitken, K. T.
  Proverbs.

  (The Daily study Bible series)
  Bibliography: p.
  1. Bible. O.T. Proverbs—Commentaries. I. Title.
II. Series: Daily study Bible series
(Westminster Press)
BS1465.3.A38 1986   223'.7077   86-15660
ISBN 0-664-21837-7
ISBN 0-664-24586-2 (pbk.)

GENERAL PREFACE

This series of commentaries on the Old Testament, to which the present volume on Proverbs belongs, has been planned as a companion series to the much-acclaimed New Testament series of the late Professor William Barclay. As with that series, each volume is arranged in successive headed portions suitable for daily study. The Biblical text followed is that of the Revised Standard Version or Common Bible. Eleven contributors share the work, each being responsible for from one to three volumes. The series is issued in the hope that it will do for the Old Testament what Professor Barclay's series succeeded so splendidly in doing for the New Testament—make it come alive for the Christian believer in the twentieth century.

Its two-fold aim is the same as his. Firstly, it is intended to introduce the reader to some of the more important results and fascinating insights of modern Old Testament scholarship. Most of the contributors are already established experts in the field with many publications to their credit. Some are younger scholars who have yet to make their names but who in my judgment as General Editor are now ready to be tested. I can assure those who use these commentaries that they are in the hands of competent teachers who know what is of real consequence in their subject and are able to present it in a form that will appeal to the general public.

The primary purpose of the series, however, is *not* an academic one. Professor Barclay summed it up for his New Testament series in the words of Richard of Chichester's prayer—to enable men and women "to know Jesus Christ more clearly, to love Him more dearly, and to follow Him more nearly." In the case of the Old Testament we have to be a little more circumspect than that. The Old Testament was completed long before the time of Our Lord, and it was (as it still is) the sole Bible of the Jews, God's first people, before it became part of the Christian Bible. We must take this fact seriously.

Yet in its strangely compelling way, sometimes dimly and sometimes directly, sometimes charmingly and sometimes embarrassingly, it holds up before us the things of Christ. It should not be forgotten that Jesus Himself was raised on this Book, that He based His whole ministry on what it says, and that He approached His death with its words on His lips. Christian men and women have in this ancient collection of Jewish writings a uniquely illuminating avenue not only into the will and purposes of God the Father, but into the mind and heart of Him who is named God's Son, who was Himself born a Jew but went on through the Cross and Resurrection to become the Saviour of the world. Read reverently and imaginatively the Old Testament can become a living and relevant force in their everyday lives.

It is the prayer of myself and my colleagues that this series may be used by its readers and blessed by God to that end.

New College   JOHN C.L. GIBSON
Edinburgh   General Editor

CONTENTS

PART TWO: THE WISE MEN'S PROVERBS (10:1–31:31)

I. TYPES OF CHARACTERS

II. WISDOM IN VARIOUS SETTINGS

A. THE HOME

B. THE COMMUNITY

CONTENTS

x   *CONTENTS*

THE DAILY STUDY BIBLE

(OLD TESTAMENT)

General Editor: John C.L. Gibson

PROVERBS

INTRODUCTION

All traditional societies have their wise men whose counsel is sought and respected by those less learned and experienced, and their proverbs in which the ripened wisdom of many generations is condensed. Israel was no exception. At all periods in Israel's history, wisdom was cultivated and counselled by the wise, and it came to form an important element in the thought and literature of the Old Testament. The Book of Proverbs is the earliest literary deposit of Israel's wisdom. It has companion volumes in Job and Ecclesiastes, and these books, together with a few Psalms (*eg* 1; 49; 73). are classified by scholars as the *Wisdom Literature*. Two further volumes are found in the Apocrypha: the Book of Ecclesiasticus, and the Wisdom of Solomon.

STRUCTURE, AUTHORSHIP AND DATE

A series of headings divides the Book of Proverbs into eight main sections:

(1)	1:1–9:18	— "The proverbs of Solomon, son of David, king of Israel"
(2)	10:1–22:16	— "The proverbs of Solomon"
(3)	22:17–24:22	— "The words of the wise"
(4)	24:23–34	— "These also are sayings of the wise"
(5)	25:1–29:27	— "These also are proverbs of Solomon which the men of Hezekiah king of Judah copied"
(6)	30:1–33	— "The words of Agur son of Jakeh of Massa"
(7)	31:1–9	— "The words of Lemuel, king of Massa, which his mother taught him"
(8)	31:10–31	— A poem on the good wife (no heading)

We usually think of Solomon as the book's author. This is certainly the impression given by its title in 1:1. However, the other headings make it clear that the book comes from many hands and that it was a long time in the making. The title comes from the final editor. It is intended to refer to the book as a whole and not specifically to the first section, which is therefore, strictly speaking, anonymous. The publication of the entire work under Solomon's name was natural enough, if a bit misleading; for the two sections directly or indirectly attributed to him (10:1–22:16; 25:1–29:27) make up its greater part. It is generally recognized that these sections contain some of the oldest material in Proverbs, but how far their contents actually go back to Solomon is debatable. Though we need not doubt that the hand of Solomon lies behind the collections, it is best not to press it too hard. Solomon came to be regarded as the wise man *par excellence* and the fountain-head of Israel's wisdom. As a result, wisdom material of much later origin came to be associated with his name (the Wisdom of Solomon was written in the first century B.C.!). There are good reasons for believing that the various sections in the book were compiled at different times, drawing upon earlier and later material, and that they stood by themselves before they were gradually brought together to form the book as we know it today. The heading in 25:1 shows that it had not yet reached its final form at the time of Hezekiah (*c.* 700 B.C.), and probably it was not completed until some time after the return from exile, perhaps in the fifth or fourth century B.C.

BACKGROUND AND GENERAL CHARACTER

Israel's wisdom had many different strands to it and as many different spokesmen. It was, for example, equally at home in the pithy proverbs of the common folk, the moral and religious instruction of parents, the sagacious advice of the elders, and the political acumen of royal counsellors. These many strands and more have left their imprint on the material in the Book of Proverbs.

But more significantly, in Israel, wisdom was also an educational discipline: a course of study taught by a teacher and learned by his pupils. The wisdom teacher seems first to have arisen after the monarchy was established; to meet its demands for a well-trained civil service. In this the Israelite court followed the example of the Egyptian wisdom schools attached to the Pharaoh's court. This development probably began under Solomon when relations between Israel and Egypt were good, and when other aspects of his administration were being modelled on the Egyptian pattern. This helps to explain several striking aspects of the book:

(a) its close connection with the figure of Solomon and the royal court over a period of three centuries (1:1; 10:1; 25:1);

(b) its educational purpose (see the comment on 1:2–6);

(c) its many sayings concerning the king and his courtiers (see the topics, *The Measure of a King, The Wise Courtier*);

(d) the many parallels between Proverbs and Egyptian wisdom literature, both in form (see the comment on 1:8–19, *The School Lesson*) and content. Most notably, the third section of Proverbs (22:17–24:22) is actually based on an Egyptian wisdom text-book, the *Instruction of Amenemopet,* dating somewhere between 1000 and 600 B.C. (see the topic, *The Words of the Wise*).

But while the primary purpose of the wisdom school was to train well-to-do individuals for a successful career in the service of the state—and the basic curriculum was much the same as in the Egyptian schools—the Israelite wisdom teachers both inherited and developed wider interests than their Egyptian counterparts, which made their teaching catch the ear of the community at large. At least by the time of Jeremiah, the sage found a place alongside the priest and prophet as an acknowledged leader and teacher in the community (Jer. 18:18); and after the return from exile, when the monarchy and its bureaucracy were things of the past, the sage's school continued to flourish and influence the life and thought of the people. In the course of this development the goal of the sage's teaching moved increasingly away from education for a good and

successful career, to become education for a good and successful life.

It was through the hands of the teachers and their schools
that the Book of Proverbs was shaped and reached its present
form. It is a text-book designed to educate young people
especially in the ways of good and wise living (1:2–7). To this
end the sage has taken up and brought together the accumulated wisdom of past generations distilled in precept and proverb,
and then cast it into the mould of a comprehensive educational
programme for future generations.

We need not dig very deeply into the book to find that the
sage looks at life from a different angle from priest or prophet.
Most strikingly, he is little concerned with the privileges of the
people as the People of God, with the richness of their faith, or
the health of their worship. He has therefore nothing to say
about the great and distinctive Old Testament themes like
election, redemption, and covenant, which resound again and
again in the teaching of both priest and prophet. Rather the
sage concerns himself with people as plain, ordinary individuals
who live in the world, and with the wisdom and folly of their
attitudes and actions in the common things of life. We will
therefore find he has much to say on a wide range of very
mundane and practical matters like bringing up children,
spreading gossip, talking too much, keeping bad company,
unscrupulous business practices, and even good table manners.
Furthermore, while prophet and priest make an unequivocal
appeal to divine authority for their teaching, the sage is
content to speak on his own account or to let his sayings speak
for themselves, making appeal to the proven canons of human
experience, good taste and common sense.

On these accounts the teaching of the wise in Proverbs has
what we would call a *secular* character. It is essentially 'this-
worldly' in its frame of reference, and prudence often appears as
the greater part of wisdom. But that is not the whole picture.
The sage has no doubts that the good and successful life is the
life lived in conformity with the order of things ordained by
God in his world for man's good and blessing. Nor has he any

doubts that the key to successful living is to fear the Lord and to trust fully in him. In Proverbs the sages have produced a full and rich tapestry in which the practical, moral and religious dimensions of human experience and endeavour are woven together, as they place before us as individual men and women the searching question: are you being wise, or foolish?

PART ONE: THE TEACHER'S INSTRUCTIONS (1:1–9:18)

PONDERING PROVERBS

Proverbs 1:1–6

¹The proverbs of Solomon, son of David, king of Israel:
²That men may know wisdom and instruction,
    understand words of insight,
³receive instruction in wise dealing,
    righteousness, justice, and equity;
⁴that prudence may be given to the simple,
    knowledge and discretion to the youth—
⁵the wise man also may hear and increase in learning.
    and the man of understanding acquire skill,
⁶to understand a proverb and a figure,
    the words of the wise and their riddles.

(i)

King Solomon is celebrated in the Old Testament as wisdom's most illustrious representative, and it is fitting that his name should stand in the title to the book, even though, as we have seen, it gives a wrong impression about its authorship. In the story of his reign in 1 Kings, Solomon's wisdom appears in several lights: by his wisdom he is enabled to rule justly (3:9, 16–28; 10:9); to negotiate advantageous treaties with other states (5:7, 12); to acquire vast knowledge about the natural world (4:33); and to compose thousands of proverbs and songs (4:32). The narrator extols Solomon's wisdom with great enthusiasm and with typical oriental exaggeration:

7

> Solomon's wisdom surpassed the wisdom of all the people of the
> east, and all the wisdom of Egypt ... His fame was in all the nations
> round about ... And men came from all peoples to hear the
> wisdom of Solomon.
>
> (1 Kings 4:30–34)

And to underscore his point he tells how Solomon dazzled the
sceptical Queen of Sheba by the sheer brilliance of his wisdom,
leaving her to exclaim, "the half was not told me" (1 Kings
10:7). It was with this episode in mind that Jesus rebuked his
sceptical contemporaries for refusing to see that in him "something greater than Solomon is here" (Matt. 12:42). Odd how
man's wisdom always seems so wise while God's wisdom
seems somehow rather foolish (cf. 1 Cor. 1:18–30).

(ii)

In verses 2–6 of Proverbs, chapter 1, the sage outlines the
purpose of his book and the benefits to be gained from
pondering it well. This passage gives us a flavour of the kind of
opening address given to new students beginning their studies
in the wisdom schools. Similar addresses are found in Egyptian
wisdom literature. Here is how the *Instruction of Amenemopet*
is introduced:

> The beginning of the teaching of life, the testimony for prosperity,
> all precepts for intercourse with elders, the rules for courtiers, to
> know how to return an answer to him who said it, and to direct a
> report to one who has sent him, in order to direct him to the ways of
> life, to make him prosper upon earth ... steer him away from evil,
> and to rescue him from the mouth of the rabble, revered in the
> mouth of the people.

But notice that our sage does not address such a distinguished
company as Amenemopet. The Egyptian sage is commending
his teaching to a professional elite of aspiring scribes, civil
servants and royal courtiers drawn from the upper classes. Our
sage is commending his to ordinary folks, especially to the
young; although he carefully adds a gentle hint that even those

who have cut their wisdom-teeth can also learn a thing or two! There is none too old to learn or too wise to become wiser. So the sage invites whoever wishes to matriculate in the school of wisdom and ponder Proverbs.

Why ponder Proverbs? By way of reply, the sage rapidly fires expression after expression, phrase after phrase, piling up words and ideas which overlap and merge into one another. The short answer is unmistakable: to become wise, or wiser still; and he is saying something here that is lost if we pause over his every word and ask exactly what he has in mind. He is trying to impress upon his students a sense of the wholeness and fullness, of the many-splendoured thing that wisdom is, and perhaps also of his own deep emotional attachment to it. Like love in the song, wisdom in this passage loses something of its lyric quality when scrutinized too closely! Nevertheless, wisdom, says the sage, is a many-splendoured thing; and he flashes before our eyes glimpses of various facets of the wisdom he wishes his students to cultivate and practise. We need therefore to look at the passage in some detail to bring these glimpses into sharper relief.

WISDOM'S MANY FACES—I

Proverbs 1:1–6 (*cont'd*)

(i)

The word "wisdom" is given pride of place, as well it might, for it is the word which best sums up the content and goal of the sage's teaching. What does it mean? The Hebrew is *chokmah,* and its meaning is not easy to pin down. It is a very rich word, and it will take the sage the rest of this passage and the rest of the book to spell it out. So to read the book is really the best way to get at its meaning. This much can be said for now: it is not a terribly sophisticated or intellectual word, but a very practical one. Its use in Exodus 35:35 is instructive. In this verse Bezalel and Oholiab are said to be filled "with *chokmah* (of heart) to do every sort of work done by a craftsman or by a designer or by an embroiderer . . . or by a weaver".

The Authorized Version has "with wisdom", but that is wooden, even misleading. Here it simply means technical know-how and skill to do a good job (RSV "ability", NEB "skill"). Similarly, sailors are deemed "wise" by dint of their navigational skills (Ezek. 27:8), as idol makers are for their expertise in wood carving and metal working (Isa. 40:20). At its simplest, then, *chokmah*—"wisdom"—is skilfulness in dealing with the matter at hand so as to get the best results. In Proverbs the matter at hand is life itself, and the best result is the good, harmonious and successful life. So for men "to know wisdom" is for them to have the skills needed to make a success of their lives. This is the first face of wisdom we catch a glimpse of in the passage: *the skilful mastery of life.* To see what this involves, however, we have to read on.

(ii)

"Instruction" has in view the way wisdom is acquired. The word is *musar.* Basically it means "discipline", and it is the word for training in the school of wisdom, whether in the classroom under the wisdom teacher or in the home under parents. Wisdom, to be sure, is the fruit of experience and is acquired through it. But the sage has no doubts that raw, individual experience alone is not up to the demands of life. It is a hard teacher and its lessons may be learned too late or—such being the vagaries of human nature—not at all. Besides experience there has to be *musar*—training in the accumulated and collective experience of many generations suitably distilled in the precepts and proverbs of the wise. Here then is a second face of wisdom in Proverbs: *learning from the experience and counsel of those who are older and wiser.* This is a face of wisdom that young people especially do well to remember.

But the word has another side to it. It also has in view the fruit of schooling in wisdom, namely *disciplined living.* This too is an important face of wisdom. In large measure the skill required for good and successful living is self-control. The man who would master life must learn to master self. That is why we will find the sage has so much to say about controlling temper and tongue, passions and appetites. In the New Testament self-control is one of the fruits of the Spirit (Gal. 5:23).

(iii)

The words "understand" and "insight" come from the same Hebrew root. Both "insight" and its sister noun "understanding" are used interchangeably with "wisdom" (see, *eg*, Prov. 2:2-3, "wisdom ... understanding ... insight"); thus the wise man is the "man of understanding (1:5). At the same time, this family of words add their own colour to what wisdom is and help to enrich it. Their hue can be seen from 1 Kings 3:9, where Solomon prays for wisdom that he "may discern between good and evil". "Discern" is the same word translated "understand" in verse 2. Wise living requires the ability to reach sound decisions and to make the right choices, and thus the *ability to discriminate* between what is right and what is wrong, wholesome and damaging, important and unimportant, wise and foolish. It is the wisdom which takes stock of life to see what matters most, and which recognizes trivialities for what they are. It is also the wisdom which knows when to turn off the television!

WISDOM'S MANY FACES—II

Proverbs 1:1-6 (*cont'd*)

(iv)

"Wise dealing" (v. 3) is now wisdom from the angle of conduct that is at once considered, circumspect and effective. A related word describes Abigail in 1 Samuel 25:3 ("intelligent", NEB), whose wise and timely intervention saved the neck of her foolish husband. But the sage has in mind men's conduct in their daily dealings with one another and spells out what "wise dealing" amounts to: "righteousness, justice, and equity" (1:3). In the Old Testament these are the great qualities of conduct

which make for the good and well-being of the community: one
in which all men play by the rules, where one man's rights are as
important as another's, and where honesty and integrity are the
only policies. Here then the *ethical and moral* face of wisdom
comes to the fore, and the sage reinforces in his own way what
the Law and the prophets have to say about how God's people
should live together. Just as the prophets warned that the
religion of a religious people who flouted God's law was empty
(Isa. 1:10–17; Amos 5:21–24; Mic. 6:6–8), so the sage would
warn that the wisdom of a wise man who has contempt for
moral values is folly.

(v)

The face of wisdom in verse 4 looks two ways in the Old
Testament. "Prudence" is the same word used in Genesis 3:1 of
the craftiness of the serpent, and in Joshua 9:4 of the cunning
deception practised by the Gibeonites. In Proverbs, however, it
is "craftiness" in a better sense. The New English Bible catches it
well by translating it as "shrewdness". This is what Jesus
commended to his disciples when he told them to be "wise as
serpents and innocent as doves" (Matt. 10:16). The Hebrew
word underlying "discretion" (NEB "prudence") basically
means the ability to plan ahead and plot a course of action with
foresight. Again it can be put to bad use (12:2; 24:8; Ps. 10:2) or
to good use.

Wisdom's face in this verse (1:4), with its complexion of
savoir faire and *savoir vivre,* looks especially in the direction of
young people. The description of the young man as "simple" is
not a comment on his lack of wits—a simpleton or half-wit—
but on his lack of experience of life and the ways of the world.
The underlying thought seems to be "open", the idea being that
inexperienced youth is "open" to suggestion and so easily
duped and led astray (see 14:15). On the other hand, the sage
does not think that the simple's openness to persuasion is
entirely a bad thing, for it also means that he is open to the
persuasion of wisdom (contrast 9:4 with 9:16). It does, however,
lend urgency to the task of teaching the young in the ways of

wisdom before it is too late (1:20–22; 8:1–5)—or, as the sage might put it, before the simple become out-and-out fools.

(vi)

The RSV takes verses 5 and 6 together and sets them apart from verse 4. But since gaining an understanding of the speech forms in which the wise expressed their wisdom was the ABC of the teacher's instruction and was not reserved for the more advanced, it is better to put verse 5 in brackets as an aside and take verse 6 following on from verse 4 (see NIV).

The most important kind of saying mentioned in verse 6 is the "proverb". We should notice that the corresponding Hebrew word (*mashal*) is not exactly equivalent to our English word, for it also covers various kinds of sayings which do not call proverbs. For example, it is used of Balaam's prophetic *discourses* (Num. 23:7; 24:15), Ezekiel's *allegory* about the great eagle (Ezek. 17:2) and Isaiah's *taunt* against the king of Babylon (Isa. 14:4). That is why the word can stand happily in the title to the book (1:1) by way of a summary of its contents, embracing both the long wisdom discourses in chapters 1–9 and the crisp sayings collected together in the other sections of the book.

Various suggestions have been made about the primary meaning of *mashal*, "proverb"; among them that it is (1) a saying which illuminates by *comparing* things, (2) a saying which *stands fast* by having passed the test of experience, (3) a saying which *rules* and so of itself commands acceptance, and (4) a saying which sets up an *example* of a type of behaviour or attitude to be followed or avoided. As ways of looking at his sayings the sage would give an approving nod to all four!

A "figure" (v.6) seems to be a figurative or allusive saying whose meaning lies below the surface and has to be thought over and teased out. The best known "riddle" in the Old Testament is Samson's (Judg. 14:12–18). There are in fact no riddles in Proverbs, although some scholars think they may underlie the numerical sayings in chapter 30.

The last face of wisdom in this passage is therefore *compe-*

tence in its literary forms of speech. They were, so to speak, the tools of the trade, the instruments of wise living. As such the real test of "understanding" them was not how well the student could explain their meaning in class but how well he could apply them in his daily life. A proverb, says the sage with typical dry humour, is about as much use to a fool as legs to a lame man (26:7); that is to say, the fool does not know how to use it properly. Understanding and application belong together. It is the same with God's word.

WISDOM'S ONE FOUNDATION

Proverbs 1:7

⁷The fear of the Lord is the beginning of knowledge;
   fools despise wisdom and instruction.

This is one of the best-known texts in Proverbs. Its words have been adopted as the motto and inscribed over the entrance of many schools and colleges. Doubtless the sage would have hung it over the door of his classroom if they had done such things in his day, for he deliberately places it here right at the outset, as the motto for schooling in wisdom. Equally deliberately he repeats the motto, with a slightly different wording, at the end of his instruction (9:10). This is his way of emphasizing that it underlies all he has to say throughout the entire section.

The "fear of the Lord" is an important theme in the Old Testament generally. There are two sides to it and they must always be held together. The *first* is deep-seated reverence and awe in recognition of the holiness of God, his utter "otherness" from men and the world he has created. This aspect is brought out most dramatically in these stories where God makes his presence known in some special way. Thus when God reveals himself to Moses at the burning bush, we read that Moses "hid his face, for he was afraid to look at God" (Exod. 3:6; cf. Gen. 28:16–17). This side of fearing God is summed up in Isaiah 8:13:

> The Lord of Hosts, him you shall regard as holy; let him be your
> fear, and let him be your dread.

The *second* side is brought out most clearly in the Book of
Deuteronomy. There fearing God is bound up with loyalty to
God's covenant and obedience to his law, with loving and
serving him and walking in his ways (cf. Deut. 6:2; 8:6;
10:12–13; 31:12–13). So "those who fear the Lord" (Pss. 33:18;
118:4) are those who are loyal and faithful to him, and who
show this by obedience to his commandments. In New Testament times, pagan converts to the Jewish faith were called
"God-fearers" (Acts 10:2). This side is well summed up in
Ecclesiastes 12:13:

> Fear God, and keep his commandments; for this is the whole duty
> of man.

Here in Proverbs, therefore, the expression "the fear of the
Lord" touches the pulse of Israel's religious faith and practice in
all its vitality, embracing reverence for and devotion to God,
and, above all, loyalty and obedience to him.

"Knowledge" is another near synonym of "wisdom". Indeed,
in 9:10 the motto is phrased, "The fear of the Lord is the
beginning of wisdom". It is the beginning, not in the sense of the
starting point which can soon be left behind, but in the sense of
the *foundation* upon which all true wisdom ultimately rests.

But it is the foundation, even the "best part" (the Hebrew
word can mean that); not the whole edifice. As we have
observed, the edifice of wisdom in Proverbs is essentially "this-
worldly". Proverbs teaches the practical lessons of experience
rather than the spiritual lessons of faith. Its counsel is one for
"wordly success" (in the best of senses) and not for spiritual
growth. The wise man in Proverbs is a man of the world, who
has his wits about him and knows how to get the best out of life
and to live out his life to its fullest potential. But a building
needs a solid foundation. And so here the sage insists that
religious faith is the essential foundation for a good, happy and
prosperous life. The truly wise man of the world will be a man of

faith. Equally, of course, a foundation is for building on. So the man of faith ought also to be a man of the world. The "fool" who despises wisdom can therefore either be the man of the world who has no time for God, or the man of God who has no time for the world—or as we might say, either people who are so earthly minded as to be of no heavenly use; or people who are so heavenly minded as to be of no earthly use.

THE SCHOOL LESSON
Proverbs 1:8–19

8Hear, my son, your father's instruction,
 and reject not your mother's teaching;
9for they are a fair garland for your head,
 and pendants for your neck.
10My son, if sinners entice you,
 do not consent.
11If they say, "Come with us, let us lie in wait for blood,
 let us wantonly ambush the innocent;
12like Sheol let us swallow them alive
 and whole, like those who go down to the Pit;
13we shall find all precious goods,
 we shall fill our houses with spoil;
14throw in your lot among us,
 we will all have one purse"—
15my son, do not walk in the way with them,
 hold back your foot from their paths;
16for their feet run to evil,
 and they make haste to shed blood.
17For in vain is a net spread
 in the sight of any bird;
18but these men lie in wait for their own blood,
 they set an ambush for their own lives.
19Such are the ways of all who get gain by violence;
 it takes away the life of its possessors.

This is the first in a series of passages in which a father instructs his son in the ways of wisdom (see 2:1ff.; 3:1ff.; 4:1ff.; *etc*). These passages form the backbone of chapters 1–9. As we shall find, they have much in common, and they are of great interest; for it is here that the sage speaks most self-consciously as a teacher of the young and allows us to see something of the style as well as the content of his teaching.

When he gives his instruction, the sage keeps very much to the same three-part outline:

(a) *He appeals for his son to pay attention and take to heart what he has to say.* It was customary for a wisdom teacher to address his pupils as a father speaking to his sons. In fact he sees himself standing in the same line as the natural father, and his teaching as an extension of the instruction given in the home (see the comment on 4:1–9). So by this form of address and appeal, the teacher claims parental authority over his pupils, matched, as it always should be, by fatherly concern for their well-being.

(b) *He counsels his son to embrace the wise course and avoid the foolish course.* Here, typically, he speaks in the imperative: "do this", "do not do that". Clearly he regards what he says not merely as a few words of fatherly advice but as directives which his son ought to obey.

(c) *He impresses upon him the benefits of obeying his counsel and the unpleasant consequences of ignoring it.* Wise 'parent' and good teacher that he is, he does not simply tell his son what he should and should not do; he also tells him why. He seeks above all to *persuade* his son to live wisely, and so appeals as much to the son's good sense as to his duty to obey his father. For at the end of the day it is his son's good sense that will count most.

Almost all the verses in this series of passages can be slotted into place within this three-part pattern. Appeal, advice and motivation form the warp and weft of the teacher's instruction. The frequency with which this pattern recurs in Proverbs suggests that it was the standard shape of a lesson in the wisdom schools of ancient Israel. By and large, teaching in the Egyptian wisdom schools was also modelled on the same pattern (*eg,* the *Instruction of Amenemopet*).

The sage fills out the pattern in a variety of ways drawing

upon a small number of stock themes, all the while driving home his central theme of the value of wisdom and the fateful consequences of folly. He gives particular attention to the need to avoid bad company, especially loose and fancy-free women. As a good teacher he knows the value of repetition and of approaching the same topic from different angles, so we will find him saying the same things over and over again in various ways. If we find his repetition excessive for our modern literary tastes, we have to remember that the teacher's instructions were given orally and were meant to be memorized by his pupils before they later became part of a written work.

SHUN EVIL COMPANIONS

Proverbs 1:8–19 (*cont'd*)

(i)

In verse 8 the sage appeals to his pupils to be attentive *and* responsive to his instruction. To "hear" rightly and wisely is to act accordingly (Matt. 7:24–27; Jas. 1:22–25), and so the Hebrew verb is often better rendered "obey" (Isa. 30:9). While he claims parental authority and expects obedience, his teaching makes its own quieter, more gentle appeal: it will adorn the obedient son's life and conduct with a dignity and a charm and beauty all its own (v. 9).

(ii)

The temptation to which the son will be exposed as he sets out to make his mark upon the world is sketched with great vigour in verses 10–14. The word "sinners" here, as very often in the Old Testament, does not bear the general sense in which it can be said that all men are sinners, but means the hardened offenders who make it their business to sin. They make no bones about what they are up to and what they want him to join in: robbery with violence, even murder; coldly calculated and as coldly carried out. These men are not a bunch of young hooligans or petty thieves, but a gang of vicious robbers and killers like those who figure in Jesus' story of the Good Samaritan (Luke 10). In verse 12 they compare themselves to Sheol. In Old Testament thought, Sheol was the abode of the dead—a dark and dreary place located in the bowels of the earth, where the departed led a feeble kind of existence (Job 10:21–22; 17:13–16; Ps. 88:3–12). It is also portrayed as a devouring monster, with gaping jaws and a hearty and insatiable appetite for human victims (Provs. 27:20; 30:15–16; Isa. 5:14; Hab. 2:5). That is the point of the comparison. Their appetite for violence and murder cannot be satisfied and they destroy their victims ruthlessly and completely.

Of course, whether they would put it to the son in quite the same way is another matter. The verb "entice" (v. 10) comes from the same Hebrew root as "the simple" in 1:4. But the inexperienced youth, gullible and morally irresponsible though he may be, is scarcely "open" to such a blatantly evil proposal. Their invitation has too much of the roaring lion and too little of the subtle serpent. Doubtless in verses 11–12 there is more of the sage impressing upon his son how evil it is to associate with such people, than their impressing upon him how appealing such a life is. But the subtlety is there. Its allurements are not far to seek: excitement (vv. 11–12), easy money (v. 13), and the *camaraderie* of being one of the gang (v. 14). These are subtle and powerful persuaders, every bit as much now as then. For, as is temptation's way, they latch on to a young man's perfectly healthy desires for adventure, independence and stout friends. This he is offered in abundance in one easy step: "Come with us" (v.11).

(iii)

But equally the sage makes no bones about what his son should do: Say no! Steer well clear of them! (vv. 10, 15). The advice is blunt and to the point. But the sage then adds two reasons why his son must respond with a resolute, no! What they invite him to join them in is wrong (v. 16); not only is it wrong, it is also foolish (vv. 17–19). A life of violence and crime, says the sage, pays a cruel dividend. It is self-destructive and its perpetrators are also its victims. To join in their company is to share in their fate. A man's friends can be his most deadly enemies.

The point of the proverb cited in verse 17 is a bit of a puzzle. Does it mean that spreading a net in the sight of birds is (1) a futile exercise for the fowler, since the birds will avoid it; or (2) a futile sign of danger to the birds, since they will swoop down into it regardless? If the *first* is intended, the point seems to be "fore-warned is fore-armed"—a comment on the value of remembering the lesson when the tempters tempt. If the *second,* the point is probably that in their eagerness for violence and ill-gotten gain they are oblivious to all signs of their own danger and plunge mindlessly to their destruction—a comment on the folly of the tempters and of those who yield to their tempting. Both points can be well taken.

LADY WISDOM'S APPEAL...

Proverbs 1:20–23

20Wisdom cries aloud in the street;
     in the markets she raises her voice;
21on the top of the walls she cries out;
     at the entrance of the city gates she speaks:
22"How long, O simple ones, will you love being simple?
     How long will scoffers delight in their scoffing
     and fools hate knowledge?
23Give heed to my reproof;
     behold, I will pour out my thoughts to you;
     I will make my words known to you".

This is an interesting passage. No longer is the teacher speaking about wisdom to his pupils, but wisdom speaks on her own account, calling all men to her devotion. There are also a few other places where Lady Wisdom (the Hebrew word is femin-ine) speaks and is spoken about as if she were a real person. In the present passage she seems to be little more than a literary and poetic personification of the sage's teaching devised to make its appeal more forceful and dramatic. But we shall find that the good Lady has some things to say about herself in chapter 8 which tell us there is more to her than that. Lady Wisdom stands more on the side of God than of men, and is a spokesman for divine wisdom and the fear of the Lord. For the moment, however, it is enough to call attention to this; but it explains why here we find Lady Wisdom in fact speaking as much like a prophet as a wisdom teacher.

(i)

Lady Wisdom, it would appear, has learned a lesson from the prophets. She lays aside her professorial gown, leaves the quiet dignity of the wisdom school, and goes to ply her wares in the streets and bazaars and at the city gates, seeking to confront and challenge men as they go about their daily lives—a lesson the Church is slower to learn and always needs to remember.

A less austere and discriminating onlooker could not help but be impressed by the colour and confusion as his eye swept the surge of humanity and took in its scenes, especially at the city gates, the hub around which the life of the city revolved. Here were to be seen farmhands going to and returning from their work in the fields; buyers and sellers haggling over prices in the shops; craftsmen displaying their skills and seeking new work; men striking business deals of all kinds, or simply passing the time of day discussing the latest news; beggars vying with buskers, and ne'er-do-wells hanging around hatching mischief. But under Lady Wisdom's withering gaze the streets and city gates become a gallery of fools.

Three kinds of fools pass before her eyes (v.22)—characters who still rub shoulders in any busy street or city centre. (1) The "simple" is the inexperienced and gullible youth we met in 1:4. (2) The "scoffer" is the person who is arrogant and self-opinionated, and always ready to debunk the views and beliefs of others. In Ps. 1:1 he takes his seat in company with the wicked and sinners. (3) The "fool" (Hebrew *kesil*) is a downright stupid person. He mistakes his folly for wisdom and seems quite insensible to what is good, right and proper. His closest companions are the *awil* and the *nabal*. Both words are also translated "fool". Indeed, all three are so well suited to one another's company that it is almost impossible to tell them apart. If anything, the *awil* is that bit more stubborn (see 27:22) and the *nabal* that bit more crude and ill-mannered (see 17:7) than the *kesil*. Lady Wisdom, like the teacher, hopes most in the simple, for his chief shortcoming is lack of instruction (1:4). For those more mature in their folly, for scoffers and fools, she is less optimistic (9:7–8; 17:10), but not entirely without hope. And so above the din and bustle of daily life she cries out and summons men to her reproof and counsel.

(ii)

The Hebrew word rendered "give heed" (v. 23) is more strictly "turn". It is the word used in the great prophetic passages which call on a sinful Israel to "[re]turn" to God (Isa. 44:22; Jer. 3:22; Hos. 6:1). It is quite possible that Lady Wisdom's summons carries these overtones of a call to repentance. At all events, the folly of the fools, their thick-headedness, is not something they were born with but something they have chosen: the simple *love* simplicity, the scoffers *delight* in scoffing, and the fools *hate* knowledge (v. 22). It has become their chosen way of life.

As we find, Lady Wisdom is no gentle persuader. She shouts, pleads, scolds, reasons, threatens, warns, even laughs (see vv. 24–33). Pulpit-bashing and hell-fire preaching if ever there were! All quite unladylike; and nowadays also quite unfashionable, even frowned upon. But the good Lady is fired by a great sense of urgency. she knows that her appeal is a critical moment of opportunity for the fools, and no-one knows better that the fool parts easier with his money than his folly. Church mission and Christian witness will never be terribly effective unless they are seen to be terribly urgent.

...AND HER REJECTION

Proverbs 1:24–33

> [24]"Because I have called and you refused to listen,
>   have stretched out my hand and no-one has heeded,
> [25]and you have ignored all my counsel
>   and would have none of my reproof,
> [26]I also will laugh at your calamity;
>   I will mock when panic strikes you,
> [27]when panic strikes you like a storm,
>   and your calamity comes like a whirlwind,
>   when distress and anguish come upon you.
> [28]Then they will call upon me, but I will not answer;
>   they will seek me diligently but will not find me.
> [29]Because they hated knowledge
>   and did not choose the fear of the Lord,
> [30]would have none of my counsel,
>   and despised all my reproof,
> [31]therefore they shall eat the fruit of their way
>   and be sated with their own devices.
> [32]For the simple are killed by their turning away,
>   and the complacence of fools destroys them;
> [33]but he who listens to me will dwell secure
>   und will be at ease, without dread of evil."

(i)

But the cajoling and browbeating of Lady Wisdom fare no better with fools than the decisive "Thus says the Lord" fared with rebels (Isa. 65:1–2, 12). So appeal gives way to accusation (vv. 24–25, 29–30). Strong verbs are used to indict the fools: "refused to listen ... no-one has heeded ... ignored ... have none of [literally 'be unwilling for'] ... hated ... did not choose ... despised". Men were not simply too busy to notice that Lady Wisdom was there and to hear her appeal. They were wilfully indifferent and even hostile. The crux of the matter, however, was their deliberate rejection of the fear of the Lord (v.29). Their rejection of Lady Wisdom amounted to rejection of God and his divine wisdom. These are the kind of people the

Psalmist has in mind when he says: "The fool says in his heart, 'There is no God'" (Ps. 53:1). These are the people who might nod at God on Sundays, but who live their lives as if God did not matter. Quite appropriately, therefore, the accusation in these verses strikes the same note as the prophets' indictment of Israel for spurning God: "they *refuse* to know me" (Jer. 9:6), "they have *not given heed* to my words" (Jer. 6:19), "they are *not willing* to listen to me" (Ezek. 3:7, "[they] *hate* the good" (Mic. 3:2),[they] *chose* what I did not delight in" (Isa. 65:12), "they have *despised* the Holy One of Israel" (Isa. 1:4).

For Lady Wisdom, the fools' response spelled rejection. That is often the way of God's man or woman in the world. His spokespeople are seldom popular figures. The prophets were not, and neither was Jesus. For the fools themselves it spelled a wasted opportunity—and more!

(ii)

As the rebellious people's rejection of God was fraught with dire consequences, so too is the fools' rejection of Lady Wisdom. So alongside accusation there is threat of judgment (vv. 26–28, 31–32). The hearty guffaw Lady Wisdom gives in verse 26 is jarring. It is meant to be. It is part of her 'shock tactics' even yet to persuade fools to depart from their folly.

Fools are rushing headlong and headstrong to their ruin! She has five things to say about the ruin of fools:

(a) *It will come when they are least expecting it and strike them with sheer terror* (v. 26). That is the thought expressed by "panic" (*ie* "sudden terror"). In Exodus 15:16 the same word is used of the paralysing "dread" that seizes the peoples of Canaan when they learn of God's victory over Pharaoh's hosts, leaving them powerless and helpless. In Isaiah 2:19 it is the divinely inspired "terror" that drives haughty men to cringe and hide in pot-holes and caves before the awesome majesty of God.

(b) *It will come with devastating and overwhelming force:* like a "storm" and "whirlwind" (v. 27). This imagery of a violent storm which sweeps aside all that lies in its path is one of the more common metaphors for judgment in the Old Testament (see Isa. 17:13; Hos 8:7; Amos 1:14). It has a special place in poetic descriptions of God's own 'coming' in judgment ("His way is in whirlwind and storm . . .", Nahum 1:3–5; see also Ps. 18:7–15).

(c) *It will bring them to their senses—too late!* (v. 28). The fools have chosen to learn the hard way, and learn they will. But by then it will be too late to undo the folly done and escape its consequences. They will find the tables turned and wisdom no longer to be had; for the spurned Lady will ignore those who ignored her. Much the same picture of futile entreaty is found in the message of the prophets (Isa. 1:15; Jer. 11:14; Hos. 5:6; Mic. 3:4). It has been said that "nine-tenths of wisdom is being wise in time". These verses add the sobering thought that wisdom is to be wise *in God's time,* and his time is always *now.*

(d) *They are bringing it upon themselves* (v. 31). What makes its way in the storm and whirlwind is not God bringing them to book for their folly, but the boomerang of their own deeds and devices. Their ruin is as much a natural outflow of their behaviour as their eating the fruit which they have planted, tended and plucked. They are reaping what they have sown (cf. Hos. 8:7; Gal. 6:7).

(e) *They will have only themselves to blame* (v. 32). "Turning away" comes from the same Hebrew root as "give heed" or "turn" in verse 23; and like it, it has echoes in prophetic passages. It is the word used of Israel's apostasy and backsliding from God (Jer. 2:19; 8:5; Hos. 11:7). The fools have had ample warning and ample opportunity to wise up and turn to Lady Wisdom's counsel. But they have chosen to turn away instead, smuggly satisfied with themselves and thinking that they know better. Little do they realize, however, that they are bent on suicide.

Verse 33 now sets in contrast with the ruin of fools the security enjoyed by those who pay attention to Lady Wisdom. Doubtless the good Lady holds out this promise as a parting appeal to the fools to give up their folly and live (cf. 8:35–36).

MAN'S QUEST...

Proverbs 2:1–5

> [1]My son, if you receive my words
>   and treasure up my commandments with you,
> [2]making your ear attentive to wisdom
>   and inclining your heart to understanding;
> [3]yes, if you cry out for insight
>   and raise your voice for understanding,
> [4]if you seek it like silver
>   and search for it as for hidden treasures;
> [5]then you will understand the fear of the Lord
>   and find the knowledge of God.

It seems Mother Eve once thought wisdom grew on trees and was there for the plucking! (Gen. 3:6). The sage knows better. In these verses he warns his pupils that it is not so easy to get. Wisdom is an object for earnest quest, a goal for diligent pursuit, the end and prize of a difficult course. Their quest, however, is to be neither a search in the dark nor a venture into the unknown. It is for them to possess and prove for themselves the tried and tested: wise words (v. 1) which lead to the fear and knowledge of God (v. 5). Through the sage's teaching his son has not only a compass bearing to set him off in the right direction, but also a guide to lead him in the way and bring him to the goal. Two things are therefore required of the son if he is to win wisdom:

(a) *He must be willing to learn* (vv. 1–2). The sage never tires exhorting his son to listen and accept his teaching. An "attentive ear" was doubly important for the Hebrew student of wisdom. There were no recommended text-books or course handouts for the inattentive to fall back on. What the student learned was what he *heard* and *remembered.* To "treasure up" has in view this need for careful memorization of the lesson. The good student was the one who learned his lessons by heart through constant repetition, or as the Rabbis had it: "One who repeats his lessons a hundred times is not like one who repeats it a hundred and one times"! There is much practical wisdom in committing Scripture portions to memory.

But if he is to learn well, an attentive ear and a retentive memory are not enough. These alone will not get a student a pass mark in wisdom. He must also "incline his heart". In Old Testament thought, the heart was the seat of the intellect rather than the emotions. Its main business was to reflect, reason, know and understand—things we do with our minds. So the student has got to apply his mind to it. There has got to be some quiet reflection and some hard thinking if wisdom is to be won.

Wisdom is a closed door to a closed mind. And that, says the sage, is why there are so many fools around. They are so self-conceited that they think they know it all and have no need to learn from anyone (12:15; 15:5). Like their namesake Nabal (*ie* "Fool"), "one cannot speak to him" (1 Sam. 25:17, 25). So they remain fools. It is always easier to see the fool in someone other than ourselves.

(b) *He must be willing to work* (vv. 3–4). The student looking for a soft option had better steer clear of the course on wisdom. It is for workers only. The quest for wisdom requires the same concerted effort, patient application and dogged perseverance shown by miners as they tunnel under the earth to extract silver ore and other precious metals (see Job 28). Neither silver ore nor wisdom is got in a day, or got without industry; but for miner and student alike, the prize is worth the toil. But toil there is; and so an earnest desire to obtain wisdom must be upper-most. His son must "cry out" and "raise [his] voice" for wisdom, matching indeed Lady Wisdom's fervent desire to be found by men (1:20–21).

We are not surprised to learn that here again the fool finds himself in all sorts of trouble. He has neither the discipline nor the patience for such a quest (17:24). He thinks he can shop around for wisdom, and expects to pick it up pre-packaged and neatly wrapped (17:16) —a bit like thinking that listening to the Sunday sermon is all it takes.

... AND GOD'S GIFT

Proverbs 2:6-8

⁶For the Lord gives wisdom;
  from his mouth come knowledge and understanding;
⁷he stores up sound wisdom for the upright;
  he is a shield to those who walk in integrity,
⁸guarding the paths of justice
  and preserving the way of his saints.

(i)

Observation and reflection were the great sources of wisdom. Pearls of wisdom were to be had walking down the street with a keen eye on what was going on round about (see 24:30-34):

³⁰I passed by the field of a sluggard,
  by the vineyard of a man without sense;
³¹and lo, it was all overgrown with thorns;
  the ground was covered with nettles,
  and its stone wall was broken down.
³²Then I saw and considered it;
  I looked and received instruction.
³³A little sleep, a little slumber,
  a little folding of the hands to rest,
³⁴and poverty will come upon you like a robber,
  and want like an armed man.

Through such insightful observations of how things are and how they turn out, the wise learned wisdom. Their's was a wisdom born of experience; and the teachers among them taught the lessons and insights of experience to their pupils, confident that a diligent, thoughtful and workmanlike study of their teaching would bear fruit in wisdom.

However, when they came to evaluate their pearls of wisdom in the light of the principle that the fear of the Lord was the beginning of wisdom (1:7), the wise came to perceive that God himself was the ultimate source of all true wisdom.

In the Old Testament we meet this thought in a variety of connections. God gives Solomon the wisdom to rule wisely and justly (1 Kings 3:12), Bezalel and Oholiab their skills as master-craftsmen (Exod. 36:1), Daniel the wisdom to interpret dreams and visions (Dan. 1:17; 2:23), and even the farmer has God to thank for knowing how to work his fields properly (Isa. 28:23–29). The Psalmist prays: "teach me wisdom in my secret heart"·(Ps. 51:6), and says again: "Thy commandment makes me wiser than my enemies" (Ps. 119:98). In Ecclesiastes the sage tells us that "to the man who pleases him God gives wisdom and knowledge and joy" (Ecc. 2:26). A later Jewish wisdom teacher introduces his book with the words, "All wisdom comes from the Lord and is with him for ever" (Ecclesiasticus 1:1). And James describes the wisdom that comes from above as "first pure, then peaceable, gentle, open to reason, full of mercy and good fruits, without uncertainty or insincerity" (Jas. 3:17).

(ii)

So here now, alongside wisdom as man's quest, the sage sets wisdom as God's gift. The man who seeks to attain wisdom finds not to what he attains, but what God gives him. What then has this to tell the wisdom seeker about his quest? At least two things:

(a) *It has to be a prayerful quest.* If Solomon came to typify the wise man among later generations, his also came to typify the prayerful attitude of the wisdom seeker. Aware of the pressing responsibilities thrust upon him and his lack of experience and ability to cope, the new king turns to God in prayer and asks for the needed wisdom (1 Kings 3:7–9). A later sage elaborates this by making the wise king say:

I went about seeking how to get her [wisdom] for
myself . . .
But I perceived that I would not possess wisdom
unless God gave her to me—and it was a mark of
insight to know whose gift she was—so I appealed
to the Lord and besought him, and with my whole
heart I said . . .
Give me the wisdom that sits by thy throne.
(Wisdom of Solomon 8:18, 21; 9:4)

And James counsels (1:5):

> If any of you lacks wisdom, let him ask God, who gives to all men generously and without reproaching, and it will be given him.

To be sure, the sage in Proverbs nowhere speaks of a prayerful quest, but that does not mean it is alien to him. Perhaps he takes it for granted. Perhaps though he is a little afraid that it could give the wrong idea: that wisdom, if not there exactly for the plucking, was there at least for the pious asking. At all events, he would be the first to remind his pupils, in the words of the old Latin saying: *Orare est laborare, laborare est orare*—"To pray is to work, to work is to pray". Perhaps one of the reasons why our prayers often go unanswered is because we are not working hard enough to answer them.

(b) *It will be a fruitful quest.* Notice how verse 6 of Proverbs 2 ties in with verses 1–5. The first four verses set out the quest as a *condition* ("If . . ."), verse 5 indicates the *result* ("Then . . ."), and verse 6 then gives the *reason* why this is bound to follow ("For . . ."). So verse 6 assures the student that his quest will not be fruitless. To seek true wisdom (vv. 1–4) is to find God (v. 5), and God gives the wisdom that leads to himself (v. 6). Those who fail and become drop-outs in the school of wisdom are not those who lack intellectual ability and academic aptitude; they are those who so lightly esteem the wisdom God gives, so as not to seek it.

Verses 7–8 describe the wisdom God gives, the fruit of the quest. "Sound wisdom" is one word in Hebrew. It lays special emphasis on wisdom's effectiveness in getting results, here as resulting in right conduct. The wisdom that leads to knowing God leads to doing right (Jas. 3:13–18); for by it, God protects the way of the upright from the pitfalls and snares of evil. The seekers of this wisdom are good, respectable people—and more: they are God's "saints" (v. 8). This is the only time this word occurs in Proverbs. It means those who are loyally devoted to God and his covenant, and who remain loyal through thick and thin (see Pss. 31:23; 37:28; 79:2; 97:10). In short then, the fruit of the quest for true wisdom is an obedient, loyal and faithful people of God.

WISDOM ON GUARD!

Proverbs 2:9–22

9 Then you will understand righteousness and justice
and equity, every good path;
10for wisdom will come into your heart,
and knowledge will be pleasant to your soul;
11discretion will watch over you;
understanding will guard you;
12delivering you from the way of evil,
from men of perverted speech,
13who forsake the paths of uprightness
to walk in the ways of darkness,
14who rejoice in doing evil
and delight in the perverseness of evil;
15men whose paths are crooked, .
and who are devious in their ways.

16You will be saved from the loose woman,
from the adventuress with her smooth words,
17who forsakes the companion of her youth
and forgets the covenant of her God;
18for her house sinks down to death,
and her paths to the shades;
19none who go to her come back
nor do they regain the paths of life.

20So you will walk in the way of good men
and keep to the paths of the righteous.
21For the upright will inhabit the land,
and men of integrity will remain in it;
22but the wicked will be cut off from the land,
and the treacherous will be rooted out of it.

(i)

In Ephesians 6:13–17 the Christian "soldier" is advised to arm himself with the whole armour of God, above all "taking the shield of faith, with which you can quench all the flaming darts of the evil one". The moral and spiritual dangers which threaten the Christian are very real and very deadly. So the Christian must take care to arm and protect himself with the equipment provided for him by God.

In this chapter of Proverbs the sage is likewise concerned with the battle of the moral life and the need for protection, although here God himself is the shield (v. 7), the armour he provides is "wisdom", "knowledge" and "understanding" (vv. 6, 9–11), and the flaming darts are the perverted words of evil men and the smooth words of loose women (vv. 12–19). To judge by the attention paid to them in the early chapters of Proverbs, the sage must have felt that they were the most deadly enemies of the man who would live wisely and against whom, above all, he needed the protection of wisdom.

(ii)

A terrible description is given of evil men (vv. 12–15). Notice the words—"perverted . . . perverseness . . . crooked . . . devious". One word sums them up: *twisted!* These twisted characters turn everything upside down and inside out. What ordinary folks call 'right' they call 'wrong', and what they call 'wrong' they call 'right'. Like Milton's Satan, their watchword is "Evil be thou my Good". "Ways" and "paths" mean their line of conduct. They plough a crooked furrow through life, abandoning straight and level ways for 'dark ways' that twist and turn in all directions. Just how low they have sunk is emphasized in verse 14. They get a great kick out of their perverseness, and do their evil deeds as much for pleasure as for profit. The sage has in mind people like the robbers and killers he warns his son against in 1:8–19. People who peddle drugs to youngsters or who try to pass off racial hatred and violence as a respectable political philosophy might more readily spring to our minds.

But more dangerous than what evil men do is what they say. For by their words (2:12; cf. 6:12–14) they seek to draw others into the moral morass of their way of thinking and behaving, and they are clever at making a wicked deed sound as if it is the right thing to do. Again they have taken a leaf out of the book of Milton's Satan:

> But all was false and hollow; though
>   his tongue
> Dropt manna, and could make the
>   worse appear
> The better reason.

The theme of the loose woman (vv. 16–19) is later developed at length in 5:1–14, 6:24–35 and 7:1–27. For the present let us simply notice that her words are called "smooth" rather than perverted. Because of the way this woman speaks, she is, if anything, more and not less deadly to the unwary than her evil male counterparts (vv. 18–19).

(iii)

In verse 20 the sage reverts again to the positive side of wisdom's protection: "So you will walk in the way of good men" (cf. vv. 7–9). Notice how often the words "way[s]" and "path[s]" occur in the chapter. Throughout, a sharp distinction is drawn between (1) the good way, walked by those who fear God and who stand for the right, and (2) the evil way, walked by those who do not fear God and who stand for the wrong. This theme of two contrasting ways is an important one in Proverbs, and we will have more to say about it later (see the comment on 4:10–27).

The last two verses round off the contrast between the two ways with a further contrast between the fate of the "righteous" and the "wicked". These are the sage's favourite terms for the two corresponding classes of people. The "land" the one will possess, and from which the other will be uprooted, is the "Promised Land" (Gen. 17:8). In Deuteronomy, the same contrasting prospects are held out before God's people as they are about to cross over the Jordan and enter the land, all depending upon whether or not they would obey God (30:10–15; see also ch. 28). It is probable that the sage has this very much in mind.

This principle that the righteous prosper while the wicked suffer holds a central position in the teaching of the wise, as represented in Proverbs. It is asserted again and again throughout the book, and so confidently that one could form the impression that they thought it invariable. It should be said in fairness, therefore, that it was a principle which was to cause Israel's sages a great deal of trouble and heart-searching. It is not difficult to see why. It contains an element of truth—a man will often reap in this life what he sows—but it is far too rigid. Unless one can think of the accounts being balanced in another world after death—which Israel's sages, living in an age which had not yet developed a belief in such a world, could not—it simply does not square with the way things are. In these circumstances what might sound like a fine principle in theory can so easily become a positive menace in practice. Job will bear witness to that when, in a book not yet written, he will reject his friends' conclusion that because he is suffering he must be a sinner—and God will support him. The conclusion of the friends of Job is the kind that could too easily be reached by anyone reading the Book of Proverbs. Fortunately it is one that the wise men who gave us that book do not themselves quite draw as they map out the rewards of wisdom and the dire consequences of folly.

THE SAGE'S TORAH

Proverbs 3:1–4

> [1]My son, do not forget my teaching,
>   but let your heart keep my commandments;
> [2]for length of days and years of life
>   and abundant welfare will they give you.

> [3]Let not loyalty and faithfulness forsake you;
>   bind them about your neck,
>   write them on the tablet of your heart.
> [4]So you will find favour and good repute
>   in the sight of God and man.

(i)

This passage is a general introduction to the instructions which follow in verses 5–12. In it the sage calls on his pupils to obey his words, and sets out the benefits which obedience brings.

"Teaching" translates that well-known Hebrew word *torah*. The Authorized Version renders it by the more familiar "law". Even so, we have to remember that "law" in the Old Testament is never simply a matter of rules and regulations. The word *torah* really means "instruction which guides and directs". So God's law or *the Torah* is the instruction he has given to guide and direct the lives of his people according to his will and purpose.

Now, in verses 1–2 the sage speaks with a voice which we might more readily associate with the law of God than with the teaching of the wise. What the sage seeks from his students is the same kind of ready and willing obedience which God requires for his law and which is so well exemplified by the psalmist:

> I hasten and do not delay
> to *keep thy commandments.*
> Though the cords of the wicked ensnare me.
> I *do not forget thy law* [*torah*].
>
> (Ps. 119:60–61)

And what he holds out as the benefits of obedience, namely enjoyment of a long and richly rewarding life (on this, see the comment on 3:16–18), are also the blessings promised to those who obey God's law:

> You shall walk in all the way which the Lord your God has commanded you, that *you may live,* and that it *may go well with you.* and that *you may live long* in the land which you shall possess.
>
> (Deut. 5:33)

Are we to suppose, then, that the sage is really a teacher of the law in the disguise of wisdom? Certainly, in the Book of Deuteronomy the people are told that obeying the law will be "your wisdom and your understanding" (4:6).There are also occasions when the sage explicitly commends observance of the law (Provs. 28:4, 9; 29:18), and his ethical teaching has much in common with it. That is to be expected. However, the language and thought of these verses are every bit as much at home in *wisdom* instruction (see 1:8; 2:1; 4:4, 10; 6:20, *etc*), and the sage seems to take great care never to identify his commandments with God's: he speaks always of *his torah* and not *God's torah*. If we remember that God's law is his instruction which—like wisdom instruction—has to be taught, explained, applied and commended to the people (in particular, see Deut.), we should not wonder that wisdom and law often speak in the same tones.

All the same, it might seem strange to us that the sage never so much as refers to the law in the course of his teaching. After all, what better way to reinforce a precept than by a divine "Thou shalt not"! But that was not his style. He much preferred to quote a popular proverb to clinch it (see 1:17; 6:27–28). There are two reasons for this:

(a) The sage is concerned with a wide spectrum of attitudes and sorts of behaviour, both practical and moral, all of which he wants to place side by side under the scrutiny of the one question: wise or foolish? But many of these did not lend themselves to becoming the subject of legal prescription.

(b) In any case, the sage approaches things from the angle of experience, and so prefers to teach on the basis, not of divine commandments, but of the "old rules" which had proved their worth and their wisdom by promoting the good and well-being of individuals and the community down through the generations—rules which when looked at from another angle, to be sure, found their expression in part in the law. As a society which has by and large abandoned God's will as the guide for its behaviour, we are slowly coming to learn that there was much wisdom in the old rules abandoned with it as outmoded.

(ii)

In verse 3 the old rules are gathered up in and capped by the words "loyalty" and "faithfulness". These are great Old Testament words which are often found linked together, for between them they express the *sine qua non* of true and lasting relations, whether between God and man, or between man and his fellow men. The *first* word (Hebrew *chesed*) expresses unswerving fidelity and constancy; the *second* expresses rock-solid integrity and trustworthiness. When applied to God, *chesed* is regularly translated "steadfast love". It is God's covenant-love (the New Testament calls it "grace") by which he never abandons his people, even in the face of their sin and unfaithfulness (see Exod. 34:6–7; Deut. 7:9; Ps. 51:1; Isa. 54:10). Applied to the people, it occasionally means their answering "devotion" (Jer. 2:2) or "love" (Hos. 6:4) for God. But far more often it means the loyalty and kindness which they should show towards one another, especially to those less fortunate than themselves (Ps. 109:16; Hos. 4:1; Mic. 6:8—see further, the topic, *Loyalty . and Faithfulness*). What God has shown and shows towards us is best answered when we "go and do likewise". On the theme of verse 4, see the topic, *A Good Name.*

TRUST IN THE LORD...

Proverbs 3:5–8

⁵Trust in the Lord with all your heart,
  and do not rely on your own insight.
⁶In all your ways acknowledge him,
  and he will make straight your paths.
⁷Be not wise in your own eyes;
  fear the Lord, and turn away from evil.
⁸It will be healing to your flesh
  and refreshment to your bones.

This is one of those wonderfully rich texts of the Bible which seem to say all that needs to be said. In plain and simple language the sage lays his finger on what is of the essence of religious faith: trusting in God. An ancient Rabbi described his words as the text upon which "all the essential principles of Judaism may be considered to hinge". His words are also well-

known and well-loved by Christian folk, and have been inscribed in the fly-leaf of many a Bible and put up on the living-
room wall of many a home as a constant reminder of what faith
in God is all about.

(i)

The call to "trust in the Lord" is heard many times over in the
Old Testament, notably in the Book of Psalms (Pss. 4:5; 37:3–5;
62:8). It is not an evangelistic call to 'outsiders', but is
addressed to those who already know what it means to have
faith in God. In Psalm 115:9–11, the whole worshipping
community, their priests and all who fear the Lord, are called
upon to put their trust in God, "their help and their shield". It is
a summons to "the faithful" to live *faith-full* lives. The sage
therefore takes it for granted that his pupils belong within the
community of faith, and he places the whole emphasis of his
teaching on the need for *whole-hearted* and *absolute* depen-
dence upon God, uncompromised by reliance on one's own
resources.

(ii)

The self-reliant attitude is celebrated in William Ernest Henley's *Invictus:*

> Out of the night that covers me,
> Black as the Pit from pole to pole,
> I thank whatever gods may be
> For my unconquerable soul.
> In the fell clutch of circumstance,
> I have not' winced nor cried aloud:
> Under the bludgeonings of chance
> My head is bloody, but unbowed.
> It matters not how strait the gate,
> How charged with punishments the scroll,
> I am the master of my fate:
> I am the captain of my soul.

These are stirring words, and there is something to admire in
the strength of character they reveal. Probably the sage would
find them less provocative than what he says here might lead us

to think. Indeed, he might well find greater difficulties with the sentiment expressed by Charles Wesley in his hymn, *Jesus Lover of my Soul:*

> Other refuge have I none;
> hangs my helpless soul on thee ...

At all events, every bit as much as Henley in *Invictus,* the sage is a strong, courageous soul, who faces life square on and without flinching. He is also absolutely clear that men are free and responsible people, who have to make up their own minds and make their own decisions, and then accept the consequences. So his counsel in this passage is not that men should abdicate their God-given freedom and responsibility for their lives and the life of their community by passing the buck to God. He would take a rather dim view of the kind of Christian who prays, "Thy will be done, On earth as it is in heaven", and who then leaves it "in God's hands" while he opts out of all political and social responsibility for the ills of a world in which God's will so badly needs to be done. In a very real sense, man is "the master of his fate". He lives in the kind of world his own hands have shaped. He is not the pawn of faceless gods, or of time and circumstance. But, our sage firmly believes, that is precisely why man dare not go it alone relying only on himself. The responsibility is too great, the stakes are too high, and his own resources are too limited for going it alone to be anything other than a recipe for disappointment and disaster.

(iii)

As we have already seen (see the comment on 2:9–22), the sage has a keen sense that the man who would live wisely finds himself in an often hostile environment. He has more foes than friends, ready at the first opportunity to knock him off course and drag him down. His situation is rather like that of a crook who leaves prison determined to go straight, but who is continually under pressure from his one-time associates to revert to a life of crime; and even as he resists, he is so worried he will slip up and land back in prison that he is unable to enjoy his new life style and make the best of it. The sage saw this as a fundamental problem of wise living, and it is in this connection that for him the question of "trust" becomes paramount.

The Hebrew verb "trust" has two related nouns which also occur in Proverbs. One appears in Lady Wisdom's promise that "he who listens to me will dwell *secure* and will be at ease, without dread of evil" (1:33); and again in 3:23: "Then you will walk on your way *securely* and your foot will not stumble". The other appears in the saying, "In the fear of the Lord one has strong *confidence*" (14:26). So here the question of "trust" is the question of a sure and firm foundation for (1) a *secure* path through life, especially in face of the temptations and snares which lurk at every step (cf. v. 6*b*), and (2) the quiet *confidence* to step boldly and to meet life's problems, difficulties and temptations without fear that all will crumble underfoot—an anxiety-free frame of mind which keeps the doctor away (cf. v. 8). The sage is quite sure that trust in oneself will hardly do as a foundation for security and confidence in the difficult business of life. Complete trust in God is the key.

(iv)

But can God be *completely* trusted? Put so baldly the question sounds almost impertinent; but it is an important one, and Israel's sages addressed themselves to it.

The faith of the fathers gives an unequivocal answer:

> In thee our fathers trusted;
>   they trusted and thou didst deliver them.
> To thee they cried, and were saved;
>   in thee they trusted, and were not disappointed. (Ps. 22:4-5)

These lines recall the epic events of the past days, the days of the exodus from Egypt and the long, hazardous journey through the wilderness, the days of the conquest of the land of Canaan and of the great Judges or Deliverers—days during which God never once let his people down.

This is the line of argument taken up by the Jewish wisdom teacher Ben Sirach in answer to the question:

You who fear the Lord, trust in him . . .
Consider the ancient generations and see:
who ever trusted in the Lord and was put to shame?
Or who ever persevered in the fear of the Lord and was forsaken?
(Ecclesiasticus 2:8, 10)

As we should expect of a sage, his argument is based upon the practical experience of the past generations, and not upon some profound theological considerations about the nature of God. This is in keeping with his whole way of thinking. In the classical statement of trust in God in the New Testament, appeal is also made to experience, though of a different kind: God's care and provision for the birds of the air and the flowers of the field (Matt. 6:25–34).

God's complete trustworthiness passes the sterling test of experience. That is good to know.

. . . IN PROSPERITY AND ADVERSITY

Proverbs 3:9–12

⁹Honour the Lord with your substance
  and with the first fruits of all your produce;
¹⁰then your barns will be filled with plenty,
  and your vats will be bursting with wine.

¹¹My son, do not despise the Lord's discipline
  or be weary of his reproof,
¹²for the Lord reproves him whom he loves,
  as a father the son in whom he delights.

The sage now brings out what whole-hearted trust in God means in two contrasting situations: in prosperity (vv. 9–10) and in adversity (vv. 11–12). The good times and the bad are part and parcel of human experience. Most folks get their fair share; some seem to be more fortunate, or unfortunate. But both in their different ways are the real tests of trust in God. For in the one it can seem to be quite unnecessary, while in the other it can seem to be quite impossible.

(i)

Verse 9 is noteworthy, because it is the only time that the teacher advises his pupils to observe a formal act of worship. The offering of the first fruits was the Israelite equivalent to our harvest thanksgiving service. But why should he single out this for special mention when he generally ignores such matters? The answer probably lies in its significance.

For the Israelites, who were mostly farmers, the land was the greatest of God's gifts and its abundant produce was evidence of his providential care for them (see Deut. 8:7–10; 11:9–15). But so bounteous was God's provision that there was always the temptation to become complacent and take it for granted or to become conceited and put it down to their own cleverness, and with their affluence forget God (see Deut. 8:11–20; 11:16–17). This was the mistake made by the rich fool in Jesus' parable (Luke 12:16–21). It is a mistake we can all make. That was why the offering of the first fruits was so important. It was an acknowledgment that all was owed to the goodness and blessing of God. God was the giver of all the good things they and their families enjoyed; and in gratitude they were giving the first fruits back to God (cf. Deut. 26:1–11). So, in effect, it was a mark of faith and trust in God—not when the barns were empty and when they were anxiously waiting for the spring rains to fall and ripen the grain, but in days of prosperity, when the harvest had been gathered in and the barns were stacked full. It put and kept the stacked barns in their proper place.

Church treasurers might wish to draw a lesson for the next time the offering plate is handed round. The lesson is one we ought to heed, although there are, of course, many different ways we can honour God by our giving. But there is a more searching challenge in this verse than to dig deeper in our pockets when occasion demands. It reminds us that how we spend our money and use the possessions God has blessed us with is a very practical and very telling test of the quality of our faith and trust in God. It is a poor faith that has nothing to do with planning the family budget and providing for the family needs.

Those who honour God by giving will find that they have

made a sound investment (v. 10). The order here is important. The man who has in mind the barns of verse 10 when he gives to God is likely to be disappointed. But in their proper order the verses are in line with the Biblical teaching that those who honour God, God will honour (1 Sam. 2:30). We must be wary of taking this in a completely spiritual sense as though it had nothing to do with material things (cf. Hag. 1:3–11; Mal. 3:10–12). On the other hand, where material things are concerned, neither must it be pressed as though it were automatically and invariably the case. We might sometimes wish it were, but we know better than that. It is a general principle which holds good for a part of what God's people experience, but only a part. The corresponding thought in the New Testament lays stress on God's abundant provision for our *needs* (see 2 Cor. 9:6–8; Phil. 4:14–19); for there are far greater blessings to be had by honouring God than stacked barns and vats bursting at the seams.

(ii)

In case we get the wrong idea that prosperity is the whole story for the man or woman of faith, the sage goes on to set against it the other, darker, side to the story: hardship and suffering (vv. 11–12). It is one thing to trust God when the horizon is bright; much more difficult when the storm clouds gather. Then the temptation is not so much to forget God as to allow our situation to alienate us from him; for the question 'why?' can stretch faith to breaking-point.

The passage has three things to say about this side of the story:

(a) *Suffering is God's means of disciplining us.* It is a necessary part of our training in God's school of discipleship, part of our spiritual education towards becoming mature and fruit-bearing disciples. The great heroes of the faith celebrated in Hebrews 11 were all called upon to suffer; and many since have found that it was the path which led them to a more vibrant faith and holier life. After quoting these verses, the writer to the Hebrews underlines the point (12:10–11):

He disciplines us for our good, that we may share his holiness. For the moment all discipline seems painful rather than pleasant; later it yields the peaceful fruit of righteousness to those who have been trained by it.

(b) *There is the proof of God's fatherly love.* It is a very human reaction to suffering to feel resentment against God— that it is just not fair, and that for some reason God must have it in for us. This, at any rate, was exactly what Job felt; and he was not slow to let God know it (see *eg* Job 7:11–21). But the lesson here is that when God disciplines us through suffering, it is a sign of his love for us as his children, and not of his unfairness, his anger, or his indifference. Again the writer to the Hebrews brings out the thought well by pointing out that to escape hardship and suffering would not be a sign of God's favour but a sign that we were not his children (Heb. 12:7–8).

(c) *We ought therefore to submit to his discipline,* and neither "spurn" it nor "take offence" at it (NEB, v.11). In his book, *The Problem of Pain,* C.S. Lewis writes: "God whispers to us in our pleasures, speaks in our conscience, but shouts in our pains". God has always something to say to us in suffering. There is always a lesson to be learned and a blessing to be received. The triumph of faith and trust in adversity is to learn the lesson and receive the blessing. That is the secret—as the Psalmist discovered it:

Before I was afflicted I went astray;
  but now I keep thy word . . .
It is good for me that I was afflicted,
  that I might learn thy statutes.

(Ps. 119:67, 71)

HAPPY IS THAT MAN!

Proverbs 3:13–20

[13]Happy is the man who finds wisdom,
  and the man who gets understanding,
[14]for the gain from it is better than gain from silver
  and its profit better than gold.

¹⁵She is more precious than jewels,
  and nothing you desire can compare with her.
¹⁶Long life is in her right hand;
  in her left hand are riches and honour.
¹⁷Her ways are ways of pleasantness,
  and all her paths are peace.
¹⁸She is a tree of life to those who lay hold of her;
  those who hold her fast are called happy.

¹⁹The Lord by wisdom founded the earth;
  by understanding he established the heavens;
²⁰by his knowledge the deeps broke forth,
  and the clouds drop down the dew.

This passage falls into two parts: (1) wisdom's benediction in verses 13–18, and (2) wisdom's credentials in verses 19–20.

(i)

Verses 13–18 begin and end on the same "happy" note. Their theme is the happiness of the man or woman who finds wisdom (v. 13) and who, having found it, does not let it go (v. 18). "Happy" is the same word which opens the Psalms (1:1) and which lies behind the Beatitudes in the Sermon on the Mount (Matt. 5:3–12).

Notice that these verses are cast in the style of a hymn in praise of wisdom and not as a father instructing his son. Nevertheless, by extolling the blessings wisdom bestows, the hymn picks up and enhances what the sage claims are the benefits of obeying his instructions (cf. 1:8; 3:1–4), and so it fits in well with his concern to commend his teaching. Notice too that here once again wisdom is presented as her own woman, the good Lady Wisdom (see the comment on 1:20–33). This becomes especially clear in verse 16. Indeed, in 8:17–21 Lady Wisdom has much the same to say about herself as is said about wisdom here. However, the personal traits of wisdom in the hymn are not nearly so pronounced as they were in 1:20–33 and are later in chapter 8. They are just sufficient to hint that this is the benediction of wisdom founded on the fear of the Lord.

Wisdom's is a four-fold benediction:

(a) Simply to find wisdom is to own its highest blessing, for it is a priceless treasure beyond all comparison (vv. 14–15). In 2:4 we met the thought that the wisdom seeker must have the grit and determination of a miner seeking to unearth silver ore. There is no question about who will be the richer for finding it— miner or wisdom seeker. Verse 14 brings out the surpassing value of wisdom in commercial language. "Gain" and "profit" are words belonging to the world of businessmen and stockbrokers. Wisdom knows the value of a good business deal—and does not despise it; wisdom also knows that the best things in life cannot be bought and sold in the markets—and does not overrate it. For the things which make a man and woman truly rich and bring real joy and happiness, money is a worthless currency. Their price is wisdom.

Verse 15 recalls the inestimable value of the good wife in Proverbs 31:10. That is probably why the RSV now suddenly switches from "it" and "its" to "she" and "her". The wisdom seeker needs not only the hardiness of a miner to dig for it; he also needs the passion of a lover to woo her! (See the comment on 4:6–9.)

(b) The depiction of wisdom in verse 16 probably owes something to portraits of the Egyptian goddess *Maat,* the goddess of Truth and Right. She is pictured holding a symbol of long life in one hand and a symbol of riches and honour in the other. Enjoyment of a long and prosperous life was prized by the wise in Egypt as well as in Israel, and was equally regarded as the "profit" of wisdom.

As wisdom's blessing, long life is not simply living threescore years and ten or more (Ps. 90:10). That is not a blessing if life is felt to be not worth living. Rather, it means living a rich and full, meaningful and fulfilled life (see v. 18). In harmony with the principle that good men prosper (see the comment on 2:20–22; but also on 3:11–12), wisdom reckons among its blessings riches and the esteem in which a man is held and the "weight" ("honour" is from a verb whose root meaning is "to be weighty") he carries in the affairs of the community. But wisdom is not blinded by the glitter of gold. Notice that wealth is held in the *left* hand. For the Hebrews, the left was the side of lesser worth (Gen. 48:14) and even misfortune (Eccles. 10:2; Matt. 25:33). Even at its most materialistic, wisdom offers a man no encouragement to give his life to making money. Only the short-sighted fool can be so stupid (28:22—see the topic, *Wisdom and Wealth*). Here too the rule is "Seek first [wisdom: the highest prize, 3:13–15] . . . and all these things shall be yours as well" (3:16–18; see Matt. 6:33). But the fact remains that, even allowing for hyperbole, in Proverbs wisdom holds out the promise of wealth (cf. 8:18, 21), and not just "daily bread". We can certainly agree that a man or woman is "better off" for doing what is wise and right and "poorer" for doing what is wrong, without insisting that the proof lies in the bank account.

(c) Wisdom leads its finders along pleasant and peaceful paths (v. 17). This is apt to make us think of a quiet stroll down a country lane on a sunny, summer afternoon. It is nothing of the kind! Wisdom's paths lead along busy main streets and through crowded city centres rubbing shoulders with the world. And "peace" (Hebrew *shalom*) is a word well able to follow hard on its heels. It is an all-embracing word. It embraces the thought of wholeness and completeness, of security and well-being, of harmony and concord—all in the manifold relationships and experiences of life. The RSV tries to catch something of this when it translates *shalom* by "abundant welfare" in 3:2.

(d) Wisdom's blessing is life itself in all it richness and fullness (v. 18). The metaphor of the "tree of life" occurs three more times in Proverbs (11:30; 13:12; 15:4). It recalls the tree in the story of the Garden of Eden in Genesis chapters 2–3. We also find the expression "fountain of life" in Proverbs (10:11; 13:14; 14:27; 16:22), and it may echo (less directly) the rivers which watered the Garden. It is perhaps significant that we also hear about "the tree of the knowledge of good and evil" in the Garden. It may be that there is some subtle interplay going on between Proverbs and Genesis at these points. On balance, however, the impression given by the use of these metaphors in Proverbs is that they are little more than vivid figures of speech used to describe things as a vital source which nourishes growth and fruitfulness and promotes fullness of life.

(ii)

High claims, then, are made by wisdom in the arena of human affairs. To find wisdom is to win life at its very best and most rewarding. But what credentials does wisdom have to authorize it to bestow such blessings upon those who find it? Wisdom's credentials are presented (in part) in verses 19–20. The wisdom which brings blessing to mankind is at one with God's design and purpose in the creation of the world. By wisdom the creation exists; by it the creature is blessed. Here we are given an appetizer for that great passage in 8:22–31.

SOME ADVICE ON NEIGHBOURLINESS

Proverbs 3:21–35

[21]My son, keep sound wisdom and discretion;
   let them not escape from your sight,
[22]and they will be life for your soul
   and adornment for your neck.
[23]Then you will walk on your way securely
   and your foot will not stumble.
[24]If you sit down, you will not be afraid;
   when you lie down, your sleep will be sweet.
[25]Do not be afraid of sudden panic,
   or of the ruin of the wicked, when it comes;
[26]for the Lord will be your confidence
   and will keep your foot from being caught.

[27]Do not withhold good from those to whom it is due,
   when it is in your power to do it.
[28]Do not say to your neighbour, "Go, and come again,
   tomorrow I will give it"—when you have it with you.
[29]Do not plan evil against your neighbour
   who dwells trustingly beside you.

³⁰Do not contend with a man for no reason,
　　when he has done you no harm.
³¹Do not envy a man of violence
　　and do not choose any of his ways;
³²for the perverse man is an abomination to the Lord,
　　but the upright are in his confidence.
³³The Lord's curse is on the house of the wicked,
　　but he blesses the abode of the righteous.
³⁴Toward the scorners he is scornful,
　　but to the humble he shows favour.
³⁵The wise will inherit honour,
　　but fools get disgrace.

From its grand task at the creation of the world, wisdom now
gets down to the humbler task of giving some advice on how to
be a good neighbour. That is the theme in the main section of
the passage. First, however, the sage drives home an earlier
lesson.

(i)

Verses 21–26 should be read alongside 2:6–19 and 3:5–8 and in
the light of the comments made there. The verses develop the
theme of the *secure* and *anxiety-free* lives of those who, assailed
by "fightings without and fear within", keep steadily before their
eyes the "sound wisdom" which God gives (v. 21; cf. 2:7), and
trust fully in him (v. 26; cf. 3:5). In these two earlier passages,
the wisdom seeker had an important lesson to learn on the need
to rely upon God and not himself. But the sage knows, as we
well know, that it is easy to learn the lesson only to let it slip out
of sight and out of mind (v. 21). Often it is when we have most
need to remember it that we are most liable to forget it. So the
lesson bears reminding.

Our homes can be treacherous places, fraught with danger
for the unsuspecting:

I left the room with silent dignity,
　　but caught my foot in the mat.
　　　　　　(George and Walter Grossmith, *Diary of a Nobody*)

Infinitely more treacherous and fraught with danger is the journey through life for the unwary traveller; and he has far more to lose than loss of face (v. 25; see the comment on 1:26–27). Travellers who think that they are wise and sure-footed enough to stay on their feet are in for a nasty tumble. The key to sure-footedness is the steadying and protecting hand of God (vv. 23, 26). To learn this lesson well is to learn the secret of real relaxation and refreshing sleep (v. 24). Psalm 4:8 sums it up beautifully:

> In peace I will both lie down and sleep;
>   for thou alone, O Lord, makest me dwell in safety.

(ii)

"Whatever you wish that men would do to you, do so to them" (Matt. 7:12) is Jesus' 'golden rule' for getting along with other people, neighbours included. So if we would like to have good neighbours, the sage has got some words of advice for us. Three things are highlighted as the marks of a good neighbour:

(a) *He is helpful* (vv. 27–28). What exactly is running through the sage's mind in verse 27 is not very clear. The difficulty lies in the odd Hebrew expression "from its owners", which the RSV paraphrases, "from those to whom it is due" (v. 27). But what does it mean? Who are these "owners of good"? The major ancient greek translation, the *Septuagint,* hazards that it means "the poor", understanding the verse as an exhortation to almsgiving. The Today's English Version follows the same line, but makes it less specific when it renders, "to those who need". On the other hand, the New English Bible takes them to be people who have done us a favour and want it returned: "Refuse no man any favour that you owe him"—a far cry from giving alms to the poor! Probably the sage intends his words to be general in scope and applicable in different kinds of circumstances where a neighbour needs our help, but laying the emphasis on his *right* to it rather than his need of it. Perhaps the best commentary on the verse is the story of the Good Samaritan, which drives home the lesson that the man in need is our neighbour, and that his need is our *obligation* to help him in whatever way we can (Luke 10:30–37). The New International

Version gives the verse a different twist: "Do not withhold good from those who deserve it"—as though to say, "Be generous with your help, but don't be a 'sucker'!"

There is an old saying, "Help which is long on the road is no help at all". That is the thought lying behind verse 28. Mostly there is nothing wrong with our intentions (Jas. 2:15–16); we simply end up giving too little (v. 27) too late (v. 28).

(b) *He is reliable* (v. 29). We noticed in connection with 3:3 that "kindness" and "faithfulness" must govern men's dealings with one another if they are to live together as neighbours. If verses 27–28 answer to kindness, verse 29 answers to faithfulness. To plot evil against a hapless victim is crime enough; but to do it and betray the victim's trust in you is the ultimate treachery: "*Et tu, Brute?*" Those who turn a word spoken in confidence into a piece of juicy gossip fall under this judgment.

(c) *He is friendly* (v. 30). This verse warns against being the kind of neighbour who is always ready to quarrel across the garden fence. This sort of unfriendly fellow is a downright menace and bears the brunt of a number of the sage's maxims (see, *eg* 15:18; 26:21).

(iii)

Unfortunately, not all men make helpful, reliable, friendly neighbours. Some quite the opposite in fact—as verse 31 observes. But men of violent and underhand ways often seem to do better out of life than good folk. Whether or not their ill-gotten wealth is "gravel" in their mouths (20:17), it is certainly 'gold dust' in the eyes of the fellow down the street. His temptation is to envy such men; worse still, to imitate them. That is what the sage now warns against in verses 31–35, developing it along much the same lines as 2:20–22. Psalm 37 deals with the same theme.

Men of honesty and integrity enjoy God's friendship ("confidence" in v. 32 is the word translated "friendship" in Job 29:4 and Ps. 25:14), but these "perverse" characters (see 2:12–15) are "an abomination to the Lord" (v. 32). This is a very strong word. It means something so hateful and loathsome that, as we might say, it 'turns the stomach'. So the wicked man is not to be envied. God's weighty word of judgment ("curse"; see Deut. 27:15–26; 28) rests upon his house and he will be utterly disgraced and shown up for the despicable creature that he is; whereas the upright will enjoy God's blessing and favour and will be held in high regard. Daniel 12:2–3 takes a long term view of the honour and shame which fall to the upright and the wicked—as destinies in the life beyond death. The sage's sights are necessarily set lower. It is a matter of the respect or lack of respect a man commands in the community. A vivid illustration of the contrast implied can be seen by comparing Job 29 and 30. It is easy to see why Job's friends thought he must be a scoundrel!

The quotation in James 4:6 and 1 Peter 5:5—"God opposes the proud, but gives grace to the humble"—rests on the *Septuagint's* rendering of verse 34.

WISDOM IN THE HOME

Proverbs 4:1–9

1Hear, O sons, a father's instruction,
   and be attentive, that you may gain insight;
2for I give you good precepts:
   do not forsake my teaching.
3When I was a son with my father,
   tender, the only one in the sight of my mother,
4he taught me, and said to me,
  "Let your heart hold fast my words;
   keep my commandments, and live;
5do not forget, and do not turn away
   from the words of my mouth.
   Get wisdom; get insight.
6Do not forsake her, and she will keep you;
   love her, and she will guard you.
7The beginning of wisdom is this: Get wisdom,
   and whatever you get, get insight.

⁸Prize her highly, and she will exalt you;
   she will honour you if you embrace her.
⁹She will place on your head a fair garland;
   she will bestow on you a beautiful crown."

(i)

In this passage the sage appeals to his pupils to pay close attention to his teaching (vv. 1–2). Such appeals are dotted throughout these chapters, but what is interesting here is the way he reinforces it by an autobiographical note. When he was a young lad he had listened carefully to his father and had learned the value of wisdom (vv. 3–9). What he has learned from him he is now passing on to them. Here we catch a view of the traditional character of wisdom instruction and the way it is passed down from one generation to the next.

We have already noticed it was the convention for the wisdom teacher to address his pupils as a father to his sons. This was also the practice in the wisdom schools of Egypt and Mesopotamia. This convention, however, rested upon the responsibility the natural father had for the education of his sons within the home. The home was and would remain the most important setting for the education of young people. The average Israelite youth had neither the leisure nor the means to pursue an education in the wisdom schools, and elementary schools were unknown in Israel before New Testament times. So during a child's formative years the home was the school and the parents were the schoolteachers, and for most this was their only schooling. There a son learned the practical skills needed to follow in his father's footsteps, but he also received moral and religious instruction (see Exod. 12:26–27; Deut. 6:6–7, 20–25). While a mother could play a part in her son's education (v. 3; 1:8; 31:1–9), her main responsibility was to teach her daughter to become a good wife and mother. The parent was an honoured member of the goodly fellowship of the wise, and the wisdom teachers quite deliberately reinforced and built upon parental instruction. Although the Book of Proverbs has come down to us from the sages and reflects their more advanced teaching, we are nevertheless still closely in touch with the kind of instruction given in an ordinary Israelite family. In Israel the wise teacher and the wise parent spoke with one voice.

Wisdom for living, like life itself, should start at home. It is there that character and habits are formed, and attitudes and values acquired, that make the man or woman—for better or worse. In good wisdom language the New Testament urges Christian parents to bring up their children "in the discipline and instruction of the Lord" (Eph. 6:4); and this responsibility is all the more pressing in an age when the Christian parent and the child's teachers outside the home do not speak as one.

(ii)

Verses 6–10 return to the theme of the need to value wisdom highly and to pursue it earnestly (see 2:1–4). Verse 7 apart, here we find the same tendency to present wisdom as a person, as we found in 3:13–18. The New English Bible places verse 7 before verse 6 since it interrupts the connection between verses 6 and 8. The Hebrew of this verse is difficult and doubtful. The first line reads, "The beginning of wisdom, [literally] get wisdom" (RSV), which does not give very good sense. The New English Bible thinks "wisdom" has accidentally been written twice and renders, "The first thing is to acquire wisdom". We have to get our priorities right. Wisdom comes first. But it is not just a question of priorities. The verb "get" really means "to acquire at a price". The second line of the verse is not saying that we must put wisdom at the top of our shopping list, so to speak, but that no price is too high to pay for it. The New English Bible expresses the sense better: "gain understanding though it cost you all you have". Discipleship in the school of wisdom is a costly affair; we should not expect it to be any less costly in the kingdom of heaven (see Matt. 13:44–45).

In 3:15 we had a hint that wisdom was a fair lady to be wooed and won for a bride. That is the thought developed here. The wisdom seeker must "love" and "embrace" her, as though the minister had just pronounced them husband and wife. The later

Jewish wisdom book, the Wisdom of Solomon, makes the wise
king say (8:2):

> I loved her [wisdom] and sought her from my youth,
> and I desired to take her for my bride,
> and I became enamoured of her beauty.

The word "exalt" (v. 8, see ftn.) is normally used of constructing
a raised highway (15:19; Isa. 57:14). Here it evidently means
"highly esteem" (NEB "cherish"). "A good wife is the crown of
her husband", says 12:4, and wisdom's crown is the most
beautiful of all (v. 9; 1:9). It was the custom at weddings for the
bride to place a garland on the head of the bridegroom, and
verse 9 may have this in mind.

THE TWO WAYS

Proverbs 4:10–27

10Hear, my son, and accept my words,
  that the years of your life may be many.
11I have taught you the way of wisdom;
  I have led you in the paths of uprightness.
12When you walk, your step will not be hampered;
  and if you run, you will not stumble.
13Keep hold of instruction, do not let go;
  guard her, for she is your life.
14Do not enter the path of the wicked,
  and do not walk in the way of evil men.
15Avoid it, do not go on it;
  turn away from it and pass on.
16For they cannot sleep unless they have done wrong;
  they are robbed of sleep unless
    they have made some one stumble.
17For they eat the bread of wickedness
  and drink the wine of violence.
18But the path of the righteous is like the light of dawn,
  which shines brighter and brighter until full day.
19The way of the wicked is like deep darkness;
  they do not know over what they stumble.

²⁰My son, be attentive to my words;
    incline your ear to my sayings.
²¹Let them not escape from your sight;
    keep them within your heart.
²²For they are life to him who finds them,
    and healing to all his flesh.
²³Keep your heart with all vigilance;
    for from it flow the springs of life.
²⁴Put away from you crooked speech,
    and put devious talk far from you.
²⁵Let your eyes look directly forward,
    and your gaze be straight before you.
²⁶Take heed to the path of your feet,
    then all your ways will be sure.
²⁷Do not swerve to the right or to the left;
    turn your foot away from evil.

The metaphor of life as a road the traveller walks from the cradle to the grave is one of the sage's favourites and it plays an important role in his teaching. We have already met it several times, but it is now developed at greater length as he sharply contrasts two ways travellers can walk: (1) "the way of wisdom" (v. 11), and (2) "the way of evil men" (v. 14). We will also find the two ways set out in Psalm 1.

(i)
The way of wisdom leads in "paths of uprightness" (cf. Ps.23:3). This has the double sense of paths which are morally upright and paths which are straight and level (3:6). It is therefore not only the *good* path to walk in (2:9); it is also the *safe* path. Two reasons are given why it is safe:

(a) *The traveller's steps will be unhampered* (v. 12). "Hampered" is literally 'narrow, cramped'. In Isaiah 49:19–20 the word is used of cramped living conditions, the lack of living space in the land resulting from a population explosion. So then, there is plenty of leg room on this road to take firm, even strides. Indeed, the traveller can break into a run without fear of taking a tumble. As the Psalmist puts it (18:36, NEB):

> Thou givest me room for my steps,
>   my feet have not faltered.

(b) *The traveller's way is bathed in light* (v. 18). The Authorized Version gives a delightful rendering to this verse:

> But the path of the just is as the shining light, that shineth more and
> more unto the perfect day.

The picture is one of the steady increase in the brightness and intensity of the daylight, from the first flickers of dawn to the brilliant radiance of the noonday sun which bathes the whole landscape in its light. With the light of wisdom to guide him (6:23; cf. Ps. 119:105) and to light up the road ahead, the pilgrim can see where he is going, and knows where, and where not, to place his feet. No loose stones, pot-holes or icy patches find shadows to lurk behind to catch him unawares. The way of wisdom is therefore the safe and secure road through life, and it leads to fullness of life (v. 10; 6:23). The sage has already stressed that it is the way of those who fear and trust fully in God (3:5–6, 21–26).

(ii)

The way of evil men is graphically set out in verses 16–17 and verse 19. It takes further the description of their 'twisted paths' in 2:12–15. At all points their way stands in sharp contrast to the way of the wise.

(a) *It is an evil way.* While those who walk in the way of wisdom sleep well at night knowing their "foot will not stumble" (3:23–24), evil men toss and turn unless they "have made some one stumble" (v. 16). This could mean unless they have managed to trap someone in the web of their wicked ways and made them bedfellows, or unless they have harmed some innocent victim. Both intents are there in the description of their activities in 1:8–19. Either way, they find there is nothing quite like a daily dose of evil to give them a good night's sleep. They do not need a sedative to dull the sting of a guilty

conscience (but see Job 33:15–18); for wrong-doing and violence come as naturally to them as eating and drinking (v. 17).

(b) *It is a dark way* (v. 19; cf. 2:13). "Deep darkness" is one
word in Hebrew, and an expressive one at that. There is always
something uncanny about this darkness. It is the darkness
which enveloped the land of Egypt as one of the plagues (Exod.
10:22); while the prophets speak of it in their descriptions of
that terrifying day of divine judgment, the "Day of the Lord"
(Joel 2:2; Amos 5:20; Zeph. 1:15). The word suggests the
dreadful extent of their moral blindness, having spurned
wisdom's light (1:23–25, 29–30). But more especially, it points
to what is bound to happen to those who walk along a twisting
road in total darkness.

(c) *It is a dangerous way*. So intent on engineering the
destruction of others (v. 16), they make victims out of themselves (v. 19). In this darkness of their own deeds they will not
even see what their foot strikes on that final, fatal step which
sends them plunging to destruction (see Ps. 73:18). This figure
for the ruin of the wicked is developed most fully and pictu-
resquely in Job 18:7–12. Jeremiah also uses it when he warns
the corrupt religious leaders of his day, of God's impending
judgment:

> Therefore their way shall be to them
>   like slippery paths in the darkness,
>   into which they shall be driven and fall.
>   (Jer. 23:12; see also Jer. 13:16; Isa. 59:9–10; Hos. 4:5)

(iii)

These then are the two ways. There is no third, middle way; far
less "labyrinthine ways", any one of which the traveller might
venture along as the fancy takes him. The fool only thinks there
are (see 12:15; 14:12). But the ways are forked; and so a *choice
of direction* has to be made (see Jer. 6:16).

The theme of the two ways serves as a warning against the
modern tendency to fudge the edges between right and wrong.
At the same time, we may feel a little uneasy with its very tidy

but rather simplistic division of people into two camps: the righteous and the wicked. It is apt to remind us a little of the line of the nursery rhyme: "When she was good she was very good, but when she was bad she was awful". But we should notice that the theme is used by the sage essentially as a teaching aid, and we have to allow that he has simplified matters in order to present his teaching as clearly and effectively as possible. In his hands the theme served well to impress upon his students that the ways of wisdom and folly (1) bear quite different practical fruits in the *life styles* of those who follow in them (cf. Matt. 7:17–19; Gal. 5:19–23), and (2) lead in quite different *directions,* one towards fullness of life and the other towards death (cf. 8:35–36; see the comment on 3:16, 18; 5:5–6). But above all, it served to impress upon them (3) how urgent it was for them to obey his words (v. 10), and so to *choose* the wise way (v. 13) and avoid the foolish way (v. 14). The Book of Deuteronomy also uses the theme of two ways, to the same effect (30:15–20), and Jesus takes it a step further at the end of the Sermon on the Mount (Matt. 7:13–14). The related contrast between walking in light and walking in darkness also finds its fullest explanation in the person and words of Jesus (John 1:4; 8:12; 11:9–10; see also Eph. 5:7–14; 1 Pet. 2:9), and it finds its most telling application in how we treat one another (1 John 2:8–11).

(iv)

It will be noticed that in Matt. 7:13–14 narrowness is connected with the way of life and broadness with the way of destruction. That is the opposite to what we find here. The way of life is the broad, spacious way that has roominess. But to correct any mistaken impression that this means the traveller is in for a comfortable stroll through life, verses 20–25 emphasize that this way calls for constant vigilance, self-discipline, and single-ness of mind and purpose. This is set out in a run-down of various parts of the body: the heart (v. 23), the mouth (v. 24), the eyes (v. 25) and the feet (v. 26). When they are healthy the whole body is healthy (v. 22). These verses can be contrasted with 6:16–18.

BEWARE THE SEDUCTRESS!

Proverbs 5:1–14

> [1]My son, be attentive to my wisdom,
>   incline your ear to my understanding;
> [2]that you may keep discretion,
>   and your lips may guard knowledge.
> [3]For the lips of a loose woman drip honey,
>   and her speech is smoother than oil;
> [4]but in the end she is bitter as wormwood,
>   sharp as a two-edged sword.
> [5]Her feet go down to death;
>   her steps follow the path to Sheol;
> [6]she does not take heed to the path of life;
>   her ways wander, and she does not know it.
>
> [7]And now, O sons, listen to me,
>   and do not depart from the words
>   of my mouth.
> [8]Keep your way far from her,
>   and do not go near the door of her house;
> [9]lest you give your honour to others
>   and your years to the merciless;
> [10]lest strangers take their fill of your strength,
>   and your labours go to the house of an alien;
> [11]and at the end of your life you groan,
>   when your flesh and body are consumed,
> [12]and you say, "How I hated discipline,
>   and my heart despised reproof!
> [13]I did not listen to the voice of my teachers
>   or incline my ear to my instructors.
> [14]I was at the point of utter ruin
>   in the assembled congregation."

This chapter enlarges on the theme of the seductress introduced in 2:16–19. The theme is also developed at length in 6:24–35 and 7:1–27. The space given to it and the vigour with which the destructive powers of the seductress are portrayed leave us in no doubt that the sage saw in her the greatest hazard lying in the path of young men. The Egyptian sages also warned their students against her. But since they were training young men for successful careers, their ethic of sexual morality was primarily an ethic for men in public life. They were anxious to point out that nothing can ruin a promising career so quickly as an illicit affair. That has still a modern ring to it, even in our more tolerant times. The sage of Proverbs, however, takes a deeper and more serious view of the matter. He is teaching his pupils wisdom for living, and in these passages he is anxious to warn that to meddle around with this woman is the height of folly, for her kiss is the kiss of death.

(i)

Though the situation is not always clear and seems to vary slightly from passage to passage, the seductress appears to be a married woman who behaves like a common prostitute, either for a fee or to gratify her own desires. She is regularly described as a "loose woman" and an "adventuress" (vv. 3, 20; see also 2:16; 6:24; 7:5). These words actually mean "strange woman" and "foreign woman", neither of which are the normal terms for an adulteress or prostitute. Does this mean that she is a non-Israelite? Away from home, a foreign woman would not be subject to the restraints of her own community nor to those imposed by Israelite society. She would therefore be free to indulge in this kind of behaviour if she so wished. The Egyptian sage is thinking of this kind of woman when he warns his pupils:

> Be on thy guard against a woman from abroad, who is not known in her [own] town . . . Do not know her carnally: a deep water, whose windings one knows not, a woman who is far away from her husband . . . She has no witnesses when she waits to ensnare thee.

But while something of the sort may lie behind the use of these terms, and most prostitutes in Israel may have been foreign woman, they probably intend that the woman belongs to another man rather than that she necessarily comes from another country. The New International Version translates the terms, "adulteress" and "wayward wife".

At all events, she is a very persuasive lady, well practised in the art of seduction. That is what makes her so dangerous. Although she knows how to make good use of her natural sex appeal to entice her victim (6:25), it is upon her honeyed words and seductive speech that she relies most. We have an example of the kind of things she says in 7:14–20. Her words have the sweetness of honey and the smoothness of oil (v. 3; see also 2:16; 6:24; 7:5, 21).

(a) *She is a sweet talker.* Honey was used by housewives to make food more palatable and was proverbial for its sweetness (16:24; 24:13–14; Judg. 14:18; Rev. 10:9–10). Delicious words, full of delectable promise, flow easily from her lips to titillate the taste buds and whet the appetite of her victim until he is completely entranced and captivated by her. In the Song of Solomon 4:11 the same figure is used of the bride's kisses.

(b) *She is a smooth talker.* The half-hearted resistance of her victim's better judgment is no bar against this woman's wiles. A little coaxing, a little flattery, a little deceit, above all the assurance that it is all completely harmless, and her prey is well and truly caught.

So the seductress holds out promise of pleasure and enjoyment more than enough to entice and captivate hot blooded young men. The reality, however, is something quite different. There is an old saying, "Honey is sweet, but the bee stings"; and this lady has a sting in her tail.

(ii)

The sting in the tail ("in the end", v. 4) comes in verses 4–6. Notice the stark contrast in verses 3 and 4 between "honey" and "wormwood", and "smoother" and "sharp". Wormwood, a type of plant, was as proverbial for bitterness as honey was for sweetness (see Jer. 9:15; Lam. 3:15; Amos 5:7; Rev. 8:10–11). Here is the lady in her true colours: (1) her honeyed words leave a bitter taste, and (2) her smooth words prove to be the thrusts of a razor-sharp sword (cf. Ps. 55:21). She is a merciless, implacable foe. There is bitter disillusionment here. The experience was not as pleasurable as she had promised. "Never again!", says he; but he will be back, expecting this time it will be. There is also the bitter and sharp pangs of remorse given voice to by the victim in verses 12–14. But this lady's sword has more than one edge; and as verses 5–6 make clear, becoming entangled in her ways leads to more than a bad taste in the mouth and a bad conscience. The seductress is travelling on the road to death, the path to Sheol (see 2:18–19; 7:27, and the comment on 1:12), reeling with the unsteady step of a drunkard, from lover to lover, obstinately blind to (or not giving a fig for: "What does she care?" NEB, v.6) the wrong she does and the harm she brings upon herself and her lovers (cf. 30:20). She is plunging recklessly to her ruin, and she is taking her victims with her. The Authorized Version renders Sheol by "hell", but in Old Testament times Sheol was not thought of as a place of torment and punishment, but as a place of inactivity and death. The seductress's path of death is the opposite of wisdom's path of life. Just as wisdom's path makes life rich and full and really worth living, and leads to ripeness of age (see comment on 3:13–18), so the seductress's path impoverishes life and robs it of meaning, and leads in the end to an untimely death.

The impoverished life of the man who becomes entangled with her is spelled out in frank and sober terms in verses 10–14. It is the antithesis of wisdom's benediction in 3:13–18. In short, he is a destroyed man—personally and socially. He loses every shred of dignity and the respect of his neighbours (v. 9); wastes all his resources—material, physical and mental (vv. 10–11); is filled with remorse when he learns too late how foolish he has been (vv. 12–13), and is exposed to public disgrace (v. 14). Perhaps behind the scenes is the woman's husband (cf. 6:34–35), denouncing the offender in a public assembly (v. 14) and pressing for as much compensation as he can get (v. 10). The irony of it all is that his energy and hard-won resources serve only to benefit a cruel-hearted woman and her family and associates, while he and his family lose out in every possible way.

More than the figurative language of verses 4–6, what the sage says in verses 10–14 carries a powerful appeal to young men living, as his pupils did, in a close-knit community, and would encourage them to weigh the transient pleasure against its terrible consequences, and ask: "Is it worth it?" This may not be the most searching question to ask, but wisdom dwells in prudence (8:12) as well as being founded on the fear of the Lord (1:7). Wisdom will always weigh up the consequences of an action before acting. Although nowadays this kind of behaviour is very often condoned and the greater sin is being caught out, adultery still exacts a high price in damaged relationships, broken homes, and hurt, lonely people.

(iii)

The seductress, then, is a very persuasive and very dangerous woman. The only safe course of action is to keep well away from her (v. 8; cf. 1:10, 15). This advice is well illustrated by the story of Joseph's escapade in Genesis 39, when he has to run away from the seductress as fast as he can, leaving his shirt-tail behind him. But better still, if you can help it, don't get near enough to let her grab your shirt-tail! And this is as much a matter of what we look at (see 4:25; Job 31:1; Matt. 5:28) and what we read, as where we go.

REJOICE IN THE WIFE OF YOUR YOUTH

Proverbs 5:15–23

15Drink water from your own cistern,
   flowing water from your own well.
16Should your springs be scattered abroad,
   streams of water in the streets?
17Let them be for yourself alone,
   and not for strangers with you.
18Let your fountain be blessed,
   and rejoice in the wife of your youth,

¹⁹a lovely hind, a graceful doe.
    Let her affection fill you at all times with delight,
    be infatuated always with her love.
²⁰Why should you be infatuated, my son,
        with a loose woman
    and embrace the bosom of an adventuress?
²¹For a man's ways are before the eyes of the Lord,
    and he watches all his paths.
²²The iniquities of the wicked ensnare him,
    and he is caught in the toils of his sin.
²³He dies for lack of discipline,
    and because of his great folly he is lost.

(i)

While the previous section had most in mind young unmarried men, this one is addressed to the married man, and advises him that the best antidote against the destructive wiles of the seductress is to remain in love with his wife and to keep alight the flame of romance in his marriage.

The Bible is often thought to take a rather dim view of sexual relations and to tolerate them as the means of procreation and no more. But that is a distortion which tells us more about the sexual hang-ups of some of its past interpreters than about what the Bible actually says on the subject. Here we have a passage which speaks enthusiastically about the joys and delights of the sexual relation between husband and wife. Enjoyment, not procreation, is its theme. This theme is taken up in the Song of Solomon, that lovely celebration of human love and fidelity between bride and bridegroom. As in that best of love songs, the language in this passage is frank and earthy, yet sensitive in its eroticism. Imagery connected with water is delicately used to express the pleasure and satisfaction a man ought to obtain through sexual intercourse with his wife (vv. 15, 18; cf. Song of Solomon 4:12, 15) in contrast to the waste which results when he is unfaithful to her (vv. 16–17). Compared to a love affair with a warm and loving wife, consorting with a cold and calculating woman is a poor counterfeit (vv. 19–20); for instead of being a physical *relation* between two people which expresses and deepens love, commitment and companionship, as God intended it to be and provided for (Gen. 2:18–24), sex is corrupted into a *thing* she gives and he gets, and so it is robbed of true meaning and fulfilment. This debased view of sex as a thing in itself, to be indulged in, played around with, and enjoyed quite separately from a faithful relationship of love and responsibility, is being insidiously promoted today as never before, and we cannot be too much on our guard against it.

(ii)

So far in this chapter the sage has appealed for a prudent weighing up of the consequences as a deterrent against becoming involved with loose women: it is simply not worth it, for there is everything to lose and nothing to gain. In verse 21, however, he shifts into a higher gear. While the foolish man may take steps to hide his sordid affair from the eyes of others (7:9; cf. Job 24:15) and may put all thought of God out of his mind, God's all-seeing eye is upon him, watching and observing, weighing and judging (see 15:3; Job 31:4; 34:21; Heb. 4:13).

But there is no thunderbolt from heaven to strike him down. Rather, by threading his path to folly's door he is threading a noose around his own neck, like a senseless bird weaving the net which will ensnare it (vv. 22–23: see 1:17–19, which are similar in thought). If we follow the New English Bible in verse 23, this foolish man weaves more than the tangled web which traps him; he also weaves his funeral shroud: "he will perish for want of discipline, wrapped in the shroud of his boundless folly". The word "wrapped in the shroud" (RSV "lost") is the same word the RSV translates "infatuated" in verses 19 and 20, but which the New English Bible renders "wrapped". So it appears that the sage makes a play on this word as the key word to underline and drive home the lesson to be learned: wrap up well in the love of your wife (v. 19), and don't become wrapped up with loose women (v. 20), for that is as good as wrapping yourself in a funeral shroud (v. 23).

TROUBLEMAKERS AND TROUBLEMAKING

Proverbs 6:12-19

12A worthless person, a wicked man,
   goes about with crooked speech,
13winks with his eyes, scrapes with his feet,
   points with his finger,
14with perverted heart devises evil,
   continually sowing discord;
15therefore calamity will come upon him suddenly;
   in a moment he will be broken beyond healing.

16There are six things which the Lord hates,
   seven which are an abomination to him:
17haughty eyes, a lying tongue,
   and hands that shed innocent blood,
18a heart that devises wicked plans,
   feet that make haste to run to evil,
19a false witness who breathes out lies,
   and a man who sows discord among brothers.

(N.B. For comment on 6:1–5 see the topic, *Underwriting Debts;* for comment on 6:6–11 see the topic, *The Sluggard*)

Like verses 1–11, verses 12–19 are more reminiscent of the proverbial sayings in chapters 10–31 than the discourses in chapters 1–9. The description of the troublemaker in verses 12–15, however, does pick up and amplify the description of evil men given in 2:12–15. Again the theme is his "twistedness" in word (v. 12) and thought (v. 14). The rather amusing description of his antics in verse 13 may suggest that he casts magic spells to accomplish his evil designs, or may simply allude to the covert and underhand way he goes about his business of destroying harmonious relations in the community and creating strife (v. 14). Verse 15 affirms that he will go the way of all fools (see comment on 1:24–33).

In verses 16–19 we have a graded numerical saying of a kind quite common in the Old Testament as well as in ancient Near

Eastern literature generally (see the comment on ch.30, *Observations on Nature and Society*). So in a Ugaritic myth about the god Baal we find this striking parallel to these verses:

> Truly there are two sacrifices Baal hates,
> three the rider on the clouds—
> a sacrifice of shame and a sacrifice of meanness
> and a sacrifice where handmaids debauch.

The saying complements verses 12–15 by listing the kind of disruptive activities the troublemaker indulges in. Notice that here, in contrast to 4:20–27, we have a run-down of an unhealthy body: "eyes . . . tongue . . . hands . . . heart . . . feet". Many of the proverbial sayings in chapters 10–31 deal with the troublemaker and his troublemaking, and we will hear much more about him and his nefarious activities later (see, especially, the topics, *The Mischief-Maker; The Liar, The Flatterer and the Slanderer*).

THE CASE AGAINST THE SEDUCTRESS

Proverbs 6:20–35

> 20My son, keep your father's commandment,
> and forsake not your mother's teaching.
> 21Bind them upon your heart always;
> tie them about your neck.
> 22When you walk, they will lead you;
> when you lie down, they will watch over you;
> and when you awake, they will talk with you.
> 23For the commandment is a lamp and the teaching a light,
> and the reproofs of discipline are the way of life,
> 24to preserve you from the evil woman,
> from the smooth tongue of the adventuress.
> 25Do not desire her beauty in your heart,
> and do not let her capture you with her eyelashes;
> 26for a harlot may be hired for a loaf of bread,
> but an adulteress stalks a man's very life.

²⁷Can a man carry fire in his bosom
  and his clothes not be burned?
²⁸Or can one walk upon hot coals
  and his feet not be scorched?
²⁹So is he who goes in to his neighbour's wife;
  none who touches her will go unpunished.
³⁰Do not men despise a thief if he steals
  to satisfy his appetite when he is hungry?
³¹And if he is caught, he will pay seven-fold;
  he will give all the goods of his house.
³²He who commits adultery has no sense;
  he who does it destroys himself.
³³Wounds and dishonour will he get,
  and his disgrace will not be wiped away.
³⁴For jealousy makes a man furious,
  and he will not spare when he takes revenge.
³⁵He will accept no compensation,
  nor be appeased though you multiply gifts.

(i)

Of the three passages where the sage treats this topic at length
(chs. 5–7), this is the most carefully reasoned. In it he argues the
case against the adulteress. He asks his pupils to consider the
matter from various angles; for if they just stop to think a while
and use a little common sense, they will see that succumbing to
her charms is sheer stupidity (v. 32).

The appeal in verse 20 suggests that once again the teacher is
deliberately latching on to and reinforcing in the classroom the
lesson his pupils have been taught in the home (see the comment
on 4:1–9). There is always a temptation for young people to
think they have outgrown the home truths they were taught as
children, when they come of age. But their parents' teaching,
says the sage, if taken to heart and kept in clear view, will prove
a reliable guide, a watchful guard, and an agreeable companion
(vv. 21–22—on the parents' part in this, see the comment on
4:1–9, and the topic, *Parental Discipline*). Indeed, it will be light
and life for them, because it will preserve them from becoming
entangled with the adulteress and reaping the terrible consequences (vv.23–24).

These verses recall earlier statements about the value of wisdom teaching and the need to take it to heart (see 1:8; 3:1–4, 21–24; 4:18). Verses 20–22, together with 3:1–3 and 7:1–3, also recall similar statements concerning God's commandments in Deuteronomy 6:6–8, and also 11:18–19:

> You shall therefore lay up these words of mine in your heart and in your soul; and you shall bind them as a sign upon your hand, and they shall be as frontlets between your eyes. And you shall teach them to your children, talking of them when you are sitting in your house, and when you are walking by the way, and when you lie down, and when you rise.

The commandments of the wise, like the commandments of God, must become part of the air they breathe and the jewellery they adorn themselves with, from morning till evening, at work and at rest. The Jews took the two passages in Deuteronomy literally, and this gave rise to the practice of wearing *tephilim* or phylacteries at morning prayers.

Nevertheless, despite this close parallel, we ought again to remind ourselves that the sage is still speaking in the idiom of the "old rules", and not of divine commandments (see the comment on 3:1–2). His teaching in the passage can indeed be seen as a commentary on the fifth commandment (Exod. 20:14)—but not in the idiom of God's "Thou shall not . . .", but rather of experiences's "Do not adultery commit; Advantage rarely comes of it" (Arthur Clough, *The Latest Decalogue.*)

(ii)

In verse 25 the sage's advice is crisp and to the point. The word "desire" is the same translated "covet" in the tenth commandment (Exod. 20:17). Here it may have the stronger meaning "to lust after" (NIV). In Jesus' teaching on the subject, the sin in thought is equated with the sin in deed (Matt. 5:27–28). The second part of the verse may refer to her eye make-up or her inviting glances. Ben Sirach probably has both in mind when he says, "A wife's harlotry shows in her lustful eyes, and she is known by her eyelids" (Ecclesiasticus 26:9).

(iii)

The sage now gets down to arguing the case against the adulteress to back up his advice. He does this by comparing her to the prostitute, to playing with fire, and to the thief. In a word, there is a price to be paid, and it is a high one at that.

(a) *The prostitute* (v. 26). The point of this comparison is none too clear. The meaning of the *first* part of the verse is obscured by a very elliptical expression resting on a very problematical preposition. A rather free paraphrase is required to make it yield sense. The modern versions are divided between the meanings: (1) a prostitute costs a man only the price of her fee (RSV, NEB, TEV), and (2) a prostitute brings a man to poverty (AV, NIV). The *second* part of the verse is clearer. The adulteress makes a prey of a man's very life. The imagery of the adulteress as a huntress is developed in 7:22–23. So the point of the comparison is either (1) that in comparison to a prostitute an adulteress exacts a heavy price, or (2) both the prostitute and the adulteress cost a man dearly. The former is certainly a much more vigorous way of emphasizing the perils of adultery. We might feel that it makes the sage take too light a view of prostitution. As a matter of fact, in the Old Testament, the common prostitute is never outrightly condemned. She is there, tacitly accepted as part of the scenery of life, although never condoned. The Old Testament reserves its condemnation for *sacral prostitution* (which made its way into Israel's worship from the Canaanite fertility cults of the day and thoroughly corrupted it; see Deut. 23:17; 2 Kings 23:7; Hos. 4:14), and for *adultery.* They were considered the most dangerous; for sacral prostitution attacked the fabric of religious life and destroyed relations with God, while adultery was targeted on the fabric of social life and destroyed family relations as well. The New Testament is clear and solemn in its warning against all forms of sexual immorality (1 Cor. 6:13–20; Gal. 5:19–21; Eph 5:5; 1 Thess. 4:1–8). But whichever way we take the comparison, the point being made is crystal clear: adultery is a costly business.

(b) *Playing with fire* (vv. 27–29). As in 1:17, the sage again appeals to a popular proverb to clinch his argument. A word-play in the Hebrew hammers the point home: to play around with another man's "wife" (*eshet*) is to play with "fire" (*esh*)! And the foolish man will burn more than his fingertips!

(c) *The thief* (vv. 30–35). Verse 30 can be translated either as a question (RSV, NEB), or as a statement (AV, NIV, TEV). If it is a question, verses 30–33 are (1) saying that the thief who steals because he is hungry is still a despicable fellow, and if he is caught he will be made to pay the penalty *in full* ("seven-fold", see Exod. 22:1–9 where the limit is actually five-fold); and (2) saying how much more despicable is the adulterer, and how much more certainly he will be made to pay up to the hilt, for he has no excuse for his behaviour.

On the other hand, if it is a statement the point of the contrast is quite different: (1) people take a lenient view of the thief in such circumstances, and once he has made complete restitution do not treat him as a social leper; (2) but the adulterer has no mitigating circumstances to tell in his favour, and will suffer lasting disgrace. Although the thief would much prefer to think verse 30 makes a statement, either way the adulterer loses.

But the adulterer has not only to reckon with public disgrace. He also has to reckon with the anger of a jealous husband. Whether verses 33–35 envisage the enraged husband taking the adulterer to court or taking the law into his own hands, is unclear. In any case, he will not be bought off, and will exact a higher price than money. He is out for blood!

WHEN THE HUSBAND'S AWAY...!

Proverbs 7:1–27

> ¹My son, keep my words
>   and treasure up my commandments with you;
> ²keep my commandments and live,
>   keep my teachings as the apple of your eye;
> ³bind them on your fingers,
>   write them on the tablet of your heart.

⁴Say to wisdom, "You are my sister,"
  and call insight your intimate friend;
⁵to preserve you from the loose woman,
  from the adventuress with her smooth words.

⁶For at the window of my house
  I have looked out through my lattice,
⁷and I have seen among the simple,
  I have perceived among the youths,
  a young man without sense,
⁸passing along the street near her corner,
  taking the road to her house
⁹in the twilight, in the evening,
  at the time of night and darkness.

¹⁰And lo, a woman meets him,
  dressed as a harlot, wily of heart.
¹¹She is loud and wayward,
  her feet do not stay at home;
¹²now in the street, now in the market,
  and at every corner she lies in wait.
¹³She seizes him and kisses him,
  and with impudent face she says to him:
¹⁴"I had to offer sacrifices,
  and today I have paid my vows;
¹⁵so now I have come out to meet you,
  to seek you eagerly, and I have found you.
¹⁶I have decked my couch with coverings,
  coloured spreads of Egyptian linen;
¹⁷I have perfumed my bed with myrrh,
  aloes, and cinnamon.
¹⁸Come, let us take our fill of love till morning;
  let us delight ourselves with love.
¹⁹For my husband is not at home;
  he has gone on a long journey;
²⁰he took a bag of money with him;
  at full moon he will come home."

²¹With much seductive speech she persuades him;
  with her smooth talk she compels him.

²²All at once he follows her,
    as an ox goes to the slaughter,
    or as a stag is caught fast
²³till an arrow pierces its entrails;
    as a bird rushes into a snare;
    he does not know that it will cost him his life.

²⁴And now, O sons, listen to me,
    and be attentive to the words of my mouth.
²⁵Let not your heart turn aside to her ways,
    do not stray into her paths;
²⁶for many a victim has she laid low;
    yea, all her slain are a mighty host.
²⁷Her house is the way to Sheol,
    going down to the chambers of death.

(i)

Just in case there are any lingering doubts about the perils of the seductress, the sage has a little story to tell. But first he repeats his plea for his students to take his teaching to heart (vv. 1–5) in much the same terms as 6:20–24. "Apple of your eye" (v. 2) is a quaint expression in the Hebrew. It is literally "the little man of your eye". It refers to the reflection we see of ourselves when we look into the pupils of someone's eyes. The thought here is explained by 6:23. Light comes through the pupil, and without it there is only darkness. So the pupil needs to be carefully guarded. The advice to claim wisdom as a "sister" is worth noting. This again reflects the tendency to personify wisdom. The word sister can sometimes mean "bride" (Song 4:9–10), and so the intention may be to suggest that Lady Wisdom is the true wife and lover in contrast with the spurious and dangerous love of the seductress. As we shall see, this contrast is brought out rather effectively in chapter 8.

(ii)

The story is presented as what the sage saw from the window of his house. This is part of the story. The sage's window looks out to the world, and he has seen this kind of thing many times before. But for dramatic effect he speaks, as all good story-tellers speak, about "once upon a time". The story develops through three scenes:

(a) *The first scene* (vv. 6–9). A young man makes his way through the darkening streets, hugging the shadows. From verse 9 we can almost feel the impending darkness closing in, threatening. It is a dark scene in every way. He is going in the direction of "her house". By chance? Probably not, although the Hebrew in verse 8 could imply a rather aimless saunter. He knows where he is headed (or thinks he does!); but he is in unfamiliar territory and is more curious than purposeful. He is not a downright immoral fellow (he takes some persuading, v. 21), but he is a downright stupid one (v. 7). This is the "simple" in all his simplicity (see the comment on 1:4, 22). Unknown to him, a wise man is peering out of his window watching him: silent, thoughtful, always learning, and knowing only too well what is going to happen.

(b) *The second scene* (vv. 10–20). Soon the young fellow is stopped by a woman whose dress shows that she at least is not aimlessly walking the streets. She is on familiar territory; an old hand at the game, well-used to hunting down young fellows at street corners. This is her real home ground (vv. 11–12). The die is already as good as cast, for she is a consummate persuader. The wise man overhears the sweet and smooth words she deploys, the chief weapons in her arsenal. She flatters him (v. 15), tells him she has a sumptuous bed for them to luxuriate in (vv. 16–17) and, very importantly, assures him that there is no chance of her husband returning unexpectedly to catch them (vv. 19–20). And what better way to start the evening than by a candlelit dinner for two (v. 14; see Lev. 7:16. The meat of this offering was shared as a meal).

(c) *The third scene* (vv. 21–23). The young fellow is like putty in her hands. He finds her quite irresistible. Soon his head is filled with fantasies of a night of pleasure. He hesitates—he knows he really shouldn't—then suddenly ("all at once"), his mind is made up. He follows her. To her house? To the vestibule of Sheol! (v. 27) For a night of pleasure? For his own funeral!

One more animal to the slaughter; one more bird caught in the trap! One more fool consigned to a living death. Her poisoned arrow has found its mark.

The lesson is unmistakable (vv. 24–27; see the comment on 5:8).

(iii)

The story is told in bold lines. The seductress is blacker than black, and the young fellow is by comparison a pale shade of white. It is a scenario which rings true enough—not all young men would have had the good sense and resolve of Joseph to run away (Gen. 39). But interestingly enough, the only story of adultery in the Old Testament gives a quite different scenario (2 Sam. 11:2–4). The blame is laid squarely at David's door (12:1–14). So as a lesson on the perils of seduction, the sage's teaching is one-sided. That is simply because he is addressing young men. Doubtless parents would have cautioned their daughters against the hunter, as well as their sons against the huntress.

LADY WISDOM PUTS HER CASE

Proverbs 8:1–21

> [1]Does not wisdom call,
>   does not understanding raise her voice?
> [2]On the heights beside the way,
>   in the paths she takes her stand;
> [3]beside the gates in front of the town,
>   at the entrance of the portals she cries aloud:
> [4]"To you, O men, I call,
>   and my cry is to the sons of men.
> [5]O simple ones, learn prudence;
>   O foolish men, pay attention.
> [6]Hear, for I will speak noble things,
>   and from my lips will come what is right;

⁷for my mouth will utter truth;
    wickedness is an abomination to my lips.
⁸All the words of my mouth are righteous;
    there is nothing twisted or crooked in them.
⁹They are all straight to him who understands
    and right to those who find knowledge.
¹⁰Take my instruction instead of silver,
    and knowledge rather than choice gold;
¹¹for wisdom is better than jewels,
    and all that you may desire cannot compare with her.
¹²I, wisdom, dwell in prudence,
    and I find knowledge and discretion.
¹³The fear of the Lord is hatred of evil.
    Pride and arrogance and the way of evil
    and perverted speech I hate.
¹⁴I have counsel and sound wisdom,
    I have insight, I have strength.
¹⁵By me kings reign,
    and rulers decree what is just;
¹⁶by me princes rule,
    and nobles govern the earth.
¹⁷I love those who love me,
    and those who seek me diligently find me.
¹⁸Riches and honour are with me,
    enduring wealth and prosperity.
¹⁹My fruit is better than gold, even fine gold.
    and my yield than choice silver.
²⁰I walk in the way of righteousness,
    in the paths of justice,
²¹endowing with wealth those who love me,
    and filling their treasuries."

Once again Lady Wisdom takes her stand in the city streets and at the city gate and cries aloud, calling upon men everywhere, the simple and the foolish especially, to pay attention and to receive her counsel (vv. 1–5, 32–36; see 1:20–33). Once more there is the note of urgent appeal and the suggestion that a critical decision has to be made. But since Lady Wisdom last raised her voice in the city streets, a deeper urgency has been lent to her words. It has now become clear that she has to compete not only with the activities and distractions of daily life and wilful folly, but also with the seductive voice of the loose woman, who lurks "now in the street, now in the market, and at every corner" (7:12), waiting to seize her victims. So Lady Wisdom and the seductress rub shoulders in the crowded streets, vying for the attention and embrace of the simple and the foolish (cf. 9:1–6, 13–18). Lady Wisdom sees in the seductress her greatest rival for men's affections, and this *femme fatale* seems to be at the back of her mind throughout the whole of this chapter as she sings her own praises loudly and eloquently. Notice that the note of reproach and condemnation so prominent in her earlier speech is lacking in this one.

The overriding concern of Lady Wisdom in this long speech is to recommend herself to men as serving their best interests, and as worthy of their undivided faithfulness and obedience. This is designed to encourage the wisdom seeker to pursue wisdom more earnestly and to value it more highly, as well as to convince the doubter. In verses 6–21 Lady Wisdom recommends herself on four counts:

(a) *Her words* (vv. 6–9). Much has been said about the perverse words of evil men and the honeyed words of loose women, which are fired at young men from all sides like poisoned arrows. But it has also been frankly recognized that the poison is in the tail and not the tip of their arrows; for they make their words sound attractive and offer their victims satisfaction of their every desire. This puts Lady Wisdom at a disadvantage. When she speaks, the attraction is in the tail and not the tip. For she has some hard things to say and some uncomfortable truths to tell, and she talks about self-discipline and not self-indulgence. The emphasis in these verses can best be seen in the light of this contrast. Deception, duplicity and perverseness mark the words of evil men and wayward women; straightforwardness, forthrightness and integrity mark the words of Lady Wisdom. She will not even stoop to bending the truth a little to make her point, far less to curry favour—a temptation all preachers face from time to time. She speaks in plain language, which can be understood where there is a willingness to understand (v. 9), and which can always be implicitly trusted. Moreover, what she says guides men in right paths (v. 20), and leads to life and God's approval (8:35).

(b) *Her value* (vv. 10–11). The pricelessness of wisdom is a theme we have met already, especially in 3:14–15 (v. 11 is almost identical with 3:15). Notice that this is a comment interjected by the teacher (Wisdom is referred to in the third person) and not part of Lady Wisdom's speech.

(c) *Her statecraft* (vv. 12–16). Here we find some old words and expressions (vv. 12–14) in a new context (vv. 15–16). In fact, verses 12–14 sound very much like a resume of 1:2–7 ["prudence . . . knowledge . . . discretion" (1:4); "fear of the Lord" (1:7); "insight" (1:2)] with 2:7 ("sound wisdom") and 1:25 ("counsel") thrown in for good measure. It is only to be expected that Lady Wisdom should lay claim to possess and bestow all of these things. But the novelty of this passage is where they are operative; in the able and just rule of the kings and princes of the earth. There is nothing parochial about Lady Wisdom. The universality of her sway matches the universality of her appeal (v. 4). Nor is there anything snobbish about her. The Wisdom who holds sway in the palace of kings offers herself to the man in the street.

Not only in Israel but in the ancient Near East generally, wisdom was closely allied with kingly rule. We see this particularly well in the story of king Solomon (see the comment on 1:1). In this connection the synonyms of "wisdom" in verses 12–14 take on the colouring of the hard-headed skills of statecraft and diplomacy a King needs in order to conduct the affairs of state efficiently and effectively, and especially of the perceptiveness he needs to govern justly; for that was above all the mark of a wise king (see the topic, *The Measure of a King*). The role which Lady Wisdom claims for herself in these verses is that of a royal counsellor, rather than a king. We can compare her to David's counsellor Ahithophel, whose counsel was reported to be "as if one consulted the oracle of God" (2 Sam. 16:23). Although the "fear of the Lord" (v. 13) nicely balances the earthy, hard-headedness of verses 12 and 14, some commentators feel that it does not suit the context very well and think it is a later addition. The New English Bible omits the first line. The verse certainly fits in better with verses 6-9 ("perverted speech 1 hate"), and it may have been displaced when the manuscripts were being copied by hand.

(d) *Her fruit* (vv. 17-21). This description of Lady Wisdom's "fruit" (v. 19) is closely paralleled by 3:13-18. But here it is underlined even more strongly that Lady Wisdom's most important bounty is not a full bank account, but first and foremost her unfailing faithfulness (v. 17) and her guidance in right paths (v. 20).

In verses 22-31 Lady Wisdom adds a fifth reason. But this is such an important passage it deserves a section to itself.

LADY WISDOM: THE FIRST OF GOD'S WORKS

Proverbs 8:22-36

> [22]"The Lord created me at the beginning of his work,
>   the first of his acts of old.
> [23]Ages ago I was set up,
>   at the first, before the beginning of the earth.
> [24]When there were no depths I was brought forth,
>   when there were no springs abounding with water.
> [25]Before the mountains had been shaped,
>   before the hills, I was brought forth;
> [26]before he had made the earth with its fields,
>   or the first of the dust of the world.
> [27]When he established the heavens, I was there,
>   when he drew a circle on the face of the deep,
> [28]when he made firm the skies above,
>   when he established the fountains of the deep,
> [29]when he assigned to the sea its limit,
>   so that the waters might not transgress his command,
>   when he marked out the foundations of the earth,
> [30]then I was beside him, like a master workman;
>   and I was daily his delight,
>   rejoicing before him always,

³¹rejoicing in his inhabited world
  and delighting in the sons of men.

³²And now, my sons, listen to me:
  happy are those who keep my ways.
³³Hear instruction and be wise,
  and do not neglect it.
³⁴Happy is the man who listens to me,
  watching daily at my gates,
  waiting beside my doors.
³⁵For he who finds me finds life
  and obtains favour from the Lord;
³⁶but he who misses me injures himself;
  all who hate me love death."

The tantalizing glimpse of wisdom given in 3:19–20 now breaks into a majestic panorama as Lady Wisdom opens out to view her relation to God and her place in his creative work. It is Lady Wisdom's final word on the credentials which authorize her to hold out promise of life and blessing to her finders, and death to those who miss her (vv. 35–36). However, as we shall see, it was not to be the last word on the subject; for this passage became the fountain head for several streams of thought on the nature and character of the Wisdom which speaks in it.

(i)

The statements in the passage about God's creation of the world echo the familiar story in Genesis 1, together with more hymnic celebrations of God as creator, such as the ones found in Psalm 104:5–13 and Job 38:4–18. However, unlike these passages, here it is not God the creator but Lady Wisdom who occupies the centre of the stage. In verses 22–26 she describes her origins as lying in the remotest antiquity before the creation of the world, and then in verses 27–31 she moves on to describe the part she played at God's side when he created the world.

Unfortunately the good Lady begins and ends on an ambiguous note, as a glance at verses 22 and 30 in other versions quickly reveals.

(a) There are three ways of taking the first phrase of verse 22: (1) "The Lord possessed me" (AV, NIV), (2) "The Lord created me" (RSV, NEB), or (3) "The Lord brought me forth" (*ie* "begot", NIV footnote). The problematic word is *quanah*. Basically it means to "acquire", and so to "possess". It is most often used of acquiring through purchasing (Gen. 47:20), but can also be used of acquiring through creating (Gen. 14:19) or begetting (cf. Gen. 4:1). All three translations are therefore possible. Alongside *qanah,* two other words speak of Lady Wisdom's origins: "set up" (v. 23) and "brought forth" (vv. 24-25). The *first* is a rare word of uncertain derivation. The RSV connects it with a root meaning "install, establish", elsewhere found only in Psalm 2:6 in reference to God installing his king on Mount Zion. However the New English Bible translates "fashioned", connecting it with a root found in Job 10:11 and Psalm 139:13, where it means fashioned (RSV "knit together") in the womb. The *second* is a more common word and means "born".

If "possessed" is right (cf. v. 22), then verses 23-25 spell out how God came by her. But the whole tone of the passage might lead us to expect that this verse also says something about her origins. If that is the case, was Lady Wisdom created or begotten by God? Some scholars come down heavily on the side of birth, and take all three expressions the same way ("begot . . . fashioned [in the womb] . . . born"). Lady Wisdom would therefore be presenting herself as a child of God rather than the first of his creative works. While this is possible and attractive, it may be wiser not to press the language into a single mould. If we follow the RSV, Lady Wisdom describes her origins from different standpoints: as created, installed (perhaps with overtones of her royalty), and born. We should notice that the ideas of creation and birth are not nearly so diametrically opposed in Old Testament thought as we might suppose— and as they later became in the Christological controversies of the early Church, as indicated in the phrasing of the Nicene creed "begotten, not made". In the Old Testament, birth can happily be described as an act of creation (Ps. 139:13; cf. Deut. 32:6), and an act of creation just as happily as a birth (Ps. 90:2). The language is in any case poetical and metaphorical, and the choice between created and born is not of terribly great importance. What is central is not the manner of Lady Wisdom's origins so much as her antiquity and precedence within God's creation.

(b) In verses 27–31 Lady Wisdom tells us that she "was there" (v. 27), "beside him" (v. 30) when God created the world. Clearly she was God's intimate companion at creation, but what was she doing? According to the RSV (also NIV) she played the role of a "master workman" (v. 30). We might picture her rolling up her sleeves and helping God to create the world, as his agent and craftsman—much like Bezalel when he was commissioned by God to build the tabernacle and its furniture (Exod. 35:30–31). This picture is perhaps in keeping with 3:19. Later sages certainly saw Wisdom's role in these terms and spoke explicitly about Wisdom as "the fashioner of all things" (Wisdom of Solomon 7:22). The difficulty with this is that there is nothing else in the passage to suggest that Lady Wisdom did anything of that sort. The RSV footnote observes that the word could in fact be "little child" (cf. AV, NEB). In that case we get a quite different picture, and one which is probably more in keeping with the context. Lady Wisdom has already spoken of her birth, and verses 30–31 read much better as a description of a child at play than a craftsman at work. The word "rejoicing" really means "to laugh, play". The same word is used of Lady Wisdom's laughter in 1:26, and of children playing together in the streets in Zechariah 8:5. The picture now is of Lady Wisdom as a child, first bringing pleasure to her father as she played at his feet (v. 30), and then making the world her playground and herself finding peculiar pleasure in his handiwork and in human beings (v. 31).

Although the details are obscure, once again the central point of the verses seems clear enough. Lady Wisdom is at home with God in his grand design of the world, but just as surely she is at home with human beings who live in his world.

(ii)

It turns out that this passage is as tantalizingly obscure as
3:19–20 was brief. At the two key points where Lady Wisdom
speaks of her origins and of her role in creation she succeeds in
hiding as much as she reveals. There is a studied ambiguity
about the whole passage, and it is difficult to escape the
impression that this is deliberate. It seems clear that Lady
Wisdom does not set out to answer the questions we might most
like to ask, and we must resist the temptation to answer them
for her with our eye on some New Testament passages (see the
next section). In any event, the lesson of the passage drawn out
in verses 32–36 is entirely practical: "listen to me: happy are
those who keep my ways" (v. 32). Here speaks a grand old Lady
of noble character and impeccable credentials. For she was
brought forth by God before the world was made, and was
present when it was created. As her ways (playful or skilful)
brought joy to God then, so they now bring happiness and life
to those who follow in them. It would be a pity to let the
ambiguities of verses 22–31 steal the thunder of verses 32–36.

WHO IS LADY WISDOM?

Proverbs 8:22–36 (*cont'd*)

(i)

Throughout chapters 1–9 the figure of Lady Wisdom is boldly
and daringly drawn. She wears a coat of many colours. She
appears like a wisdom teacher giving counsel, a prophet
pronouncing doom, and a hostess fêting her guests (see 9:1–6).
She is a bride to be wooed and a faithful lover, a tree of life; who
leads in straight and peaceful paths and in the fear of the Lord,
and who brings riches and honour in her train. She was brought
forth in the dim and distant past before the world was, and was
God's intimate at creation. She belongs to God and is at home
at his side; yet belongs to the world and is at home in the streets.
What are we to make of all this? Who is Lady Wisdom?

The simple answer is that she is a personification of wisdom. Personification is a literary and poetic device which serves to create atmosphere, and to enliven abstract ideas and inanimate objects by representing them as if they were human beings. It is found elsewhere in the Old Testament, notably in the elevated style of the Psalms (85:10–13; 96:11–12). At the same time, the figure of Lady Wisdom is much more elaborate and goes far beyond anything we find in the Psalms. Evidently Israel's sages found in personified wisdom a very useful figure and developed it beyond the normal bounds of a literary personification in a variety of ways and drawing upon a variety of figures—both traditional Israelite figures like the wisdom teacher and the prophet, and figures further afield (see the comment on 3:16)— to help flesh out and give greater vigour to it. That said, however, the varied colours in which Lady Wisdom is depicted warn us against looking for any simple answer to her identity.

It should be noticed that at all points Lady Wisdom is rooted in the teaching situation. The sage is not indulging in abstract, speculative thought, but always has the wisdom seeker in mind and the need to direct and encourage him in his pursuit of wise living. Even at her most universal (8:4, 15–16) and most exalted (8:22–31), Lady Wisdom reinforces the teacher's appeal to accept his instruction (8:10–11), and slips easily into speaking exactly like a wisdom teacher herself (8:32). There is therefore a close connection between Lady Wisdom and the sage's instruction. Indeed, to keep the sage's commandments and to embrace Lady Wisdom come to the same thing (7:1–4), and the value and rewards of both are the same (cf. 3:1–2 with 3:16–18). Again, the striking depiction of Lady Wisdom as a bride to be wooed and won likewise reinforces the teacher's warnings against the adulteress by presenting Lady Wisdom as the true bride and lover, whose embrace spells life and not death; and who, in more general terms, is designed to make what the sage recognizes as a difficult and demanding pursuit (2:1–4), as attractive and alluring as possible. But the voice of Lady Wisdom does not only echo the voice of the wisdom teacher and counter the voice of the seductress; it is also hedged with divinity. She was brought forth by God and dwelt beside him before the world was created (8:22–31); she speaks in prophetic tones, and to spurn her amounts to spurning God (1:24–30).

Who then is Lady Wisdom? Probably she began life rather modestly as a personification of the sage's teaching, but soon outgrew the role of a wisdom teacher, particularly as her feminine characteristics were developed. Ultimately she begins life in primeval times, grows up at God's side and witnesses his creation of the world. This significant development in how she is depicted was probably designed to express the conviction of the wise that the rules of good and wise living which they learned through experience of the world were written large in its structure and order from the first, and that the wisdom of experience therefore rests upon the divine wisdom which created the world. So Lady Wisdom is an ambivalent figure. She comes to bear two birthmarks: the mark of human wisdom learned through experience, and the mark of the divine wisdom of God, revealed by God through his creation. These are laid side by side in the Book of Proverbs and sometimes one, sometimes the other, is most visible. However, when later sages took up the theme, it was Wisdom's mark of divine origin and proximity to God which most impressed.

(ii)

The figure of Wisdom is developed in the Apocryphal books of Ecclesiasticus and the Wisdom of Solomon. Here is how Wisdom describes herself in Ecclesiasticus, chapter 24:

> I came forth from the mouth of the Most High,
>   and covered the earth like a mist.
> I dwelt in high places,
>   and my throne was in a pillar of cloud.
> Alone I have made the circuit of the vault of heaven
>   and have walked in the depths of the abyss.
> In the waves of the sea, in the whole earth,
>   and in every people and nation I have gotten a possession.
> Among all these I sought a resting place;
>   I sought in whose territory I might lodge.

Her restless search for a permanent dwelling place came to an end:

Then the Creator of all things gave me a commandment,
    and the one who created me assigned a place for my tent.
And he said, "Make your dwelling in Jacob,
    and in Israel receive your inheritance".
From eternity, in the beginning, he created me,
    and for eternity I shall not cease to exist.
In the holy tabernacle I ministered before him,
    and so I was established in Zion.
In the beloved city likewise he gave me a resting place,
    and in Jerusalem was my dominion.
So I took root in an honoured people,
    in the portion of the Lord, who is their inheritance.

And once in Jerusalem, among God's chosen people, divine Wisdom assumes concrete shape in a written book:

All this is the book of the covenant of the Most High God,
    the law which Moses commanded us
    as an inheritance for the congregations of Jacob.

So in Judaism the divine Wisdom by which the world was created comes to be identified with the Torah; the wisdom school becomes the *Beth Midrash* (House of Study [of the Torah]) and the wisdom teacher becomes the Rabbi.

In the Wisdom of Solomon a more philosophical note is struck, and the divine wisdom becomes an emanation of God's attributes, identical to or barely distinguishable from God's Spirit (7:22-26):

In her there is a spirit that is intelligent,
holy, unique, manifold, subtle, mobile, clear,
unpolluted, distinct, invulnerable, loving the
good, keen, irresistible, beneficient, humane,
steadfast, sure, free from anxiety,
all-powerful, overseeing all, and penetrating
through all spirits that are intelligent and
pure and most subtle . . . .

She is a breath of the power of God,
and a pure emanation of the glory of the Almighty;
therefore nothing defiled gains entrance into her.
For she is a reflection of eternal light,
a spotless mirror of the working of God,
and an image of his goodness.

(iii)

Whereas the Jewish sages came to identify the divine Wisdom with the Law or the Spirit of God, the early Christians identified it with a person: "Christ the power of God and the wisdom of God . . . whom God made our wisdom, our righteousness and sanctification and redemption" (1 Cor. 1:24, 30). The New Testament writers therefore found in the figure of Wisdom a ready-made category of thought through which they could express and deepen their understanding of the pre-existence and cosmic significance of Christ, the Son of God, in creation and redemption. So the apostle Paul writes:

He is the image of the invisible God, the first-born of all creation; for in him all things were created, in heaven and on earth . . . all things were created through him and for him. He is before all things, and in him all things hold together.
(Col. 1:15–17; see also John 1:1–3; Heb. 1:2–3; Rev. 3:14)

And the one by whom the world was created and is sustained, is the one by whom it will be redeemed:

He is the head of the body, the church; he is the beginning, the first-born from the dead, that in everything he might be pre-eminent. For in him all the fullness of God was pleased to dwell, and through him to reconcile to himself all things, whether on earth or in heaven, making peace by the blood of his cross.
(Col. 1:18–20)

For the New Testament writers, all that the Jews (and Greeks) looked for in divine Wisdom is found in Christ. Hence wisdom which ignores God's revelation through Christ is either ineffective when it really counts (1 Cor. 1:17; 2:4), or else it is downright foolishness (1 Cor. 1:18–25).

LADY WISDOM AND DAME FOLLY

Proverbs 9:1–18

1Wisdom has built her house,
  she has set up her seven pillars.
2She has slaughtered her beasts,
  she has mixed her wine,
  she has also set her table.
3She has sent out her maids to call
  from the highest places in the town,
4"Whoever is simple, let him turn in here!"
  To him who is without sense she says,
5"Come, eat of my bread
  and drink of the wine I have mixed.
6Leave simpleness, and live,
  and walk in the way of insight."

7He who corrects a scoffer gets himself abuse,
  and he who reproves a wicked man incurs injury.
8Do not reprove a scoffer, or he will hate you;
  reprove a wise man, and he will love you.
9Give instruction to a wise man, and he will be still wiser;
  teach a righteous man and he will increase in learning.
10The fear of the Lord is the beginning of wisdom,
  and the knowledge of the Holy One is insight.
11For by me your days will be multiplied,
  and years will be added to your life.
12If you are wise, you are wise for yourself;
  if you scoff, you alone will bear it.

13A foolish woman is noisy;
  she is wanton and knows no shame.
14She sits at the door of her house,
  she takes a seat on the high places of the town,
15calling to those who pass by,
  who are going straight on their way,
16"Whoever is simple, let him turn in here!"
  And to him who is without sense she says,
17"Stolen water is sweet,
  and bread eaten in secret is pleasant."

[18]But he does not know that the dead are there,
   that her guests are in the depths of Sheol.

(i)

We might have expected that 8:22–31 would have formed the grand climax to the passages describing the activities of this industrious lady. But here we find her well and truly down to earth again, now doing a little building for herself. She builds a house across the street from her great opposite and rival, Dame Folly (v. 1). Much ingenuity was exercised by earlier commentators on the significance of the seven pillars. They have been linked with, among other things, the seven days of creation, the seven planets, the seven gifts of the Holy Spirit, the seven sacraments, the seven beatitudes, the seven churches in Revelation, and even the seven liberal arts! The suggestion that they have cosmological overtones of one kind or another has been revived by some modern commentators, but is not very apt. The seven pillars probably means no more than that her house is a rather splendid one with ample room to seat at her table all who accept her invitation.

The passage itself is almost as well designed as Lady Wisdom's house, although it has five and not seven "pillars":

A. Lady Wisdom's invitation (vv. 1–6)
  B. The wise man and the scoffer (vv. 7–9)
    C. The fear of the Lord (vv. 10–11)
  B[1]. The wise man and the scoffer (v. 12)
A[1]. Dame Folly's invitation (vv. 13–18)

(ii)

(a) *The invitations.* While in 1:20–21 and 8:1–3 Lady Wisdom took a leaf from the book of the prophet and became an open-air preacher, here she takes a leaf from the book of the adulteress and becomes a hostess inviting guests to her house. She prepares a sumptuous spread, sets the table, and sends out her maids with the party invitations (vv. 2–3). The industry and care with which she prepares for her guests contrast markedly with the casual and brash way Dame Folly (v. 13, NEB "Lady

Stupidity") sets about soliciting her clients (vv. 13–15). Both however have the same invitation to extend: "come, eat . . . drink"; and seek the same clientele: the simple and the foolish, that is, those who most need to dine with Lady Wisdom, and who can be most easily induced to dine with Dame Folly.

Lady Wisdom offers a tasty meal of steak (a better translation than "bread"; cf. v. 2) washed down by wine laced with spices (v. 5). This figurative use of food and drink for Wisdom's instruction is taken up by Ben Sirach in Ecclesiasticus:

> She [wisdom] will feed him with the bread of understanding,
>   and give him the water of wisdom to drink.
>
> (15:3)

> Come to me, you who desire me,
>   and eat your fill of my produce . . .
> Those who eat me will hunger for more,
>   and those who drink me will thirst for more.
>
> (24:19–21)

The same imagery is applied to the prophetic word in Isaiah 55:1–3.

The fact that Dame Folly offers her guests water instead of wine (v. 17) does not imply that by comparison she is stinting in her hospitality. She appears to be citing a popular proverb on the magnetic power of forbidden fruit ("water"). There is an old saying, "Forbid a fool, and he'll do it directly". Dame Folly knows the truth of this and is using it to the fullest advantage. In the present context the forbidden fruit is a night of illicit love play. "Water" may therefore also contain a glance back at 5:15–16.

As different as the menus are, they are different in the eating. Lady Wisdom's is food which nourishes life, while Dame Folly's brings death (vv. 6, 18; see 8:32–35; 7:24–27). This theme of life-giving food finds its deepest exposition in John 6.

Although the figure of Dame Folly clearly represents the flesh and blood adulteress of the earlier chapters, she embraces more than the adulterer. As personified Wisdom's opposite number she is herself the personification of folly. She is therefore a symbolic figure who embraces all kinds of folly and every kind of fool. So the contrast between the two banquets is not so much designed to repeat the warnings against the adulteress as to reinforce the teaching about the "two ways" (see 4:10–19). Here again we are confronted in the sharpest and most dramatic way with the stark alternatives we must choose between, the choice of direction we must decide: the way of wisdom or folly, the path of life or death. The contrast between the two banquets is therefore a fitting climax to the first section of Proverbs.

(iii)

(b) *The wise man and the scoffer.* Verses 7–9 strike a rather pensive note. They appear to be a commentary on Lady Wisdom's invitation. While she spreads her net wide (8:4), it is sadly true that not all men can benefit from her instruction. Some men are unteachable. Simply to need instruction is not sufficient qualification to eat at her table; there must be a willingness to accept reproof as well. Her guests must be prepared to hear some unsettling truths about themselves which rub against the grain of well-grooved habits of thought, word and deed, and be willing to change their habits. The "scoffer", as we have seen, is the unteachable man at his most mature (see the comment on 1:22). He is so full of himself and so contemptuous of others that his case is practically hopeless. The root of his trouble is pride (21:24). To reprove him will do him no good and may do you some harm. He is best left alone to learn the hard way. By contrast, the wise man is the teachable man at his most mature. For it is the mark of maturity in wisdom to know there is always room for progress and improvement, and to have the humility to be stung by rebuke and thank the rebuker. Verse 12 adds the sobering thought that how we accept reproof is a test of character, and tells whether we are beating a path to Lady Wisdom's or Dame Folly's door. The humility that learns wisdom or the pride that puts us above it decides what kind of people we are, and will make us or break us.

(c) *The fear of the Lord.* As the above outline shows, the motto for learning in the school of Wisdom (v. 10) stands highlighted right in the centre of this, the last chapter of the section, much as it was highlighted in the opening chapter (see the comment on 1:7). The implication is clear. The option of dining at the table of Lady Wisdom or Dame Folly, and eating the food of life or death, depends finally and most fully upon a person's response to God. That is the fundamental, decisive factor. None who reject the fear of God can walk too far in the way of Wisdom, for that rejection is itself the greatest and the ultimate folly (see 1:29–31). In the course of time this truth was to be caught up and the invitation to dine at Wisdom's banquet was to find deeper realization in Jesus' invitation to the banquet in the kingdom of God (Luke 14:15–24).

PART TWO: THE WISE MEN'S PROVERBS (10:1–31:31)

(N.B. The topical arrangement of the sayings we have devised in these chapters is solely for the convenience of the reader. Other ways of arranging them are equally possible.)

I. TYPES OF CHARACTERS

THE SIMPLE

Proverbs

14:15 The simple believes everything,
           but the prudent looks where he is going.

22:3   A prudent man sees danger and hides himself;
           but the simple go on, and suffer for it.

27:12 A prudent man sees danger and hides himself;
           but the simple go on, and suffer for it.

14:18 The simple acquire folly,
           but the prudent are crowned with knowledge.

These proverbs recall the note struck at the beginning of the book: the simple badly needing to be instructed in the ways of wisdom (1:4). We saw then that the simple referred to is the young person who lacks experience of life and knowledge of the ways and wiles of the world, and who is easily impressed and manipulated by others to their own ends. He therefore becomes the prime candidate for the beckoning of Dame Folly (9:16). Here we find two reasons why the simple is such easy game for this lady in all her appearances:

(a) He readily accepts what people tell him as the "gospel truth" (14:15). It would never occur to him to stop and ask whether this man or woman is a person to be believed; or to carefully weigh up what they say; or to go and find out the facts for himself. In a word, he has not learned to think for himself. To let others do our thinking for us is always easier and much less troublesome than doing our own thinking, and it is especially tempting when we hear what we want to hear. But we do it at our peril and often the peril of others as well. Untold mischief has been done and untold misery caused, inside as well as outside the Church, by people giving credence to someone as foolish as themselves. The demagogue, the slanderer and the talebearer, all prize rather than pity our credulity.

The second line contrasts the credulity of the simple with the circumspection of the prudent. The point here may be that the prudent keeps a wary eye on the road ahead as he walks through life; or, more specifically, that he looks very carefully at what anyone tells him to see where it leads to. The New English Bible gives an alternative translation which sharpens the contrast: "A simple man believes every word he hears; a clever man understands the need for proof".

(b) He lacks any real awareness of the deadly perils to which he is exposed, and which will destroy him sooner than he will avoid them (22:3; 27:12). The tell-tale signs of danger are posted everywhere, but he blithely ignores them and rushes on, mistaking his simplicity for bravado. Today this side of him is perhaps most conspicuous in the youngster who dabbles in drugs. On the other hand, the prudent man not only has the wisdom to "look before he leaps", but also the wisdom to know when it is time to be a coward and run away for dear life and hide himself.

The simple's credulity and bravado make a heady cocktail, and it is not surprising that he finds folly so easy to come by (14:18). The story of his encounter with the seductress in chapter 7 is intended to underline just *how* easily, and it reads almost like a commentary on these sayings. There the young fellow wended his way through the streets towards her house oblivious to the signs of danger, believed every honeyed word which oozed from her lips, went off with her—and suffered for it. He became a fool (14:18). But Dame Folly does not have it all her own way with the simple; for Lady Wisdom too beckons him and offers him her life-saving and life-giving counsel (1:22–23; 8:5; 9:4–6). So the question facing the simple is: whose voice will he heed, Lady Wisdom's or Dame Folly's? Although addressed by Proverbs particularly to young people, it is a question none of us will ever outgrow.

THE FOOL:
HALLMARKS OF A FOOL—I

Proverbs

17:16 Why should a fool have a price in his hand to buy wisdom,
     when he has no mind?

17:24 A man of understanding sets his face toward wisdom,
     but the eyes of a fool are on the ends of the earth.

17:10 A rebuke goes deeper into a man of understanding
     than a hundred blows into a fool.

27:22 Crush a fool in a mortar with a pestle
      along with crushed grain,
     yet his folly will not depart from him.

15:14 The mind of him who has understanding seeks knowledge,
     but the mouths of fools feed on folly.

26:11 Like a dog that returns to his vomit
     is a fool that repeats his folly.

18:2 A fool takes no pleasure in understanding,
     but only in expressing his opinion.

28:26 He who trusts in his own mind is a fool;
           but he who walks in wisdom will be delivered.
12:15 The way of a fool is right in his own eyes,
           but a wise man listens to advice.
14:33 Wisdom abides in the mind of a man of understanding,
           but it is not known in the heart of fools.

Israel's wise did not suffer fools gladly. While they had every hope that the simple would heed their instruction and become wise, they expected nothing of the sort from the fool. His was a matured attitude of mind and fixed disposition towards life which were the opposite of all that the wise stood for. But like a good wine, a fool does not mature overnight. And doubtless the wise intend their proverbs about the fool and his folly to be a series of snap-shots for people to take a very hard look at to see if they can spot themselves—and be warned!

(i)

There is an old saying, "A fool in a gown is none the wiser". These sayings clothe the fool in the gown of a student in the school of Wisdom, and show why he remains a fool.

In 17:16 we have a close-up of the fool at the entrance paying his fees, accompanied by the sardonic comment of a discerning onlooker that this fellow is just wasting his money, for he does not have the resolve to apply his mind to learning wisdom but expects it to be handed to him on a plate. Not surprisingly, then, when we get a picture of the fool inside the classroom, while the other students pay rapt attention to the teacher, he is busy looking out the window, around the room and up at the ceiling, as his mind flits from one thing to another (17:24).

To be sure, lack of attentiveness and application are not uncommon student weaknesses. So it might be thought that all that was needed was a good telling-off or a few strokes of the belt to beat some of the foolishness out of him and drum some wisdom in. But while this works wonders with children (see the topic, *Parental Discipline*), and a word of rebuke is enough for the wise, even a hundred strokes makes not the slightest impact on a fool (17:10). The fool is incorrigible and his folly well nigh ineradicable (27:22).

Clearly, the fool's failure to learn wisdom does not stem simply from the fact that he is a feckless kind of student. It stems from something much more deep-seated. In the *first* place, he just does not have an appetite for wisdom. Folly is much more to his taste (15:14). And even the effects of 'food poison', which might have taught him better, seem not to curb his appetite for it (26:11). *Second,* he does not think that he has anything to learn about wisdom anyhow. He believes there is nothing to be gained, and certainly no enjoyment to be had, from thinking hard about anything and trying to learn—at least, not for someone like himself who has already got all the answers on the tip of his tongue and is just bursting to pass on his words of wisdom (18:2). He is living in a fool's paradise, of course; but no-one can tell him that (28:26; 12:15). And so, while Wisdom finds a warm welcome in the mind of the wise ("is at home", 14:33, NEB), she gets the cold shoulder from the fool ("ill at ease", NEB).

HALLMARKS OF A FOOL—II

Proverbs

13:16 In everything a prudent man acts with knowledge,
     but a fool flaunts his folly.

12:23 A prudent man conceals his knowledge,
     but fools proclaim their folly.

17:28 Even a fool who keeps silent is considered wise;
     when he closes his lips, he is deemed intelligent.

26:7 Like a lame man's legs, which hang useless,
     is a proverb in the mouth of fools.

26:9 Like a thorn that goes up into the hand of a drunkard
     is a proverb in the mouth of fools.

15:2 The tongue of the wise dispenses knowledge,
     but the mouths of fools pour out folly.

15:7 The lips of the wise spread knowledge;
     not so the minds of fools.

24:7   Wisdom is too high for a fool;
       in the gate he does not open his mouth.

29:11 A fool gives full vent to his anger,
       but a wise man quietly holds it back.
12:16 The vexation of a fool is known at once,
       but a prudent man ignores an insult.
20:3   It is an honour for a man to keep aloof from strife;
       but every fool will be quarrelling.
14:16 A wise man is cautious and turns away from evil,
       but a fool throws off restraint and is careless.
13:19 A desire fulfilled is sweet to the soul;
       but to turn away from evil is an abomination to fools.
10:23 It is like sport to a fool to do wrong,
       but wise conduct is pleasure to a man of understanding.
15:21 Folly is a joy to him who has no sense,
       but a man of understanding walks aright.

14:24 The crown of the wise is their wisdom,
       but folly is the garland of fools.
14:8   The wisdom of a prudent man is to discern his way,
       but the folly of fools is deceiving.
14:12 There is a way which seems right to a man,
       but its end is the way to death.
16:25 There is a way which seems right to a man,
       but its end is the way to death.

(ii)

Outside the school of Wisdom the fool quickly shows the stuff of which he is made. Everything he says and does trumpets his folly, and he seizes every opportunity to blow it—quite the reverse of the prudent man, who knows there is a time to speak and act, and a time to stand back and be silent (13:16; 12:23).

(a) *His words.* "Silence is the virtue of fools". It is also a virtue of the wise (see 17:27). So a silent fool and a wise man can very seldom be told apart. As long as a fool keeps quiet and nods wisely now and again, he can enjoy the esteem held out to a wise man of sound judgment and few words (17:28). But if the fool picked up this pearl of wisdom in a rare moment of attention in the classroom, we should not be too hopeful that he will keep his mouth shut. He could not possibly conceive that it applied to him. In any case, he has a happy knack of picking up words of wisdom and letting them drop at all the wrong times and places. He thinks he is being very clever when he can come out with a pithy saying, but it invariably falls flat on its face (26:7) and makes not the slightest impact (26:9). So even if the fool says something wise, his sense of timing will usually give him away.

More typically, however, what a fool says is just plain stupid or malicious; and it fairly gushes out of him like water from a copious spring (15:2). It springs from his "mind" (15:7). His words betray the worthlessness of his mind and character. At his best, he talks too much (see 13:3; 18:7), and talks without thinking or listening (see 18:13); while at his worst, slander and the like flow easily from his lips (see 10:18; 20:19).

The saying in 24:7 observes that there are in fact times when a fool keeps quiet. The "gate" was the place where matters and issues affecting the community were pondered and decided by the elders. To make a sensible contribution to these discussions is beyond the capacity of the fool, and he knows that nobody would listen to what he said. So he muzzles himself. The sage of Ecclesiasticus suggests another time when a fool might keep quiet: "There is one who keeps silent because he has no answer, while another keeps silent because he knows when to speak" (20:6).

(b) *His behaviour.* Apart from by what he says, the fool gives himself away by his outbursts of anger (29:11), often at the slightest provocation (12:16), and by his quickness to pick a quarrel and come to blows (20:3—see the topic, *The Hothead*).

The next few sayings strike the darkest note. Whereas the wise conducts himself cautiously and avoids doing anything harmful and wrong, the fool conducts himself recklessly without the slightest degree of restraint, unmindful of the wrong he does and the harm he causes (14:16). "Careless" is from the same root as the word rendered "secure" in 1:33 and "confidence" in 14:26. His recklessness is fed by his unbounded confidence in his own capabilities, always to come out on top. The very idea that he should behave in any other way is unthinkable to him, quite abhorrent in fact (13:19); for he thinks it would spoil his fun (10:23) and make life very drab (15:21). It goes without saying that he "has no sense". The reference to the straight and upright course which the wise man walks through life (15:21—and who therefore knows what "pleasure" really is, see 10:23) recalls the theme of the "two ways" developed throughout the first section of Proverbs (see, especially, the comment on 4:10–19). Here, then, the fool finally finds himself in the company of the evil and the wicked, who walk the dark and slippery path leading to death.

The Hebrew text in the second line of 14:24 reads "the folly of fools is folly", which does not say terribly much. The RSV assumes a slight modification in the Hebrew by rendering once, "garland" for "folly". Folly crowns all the fool's efforts and "adorns" his life like a wreath around his head (cf. 1:9). The trouble is that the fool believes his garland is becoming and sports it proudly. But "the folly of fools is deceiving" (14:8), and it deceives none more than themselves. Sooner or later he will discover that he has been sporting around a wreath of a different kind (14:12; 16:25).

(iii)

For the most part, the proverbs detailing the hallmarks of the fool speak about him in general terms. They embrace many assorted kinds and shades of fool. At one extreme the fool is the person who simply has too much to say for himself, and who is little more than irritating; at the other he is the person who is downright wicked, and who is positively dangerous. The other character types we will be looking at focus on one or other of the many kinds of fools and sorts of folly, although the fool now goes under a different name. There are two things, however, which all fools of whatever complexion have in common, and they emerge very clearly in these proverbs: (1) *an unwillingness to learn*—whether through formal instruction (17:16), disciplining (17:10), a word of advice (12:15), or his own experience

(26:11), however harsh (27:22); and (2) *lack of self-control*—
whether in what they say (15:2), how they react (12:16), or what
they do (14:16). These are really the cardinal hallmarks of the
fool wherever he is found, and what make him well and truly a
fool. They are also the kind of things which can just as quickly
make fools of the wise if they are not careful.

A FOOL'S LOT

Proverbs

10:13 On the lips of him who has understanding wisdom is found,
     but a rod is for the back of him who lacks sense.
10:14 Wise men lay up knowledge,
     but the babbling of a fool brings ruin near.
14:3 The talk of a fool is a rod for his back,
     but the lips of the wise will preserve them.
18:7 A fool's mouth is his ruin,
     and his lips are a snare to himself.
18:6 A fool's lips bring strife,
     and his mouth invites a flogging.
26:3 A whip for the horse, a bridle for the ass,
     and a rod for the back of fools.
10:8 The wise of heart will heed commandments,
     but a prating fool will come to ruin.
16:22 Wisdom is a fountain of life to him who has it,
     but folly is the chastisement of fools.
10:21 The lips of the righteous feed many,
     but fools die for lack of sense.
19:3 When a man's folly brings his way to ruin,
     his heart rages against the Lord.

"He who keep his mouth and his tongue keeps himself out of
trouble" (21:23) is a lesson learned by the wise. He knows how
to speak wisely and judiciously (10:13); he also knows when to
remain silent and await the opportune time to speak ("lay up",
10:14). His wise and disciplined speech enables him to navigate
his way through many a minefield and come out safe and sound
(14:3). The fool is not so fortunate. His mouth is a minefield,

and every time he opens it he put his foot on a mine (18:7).
Through his careless or malicious words, he invariably either
gets people's backs up and as much as asks for a good punch on
the nose, or else he falls foul of the authorities and as much as
asks for a public flogging (18:6). Indeed, to get a "bloodied
nose" is the only language the fool understands. If he is going to
learn anything at all, he is going to learn the hard way. For one
can no more reason with him than with a horse or an ass (26:3;
see Ps. 32:9). And even an ass can put some fools to shame (see
Isa. 1:3). The fool is therefore his own worst enemy. While
creating wreck and ruin around him, he brings calamity upon
himself and sows the seeds of his own ruin (10:8), in lesser
(16:22) or greater (10:21) measure.

The last saying observes the typical reaction of a fool when he
has to eat the fruits of his folly: he throws a temper tantrum and
blames his calamity on God. This is the ultimate comment on
his unwillingness to learn his lessons. Nothing is ever his own
fault. When misfortune befalls him, he is the hapless victim of
the envy of men, the cruel chance of fate, or the whim of God—
a quirk of human nature captured in the following lines:

> Perverse mankind! whose will created free,
> Charge all their woes on absolute decree;
> All to the dooming gods their guilt translate,
> And follies are miscalled the crimes of fate.

When things go badly for us, we are all too prone to protest,
'It's not my fault,' and to lay the blame elsewhere. In that way
we often fail to learn the valuable lessons our unhappy experiences have to teach us about ourselves.

NEXT TIME YOU MEET A FOOL...!

Proverbs

27:3   A stone is heavy, and sand is weighty,
          but a fool's provocation is heavier than both.
17:12 Let a man meet a she-bear robbed of her cubs,
          rather than a fool in his folly.

23:9   Do not speak in the hearing of a fool,
         for he will despise the wisdom of your words.
26:4   Answer not a fool according to his folly,
         lest you be like him yourself.
26:5   Answer a fool according to his folly,
         lest he be wise in his own eyes.
29:9   If a wise man has an argument with a fool,
         the fool only rages and laughs,
         and there is no quiet.
26:6   He who sends a message by the hand of a fool
         cuts off his own feet and drinks violence.
26:10   Like an archer who wounds everybody
         is he who hires a passing fool or drunkard.
14:7   Leave the presence of a fool,
         for there you do not meet words of knowledge.
13:20   He who walks with wise men becomes wise,
         but the companion of fools will suffer harm.
26:1   Like snow in summer or rain in harvest,
         so honour is not fitting for a fool.
26:8   Like one who binds the stone in the sling
         is he who gives honour to a fool.

A fool is a thoroughly provocative and burdensome fellow because of his undisciplined and unrestrained outbursts (27:3). It is less tiresome to heft around a boulder or a bag of sand than to have to put up with him. Misfortunate indeed is the man who encounters a fool bent on his folly (17:12). He is much more dangerous and much less restrainable than a maddened bear (cf. 2 Sam. 17:8; Hos. 13:8). But since, in any case, a person is more likely to meet a fool than a bear, it is concerning how best to deal with him that the sage now passes on some words of advice:

(a) *Keep quiet!* (23:9). The expression "in the hearing [literally, "ears"] of" implies speaking directly the the fool rather than speaking when he can overhear. Many years of experience trying to drill some wisdom into fools lies behind the sage's advice. Because he refuses to learn or profit from wise words, all they do is give him an opportunity to curl his lips and confirm himself in his folly. Jesus' saying about not casting pearls before swine makes a similar point (Matt. 7:6). There comes a time when fools are best left alone to learn the hard way.

(b) *Watch how you answer him!* (26:4, 5). Perturbed by the apparent contradiction between these verses, the Rabbis hesitated over accepting the Book of Proverbs as Scripture. They solved the problem by making verse 4 refer to worldly, and verse 5 to spiritual, matters. But there is no more of a contradiction between them than between the proverbs "Look before you leap" and "He who hesitates is lost". Which is best? Clearly the answer is: it all depends! Knowing how best to respond to a fool is a tricky business. Do you keep silent? If you don't, you may quickly find yourself talking at his level and making a fool out of yourself (26:4). On the other hand, if you don't speak up, the fool's conceit will go unchecked; worse still, he might be impressing others as well as himself with his vaunted wisdom. Whenever a fool opens his mouth, the wise man is caught on the horns of this dilemma, as the apostle Paul was acutely aware (see 2 Cor. 11:1–12:11). It is a test of wisdom and sound judgment to know which course, silence or reprimand, will do the least damage in the circumstances.

(c) *Don't argue with him!* (29:9). This saying refers specifically to disputes which are settled in the law court (see NEB), and observes that to enter into litigation with a fool is often more trouble than it is worth, and will seldom be satisfactorily resolved. This is equally true of arguments in general. The fool is incapable of quiet discussion and debate. He will not listen to reason nor be persuaded by argument. Instead he will either fly off the handle or try to laugh your point of view out of court. So an argument with a fool gets nowhere and achieves nothing beyond getting all concerned hot under the collar.

(d) *Don't trust him to do anything for you!* (26:6; 26:10). To ask a fool to do something for you is to make sure that it will not be done properly. And as for the mischief he will create in the process . . . ! Send a message with a fool, and instead of getting the help of an extra pair of legs, you are as good as cutting off your own (26:6); give him a job to do, and you may as well go on the rampage with your bow and arrows (26:10). That, at least, is how the RSV takes this saying. The Hebrew text, however, is quite impossible. The scale of its difficulties can be seen by comparing the Authorized Version's rendering: "The great God that formed all things both rewardeth the fool and rewardeth transgressors". But there is no word for "God" in the text. The word rendered "great" (Hebrew *rav*) means "archer" in Job 16:13 and Jeremiah 50:29, and is so rendered by most modern versions (NEB, NIV, JB; but TEV, "employer"); and while they differ in detail, most are also agreed that this is a proverb about the folly of employing a fool.

(e) *Avoid his company!* (14:7; 13:20). The fool is generous in sharing his folly with his friends, and Israel's sages were sure that to keep company with him was the quickest way to become like him. Hence their repeated warnings to watch the company we keep (*eg* 22:24–25; 23:20; 28:7; cf. 1 Cor. 15:33). Neither by word nor example is wisdom to be learned in the company of fools. The only lesson in wisdom the fool can teach is when he comes to grief (cf. 19:25). But his companions will find themselves part of the object-lesson!

(f) *Don't honour him!* (26:1; 26:8). These verses have in mind the bestowal of honour upon a fool by promoting him to some position of public responsibility in the community. Fools are neither worthy of such honour nor are they capable of discharging their public duties responsibly. So to honour a fool in this way (or any other way) is as much a distortion of what is seasonable and fitting as snow falling in the summer or rain during the harvest (*ie*, the long, dry season from March to October); and it is quite as absurd as if David had faced up to Goliath not knowing how to fit the stone in the fold of his sling properly. Some of the hero-worship of the present day falls under the same verdict.

THE HOTHEAD

Proverbs

> 17:27 He who restrains his words has knowledge,
>   and he who has a cool spirit is a man of understanding.

14:17 A man of quick temper acts foolishly,
        but a man of discretion is patient.
14:29 He who is slow to anger has great understanding,
        but he who has a hasty temper exalts folly.
29:22 A man of wrath stirs up strife,
        and a man given to anger causes much transgression.
15:18 A hot-tempered man stirs up strife,
        but he who is slow to anger quiets contention.
19:11 Good sense makes a man slow to anger,
        and it is his glory to overlook an offence.
19:19 A man of great wrath will pay the penalty;
        for if you deliver him, you will only have to do it again.
14:30 A tranquil mind gives life to the flesh,
        but passion makes the bones rot.
25:28 A man without self-control
        is like a city broken into and left without walls.
16:32 He who is slow to anger is better than the mighty,
        and he who rules his spirit than he who takes a city.

22:24 Make no friendship with a man given to anger,
        nor go with a wrathful man,
22:25 lest you learn his ways
        and entangle yourself in a snare.
15:1 A soft answer turns away wrath,
        but a harsh word stirs up anger.
30:32 If you have been foolish, exalting yourself,
        or if you have been devising evil,
        put your hand on your mouth.
30:33 For pressing milk produces curds,
        pressing the nose produces blood,
        and pressing anger produces strife.
27:4 Wrath is cruel, anger is overwhelming;
        but who can stand before jealousy?

(i)

This fellow is like a bomb with a short fuse. He is literally "the heated man" ("hot-tempered", 15:18). The word "heat"·is a strong one. It is the word used of the "venom" of serpents (Ps. 58:4) and of the "fiery" effects of wine (Hos. 7:5). He is also the "short-nosed" man ("quick-tempered", 14:17). In Hebrew the one word has the double meaning of "nose" and "anger". The common link between them is perhaps "snorting [with anger]". There is a play on the two meanings in 30:33. The hothead's opposite is the man who has a "cool" head (17:27)—as "cool" and as apt to refresh as the water which slakes the thirst of the traveller (25:25)—and who is "long-nosed" ("slow to anger", 14:29). This is the man who knows how to restrain his temper and his tongue.

The contrast between the hotheaded and the coolheaded man drawn in these proverbs was also a standard theme in Egyptian wisdom teaching. Indeed, there the ideal man is presented as the "cool" or "silent man": the man who keeps his cool and who shows disciplined restraint in all that he says and does. His opposite number is the "heated man", whose lack of self-control is unbecoming, disruptive and injurious. Of these two sorts of people, the Egyptian sages entertained the thought that the silent, self-controlled man would enjoy life, prosperity and health, while the heated man would come to an unhappy end. The *Instruction of Amenemopet* contrasts the two types and their respective fates in terms strikingly reminiscent of the contrast between the righteous and the wicked in Psalm 1 and Jeremiah 17:5–8:

> As for the heated man . . .
> He is like a tree growing in the open.
> In the completion of a moment [comes] its
>   loss of foliage,
> And its end is reached in the shipyards;
> [Or] it is floated far from its place,
> And the flame is its burial shroud.
> [But] the truly silent man holds himself apart.
> He is like a tree growing in a garden.
> It flourishes and doubles its yield;
> It [stands] before its lord.
> Its fruit is sweet; its shade is pleasant;
> And its end is reached in the garden.

As we know, the Egyptian sages were concerned with training high level officials and civil servants for careers in the service of the state, where keeping a cool and clear head at all times regardless of the provocation was absolutely essential. Perhaps some of these proverbs by Israel's sages were likewise originally intended as a counsel for those entering positions of responsibility in government service. The more power a man wields the more destructive his anger can be, and the more he has need of a cool head. But hotheads are not thin on the ground wherever we look, and the proverbs have an equally wide application.

(ii)

We have already seen that one of the hallmarks of the fool is that his anger is easily kindled and is completely ungovernable (see 12:16; 29:11). The hothead is therefore his near relative. Here several acute observations are made on this kind of person:

(a) *He acts foolishly* (14:17; 14:29). In the heat of his anger the hothead invariably displays folly. His anger clouds his judgment and robs him of all sense of perspective; so he reacts and acts impetuously in ways which are out of all proportion to the situation, which are completely unpredictable, often quite terrifying, and which in a calmer frame of mind he himself will probably regret. It is the man who keeps a tight rein on his temper who is able to think clearly and act rationally. He is able to take a long, cool look at the situation and weigh it up judiciously, and will not allow himself to be provoked into saying or doing anything hastily.

(b) *He causes trouble* (29:22; 15:18; 19:11). If it takes two to make a quarrel, the hothead generates heat enough, and more to spare. It takes only one to stir up a hornets' nest. We can all remember the sensible discussion becoming a war of words because someone lost his temper. Regrettably, it is not unknown for this to happen at the church business meeting. The saying in 19:11 puts its finger on one of the hothead's 'quicks': he is quick to take offence (cf. 12:16). At the slightest prickle to his self-esteem he will flare up and lash out with abuse or violence. And once he cools down he will still nurse a smouldering grudge against the offender. The man who is short in temper is usually also short in forgiveness. His opposite is much more thick-skinned and is sensitive to chiefly "sticks and stones"; and even when an offence bites deep, he has the good sense and the moral fibre to remain composed and to forgive and forget.

(c) *He is incorrigible* (19:19). The hothead frequently lands himself in trouble enough to show him the error of his ways. But, fool that he is, he will not learn the lesson. The point this saying makes is that to bale him out of trouble is counter-productive; for it will only encourage him to think that he will always get away with it and make him worse.

(d) *He is unhealthy* (14:30). The hothead is not only unhealthy company to be in (22:24–25), but his own health is none too good. "Passion" is a fairly general word for getting "worked up", and it includes envy and jealousy (6:34; 27:4) as well as anger. Here Israel's sages show a fine insight into the effect of mental states and emotions on a person's health (cf. 3:8).

(e) *He is defenceless* (25:28; 16:32). The saying in 25:28 speaks of lack of self-control in general, although its companion in 16:32 speaks of anger in particular. The undisciplined man is likened to a city whose walls have been razed to the ground. He has no protection from the destructive power of passion from within, or temptation from without. Indeed, he is already defeated and strewn with ruins. The other saying puts the opposite side. It recognizes that self-control does not come easy to a man—no easier and no less taxing than conquering a city. But he fights a greater battle, and his victory deserves the better medal.

(iii)

In the last three sayings, the sage passes on some practical words of advice: (1) avoid making friends with a hothead at all costs. His anger is infectious and can be lethal (22:24–25). The *Instruction of Amenemopet* passes on the same wise advice: "Do not associate to thyself the heated man, Nor visit him for conversation"; (2) if you find yourself confronted by a hothead, try a gentle word (15:1)—it often works; (3) above all, make sure you are not the culprit (30:32–33). This last saying warns against indulging in the kind of arrogant and wrongful behaviour which provokes other people to anger. Better to *suppress* it ("put your hand on your mouth"), says the sage, than *press* on with it; for you will only cause strife and you may get a bloody nose.

Once anger is given free rein, there is no telling where it will stop. That is its real danger. The ancient tribal saying about Simeon and Levi is horrific (Gen. 49:5–7; cf. ch. 34). Jesus condemns anger as equivalent to the murder to which it can lead (Matt. 5:21–22). There may well be times when 'righteous anger' is fully justified. We might think, for example, of David's anger upon hearing Nathan's parable (2 Sam. 12:5–6). What right-thinking person's anger would not be stirred against such a callous man as the fellow in this story? But nowhere in the Bible is anger commended to us as the desirable response to any situation. Ephesians 4:26 does not recommend it, but warns about it. Even righteous anger can cloud the judgment and lead to impulsive actions which might be regretted later. And the example of David shows how easily it can be hypocritical and misdirected. Righteous anger may sometimes be justified; but it can never be fully redeemed.

THE SCOFFER

Proverbs

21:24 "Scoffer" is the name of the proud, haughty man
           who acts with arrogant pride.
24:9   The devising of folly is sin,
           and the scoffer is an abomination to men.
14:6   A scoffer seeks wisdom in vain,
           but knowledge is easy for a man of understanding.
15:12 A scoffer does not like to be reproved;
           he will not go to the wise.
26:12 Do you see a man who is wise in his own eyes?
           There is more hope for a fool than for him.
19:29 Condemnation is ready for scoffers,
           and flogging for the backs of fools.

19:25 Strike a scoffer, and the simple will learn prudence;
      reprove a man of understanding,
      and he will gain knowledge.
21:11 When a scoffer is punished, the simple becomes wise;
      when a wise man is instructed, he gains knowledge.
29:8 Scoffers set a city aflame,
      but wise men turn away wrath.
13:10 By insolence the heedless make strife,
      but with those who take advice is wisdom.
22:10 Drive out a scoffer, and strife will go out,
      and quarrelling and abuse will cease.

The scoffer is one of the worst kinds of fool. The first saying lays its finger on his pulse: he pulsates with pride and arrogance. He is the fool at his most conceited and self-opinionated. At his best, he will never try to see, far less respect, someone else's point of view. He is always right and the other fellow is always wrong. At his worst, he walks around with a supercilious sneer on his face which speaks volumes of contempt for other people and for the things which they hold to be of value and worth, whether in their lives as individuals, or together as a community. The scoffer's vanity is made the measure of all things, and it is fed by putting others down. He never has a positive or a good word to say about anybody or anything; but he is always quick to let drop the cynical comment and snide remark to pour cold water on what anyone else says.

Lady Wisdom's appeal to the scoffer in 1:20–33 made it clear that his outlook on the human race and its endeavours springs from his wilful rejection of the wisdom resting on the fear of the Lord. So while nothing escapes his contemptuous look and derisive remark, he takes especial pleasure in debunking the religious faith and the moral values he has rejected. It is this darker side to the scoffer which mark him out wherever he appears in the Psalms or the Prophets (Pss. 1:1; 123:4; Isa. 28:14; 29:20; Hos. 7:5). So he finds the wicked and sinners congenial company (Ps. 1:1). Indeed, the company of the wise is irksome to him and he does all he can to avoid it (15:12). He does not see it in these terms, of course. He neither recognizes himself nor his companions for the fools they are, but deceives himself that he knows where real wisdom is to be found, as against the shallow wisdom of the so-called wise. The scoffer may well seek his sort of 'wisdom' industriously and promote it vigorously; but at bottom it is empty (14:6); for he has also made his vanity the measure of wisdom, and his bold radicalism in which he takes such perverse delight is nothing short of an ego trip. That is what makes him so unteachable (see the comment on 9:7–12). It is probably him the sage has in mind when he entertains the thought that, hopeless as the fool's case is, it is not so hopeless as in the case of the man who is wise in his own eyes (26:12). The scoffer, every bit as much as the fool, invites harsh treatment (19:29); and though he may learn nothing from it, it is a wonderful object lesson for the simple to learn from (19:25; 21:11).

The scoffer's arrogance and unteachability are matched only by his adeptness at stirring up argument and strife (29:8; 13:10; 22:10). He thrives on party quarrels and never misses an opportunity to fan any dispute into full flame, and to set men's passions ablaze. The wise man will assume the role of a peacemaker (29:8). The scoffer leaves a trail of destruction behind him, and others must pick up the pieces and put them together again, often with great difficulty. The sage is clear where the solution lies: drive him out before he does any further damage. There is no place for scoffers among serious and sensible-minded folks (22:10; 24:9).

But there is more in store for the scoffer than being despised by others and expelled from their company. Wisdom will have the last laugh at his expense (1:26) and God himself will turn the tables on him, for "toward the scorners he is scornful" (3:34).

THE PROUD

Proverbs

30:13 There are those—how lofty are their eyes,
how high their eyelids lift!

16:18 Pride goes before destruction,
         and a haughty spirit before a fall.
11:2   When pride comes, then comes disgrace;
         but with the humble is wisdom.
29:23 A man's pride will bring him low,
         but he who is lowly in spirit will obtain honour.
18:12 Before destruction a man's heart is haughty,
         but humility goes before honour.

21:4   Haughty eyes and a proud heart,
         the lamp of the wicked, are sin.
16:5   Every one who is arrogant is an abomination to the Lord;
         be assured, he will not go unpunished.
15:33 The fear of the Lord is instruction in wisdom,
         and humility goes before honour.
22:4   The reward for humility and fear of the Lord
         is riches and honour and life.

(i)

"There are those—how lofty are their eyes, how high their
eyelids lift!" (30:13). And notice has already been served that
they are detested by Wisdom (8:13) and abhorred by God
(6:16–17). These proverbs look at pride from two corresponding points of view: as foolish, and as sinful.

(a) *The Folly of Pride.* 16:18 sums it up: "Pride goes before a
fall". The words "pride" and "haughty" come from roots whose
basic meaning is "to be high, raised up". That puts it in a
nutshell: the proud man reckons he is a *cut above* other people.
Invariably too, he disdains those he considers are a cut below
him. Pride and contempt go hand in hand. The one feeds on the
other. The "Pharisee" will always thank God that he is not like
someone else. Of course, the proud man may well be more
highly talented, make more money, wield greater power,
achieve greater success or whatever than many another. But
one thing is certain, and that is that his self-esteem is out of all
proportion to what he actually has achieved or can achieve. He
has an inflated sense of his own worth and importance, and
foolishly expects other people to think of him as highly as he

does. But he is on course for a fall which will expose him to the contempt he so richly deserves (11:2). For pride more surely than ambition overstretches itself; and sooner or later the inflated bubble is bound to burst—as Shakespeare's Wolsey bitterly discovered:

> . . . I have ventur'd,
> Like little wanton boys that swim on bladders,
> This many summers in a sea of glory;
> But far beyond my depth. My high-blown pride
> At length broke under me, and now has left me,
> Weary and old with service, to the mercy
> Of a rude stream, that must for ever hide me.

(b) *The Sin of Pride.* The connection between the first and second lines of 21:4 is obscure. If "lamp" is right (AV "plough-ing"), it could be a symbol of well-being (13:9) or of the guide to conduct (6:23). So the saying may be condemning as sinful the pride which is either self-satisfied or self-seeking. The New English Bible is unhappy with the Hebrew text, and proposes the reading, "Haughty looks and a proud heart—these sins mark a wicked man". The sinfulness of pride is underlined in 16:5: it is abhorrent to God; and the proud will be punished. The Hebrew phrase rendered "be assured" is interesting. It is literally "hand to hand"—as if God has said, "Here's my hand on it", and sealed the contract (cf. 11:21).

Throughout the Old Testament, pride is seen first and foremost as sinful rebellion against God. Interestingly enough, most of the Hebrew words for human pride are also words for the exaltation and majesty of God. For example, the word "pride" in 16:18 is the same rendered "majesty" in Exodus 15:7; Isaiah 2:10; 24:14; Micah 5:4 and other passages. It is to God alone that "height" belongs. Between human pride and divine majesty there is a conflict of interests. And whether they realize it or not, proud and arrogant men and nations are usurping for themselves what rightfully belongs to God the Creator and not to man the creature. In the final analysis, the height of human pride is not that it foolishly presumes itself to be a cut above other human beings, but that it sinfully presumes itself to be a cut above God. That is the essence of pride and the ultimate sin.

This is a note sounded strongly in many passages in the prophets. Notice in particular Ezekiel 28, where the pride and punishment of the historical king of Tyre is described in mythological language which makes him representative of the proud of every age and description. See also Isaiah 10:12–14; 47; Jeremiah 50:29–32; Amos 6:8; Obadiah, verses 3–4; Zephaniah 3:11–13. In these passages, pride is seen as the root of all kinds of wickedness. But pride need not always be openly rebellious and breed lawlessness. For men to relegate God to the touchlines of the human scene as a grand irrelevancy for how they live their lives, is enough. The classic prophetic statement of God's judgment on human pride comes in Isaiah 2:6–22, and they are words our generation would do well to heed (vv. 12–17):

> For the Lord of hosts has a day
>   against all that is proud and lofty,
>   against all that is lifted up and high;
> against all the cedars of Lebanon,
>   lofty and lifted up;
>   and against all the oaks of Bashan;
> against all the high mountains,
>   and against all the lofty hills;
> against every high tower,
>   and against every fortified wall;
> against all the ships of Tarshish,
>   and against all the beautiful craft.
> And the haughtiness of man shall be humbled,
>   and the pride of men shall be brought low;
>   and the Lord alone will be exalted in that day.

(ii)

Alongside the condemnation of pride we find the commendation of humility. Humility is not rated very highly in our competitive society, being seen as a sign of weakness rather than of strength of character, and as almost an open invitation to be stepped on by those with ambition to get on in life and get to the top. With far keener insight, Israel's sages took a different view. For them humility was as much a mark of wisdom (11:2) as pride was of folly. They highly valued the humble, modest man, who quietly went about his business, who was aware of his limitations, and who did not thrust himself forward and seek self-aggrandizement. As they see things, the humble man is the wise man on four counts: (1) he is teachable (see the topic, *The Scoffer*), (2) he avoids needless conflict and strife (see again, *The Scoffer*), (3) he does not get trapped in the snare of his own pretensions—he has no inflated bubble to burst and need fear no fall (11:2); and (4) he walks the safe and sure path to solid and enduring honour and advancement, since it rests upon recognition of his genuine worth and not his pretensions. One way the sages saw this working out in practice was in the presence of the king (see the comment on 25:6–7, *The Wise Courtier*). The point is underlined in 29:23 by a word-play in the Hebrew, which happily is preserved in translation: the proud will be brought *low,* while the *lowly* will receive honour.

But humility is not only approved by wisdom and wins the favour of men; more importantly, it is also approved by God and wins his favour (see 3:34). In 11:2 "humble" is a rare word, otherwise found only in Micah 6:8, a verse which sums up God's requirements of man as being "to do justice, and to love kindness, and to walk *humbly* with your God". Humility is the proper bearing of men before God. Thus in 15:33 and 22:4 it is very closely linked with fear of the Lord, its true source and spring. The man who walks humbly before God will not walk proudly before men (1 Pet. 5:5–6).

THE SLUGGARD

Proverbs

> 26:14 As a door turns on its hinges,
>   so does a sluggard on his bed.
> 26:13 The sluggard says, "There is a lion in the road!
>   There is a lion in the streets!"
> 22:13 The sluggard says, "There is a lion outside!
>   I shall be slain in the streets!"

19:24 The sluggard buries his hand in the dish,
    and will not even bring it back to his mouth.

26:15 The sluggard buries his hand in the dish;
    it wears him out to bring it back to his mouth.

10:26 Like vinegar to the teeth, and smoke to the eyes,
    so is the sluggard to those who send him.

13:4 The soul of the sluggard craves, and gets nothing,
    while the soul of the diligent is richly supplied.

16:26 A worker's appetite works for him;
    his mouth urges him on.

21:25 The desire of the sluggard kills him
    for his hands refuse to labour.

20:4 The sluggard does not plough in the autumn;
    he will seek at harvest and have nothing.

12:27 A slothful man will not catch his prey,
    but the diligent man will get precious wealth.

26:16 The sluggard is wiser in his own eyes
    than seven men who can answer discreetly.

19:15 Slothfulness casts into a deep sleep,
    and an idle person will suffer hunger.

12:24 The hand of the diligent will rule,
    while the slothful will be put to forced labour.

15:19 The way of a sluggard is overgrown with thorns,
    but the path of the upright is a level highway.

18:9 He who is slack in his work
    is a brother to him who destroys.

20:13 Love not sleep, lest you come to poverty;
    open your eyes, and you will have plenty of bread.

24:30 I passed by the field of a sluggard,
    by the vineyard of a man without sense;

24:31 and lo, it was all overgrown with thorns;
    the ground was covered with nettles,
    and its stone wall was broken down.

24:32 Then I saw and considered it;
    I looked and received instruction.

24:33 A little sleep, a little slumber,
    a little folding of the hands to rest,

24:34 and poverty will come upon you like a robber,
    and want like an armed man.

6:6   Go to the ant, O sluggard;
          consider her ways, and be wise.
6:7   Without having any chief,
          officer or ruler,
6:8   she prepares her food in summer,
          and gathers her sustenance in harvest.
6:9   How long will you lie there, O sluggard?
          When will you arise from your sleep?
6:10 A little sleep, a little slumber,
          a little folding of the hands to rest,
6:11 and poverty will come upon you like a vagabond,
          and want like an armed man.

Clearly the sages enjoyed poking fun and pouring ridicule on
this lazy fellow. They have saved some of their best humour and
liveliest imagery for him. As we read their proverbs we are
meant to smile. We are also meant to recall when *we* got out of
our beds this morning and how *we* spent our time today!

(i)

The sluggard's day follows a well-worn routine. It begins,
naturally enough, in bed (26:14). That is where he feels most at
home. The early morning noises outside his window waken him
and tell him it is time to get up. But he is "hinged" to his bed,
and, with well-oiled movements, he turns over, and back again,
and over again—all the while sleepily muttering 'five minutes
more, just a *little* longer' (6:9–10; 24:33). The sluggard's 'five
minutes' before he does anything is usually interminable, but
even he has to get out of his bed eventually. So next we find him
'up', if not exactly 'and about', looking out of his window
contemplating what is left of the day ahead and the work to be
done (26:13; 22:13). He will swear blind to his dying day that he
really did see a lion! And what better reason could a man have
for staying at home and not going to work? He decides instead
he may as well enjoy a leisurely meal. He makes a promising
start: he gets his hand into the dish (19:24; 26:15); but it is such a
wearisome business getting the food into his mouth. So either
he gives up (19:24), or needs a nap afterwards to get his strength

back (26:15). Late afternoon may find the sluggard sitting on the door-step watching the world go about its work. He is on hand should folk need an errand run. But they would be well-advised to do it themselves. That way they will spare themselves a lot of irritation (10:26). For the sluggard will just dilly-dally around until he forgets what he was supposed to do.

These proverbs are, of course, caricatures of the lazy person. In an exaggerated and amusing way, however, they put their finger on the marks of the lazy man and woman: (1) their sheer indolence (26:14); (2) their remarkable ability to think up excuses for themselves and actually to believe them no matter how patently ridiculous they are (26:13; 22:13); (3) their inability to make a decisive start at anything (always "a little longer", 6:9–10; 24:33); and (4) once started, their inability to take the task firmly in hand and see it through to its conclusion (19:24; 26:15; 10:26).

(ii)

The extraordinary thing is that the sluggard is every bit as ambitious to get on in the world as the next man; he is also better than most at lying in bed dreaming about how he will do it! In 13:4 "soul" would have been better translated "appetite", as it has been in 16:26. There it is what drives the worker to action; here it is what drives the sluggard to frustration. He has the will for the rewards of hard work, but not the will to work hard. So he "gets nothing". His "desire" in 21:25 may be his desire to stay in bed and do nothing, or for the things this puts beyond his reach. Either way, it is the death of him—if not literally, then in every other imaginable way. The short and inevitable step from laziness to frustration is shown in 20:4. The sluggard stands idly by, watching while others are busy plough-ing their fields. But ever the optimist, he will turn out at harvest time expecting to find a bumper crop. The fellow lives in cloud-cuckoo land! So does any lazy person who thinks he deserves to get anything without working for it. The saying in 12:27 appears to make much the same point, although the Hebrew is none too clear: the lazy hunter will fail to "catch" (RSV—or is too lazy to "roast", AV, NIV) his prey; that is, to secure the rewards of hard work. For that, diligence is required.

The sluggard is one of that unhappy brood in Proverbs who are wise in their own eyes. He will pit the wisdom of his lazy ways and his pipe-dreams against the earthy realism of any group of intelligent people, and prove he is wiser (26:16). Self-conceit is, of course, a luxury all who live in a fool's paradise can enjoy undisturbed; but the real world has little time for the conceit of fools or sluggards. And if his antics sometimes give amusement to others (so long as they do not rely on him for anything, 10:26), the fellow's unhappy lot is anything but amusing for him: he will suffer poverty and want (19:15; 6:11; 24:34), loss of independence (12:24), and perpetual frustration at getting nowhere (15:19). In a word, he destroys himself by his lethargy just as surely as another destroys by his violence (18:9; cf. 6:11). The contrast between him and "the upright" in 15:19 is unexpected. Is it being suggested that laziness is a kind of dishonesty? The New English Bible follows the Greek translation and reads instead, "the diligent".

The "diligent" is the sluggard's opposite number. The word literally means "sharp, keen". He is the man who puts his back into his work and reaps its rewards (12:27), who is able to provide richly for himself and his family (13:4), and who climbs to the top of the social ladder (12:24). But even if the satisfaction and rewards of honest work are less generous than that, he will work just as hard to keep hunger away from the door (16:26).

(iii)

Knowing human nature only too well—its fondness for siesta and manyana, and the cost of this in missed opportunities—the sages take care to spell out the lesson: "love not sleep, lest you come to poverty; open your eyes, and you will have plenty of bread" (20:13). The same lesson is drawn in 24:30–34, although it is now reinforced by an anecdotal "once upon a time" to make the point crystal clear. We found the lesson about the seductress being reinforced in much the same way (see 7:6–23). While in

24:30–34 the lesson is reinforced from observation of a man's laziness, in 6:6–11 it is reinforced from observation of an ant's industriousness. Needing neither to be goaded nor organized, the ant displays industry, discipline and foresight in providing for itself. For good measure the Greek *Septuagint* version adds a passage on the industriousness of the bee:

> Or go to the bee, and learn how diligent she is, and how earnestly she is engaged in her work; whose labours kings and commoners use for health, and she is desired and respected by all: though weak in body, she is advanced by honouring wisdom.

That we human beings can learn wisdom from observing how animals behave is a sobering thought (see 30:24–28; Job 12:7).

THE DRUNKARD

Proverbs

20:1 Wine is a mocker, strong drink a brawler;
      and whoever is led astray by it is not wise.

23:29 Who has woe? Who has sorrow?
      Who has strife? Who has complaining?
      Who has wounds without cause?
      Who has redness of eyes?
23:30 Those who tarry long over wine,
      those who go to try mixed wine.
23:31 Do not look at wine when it is red,
      when it sparkles in the cup
      and goes down smoothly.
23:32 At the last it bites like a serpent,
      and stings like an adder.
23:33 Your eyes will see strange things,
      and your mind utter perverse things.
23:34 You will be like one who lies down
      in the midst of the sea,
      like one who lies on the top of a mast.

23:35 "They struck me," you will say,
    "but I was not hurt;
    they beat me, but I did not feel it.
    When shall I awake?
    I will seek another drink."

23:19 Hear, my son, and be wise,
    and direct your mind in the way.
23:20 Be not among winebibbers,
    or among gluttonous eaters of meat;
23:21 for the drunkard and the glutton will come to poverty,
    and drowsiness will clothe a man with rags.

(i)

The brief saying in 20:1 sets the tone for the longer passages that follow. "Mocker" is the same word translated "scoffer" in the passages we looked at earlier. The personification of "wine" and "strong drink" is a vivid and poetic way of saying that they turn the man who over-indulges in them into a mocker and a brawler. He might be a quiet, unassuming person when he is sober, but under the influence of drink he creates around him an atmosphere of strife and quarrelling and becomes a public menace. "Led astray" is the word rendered "infatuated" in 5:19, 20, although we saw that it might rather mean "wrapped". It occurs again in the context of drunkenness in Isaiah 28:7, where the RSV translates "reel". But probably, both here in 20:1 and in Isaiah, it means having the senses wrapped round by wine, utterly bemused by it (cf. NEB). Note in passing that in Isaiah 28 we also find drunkenness going hand in hand with scoffing (see vv. 1–3, 7–8, 14). The point of the last phrase may be either that to drink wine to excess is not wise, or that it makes a man act unwisely. Both are true. The drunkard's folly is compounded by folly.

The folly of drunkenness is developed at length in 23:29–35. For its sheer vividness and descriptive power, this portrait of the drunkard is matched only by the portrayals of the seductress and the sluggard. Laziness, drunkenness, adultery! They make a fearsome trio, and are often to be found together. But by themselves, each one is just as impoverishing and deadening as the others, and just as ready to pounce and seize its unwary prey. Israel's sages were sure that all three had to be equally guarded against.

In the middle of the passage is a warning against becoming hypnotized ("look") by the full-blooded redness and the sparkle of the wine in the glass, and its delectable taste as it glides smoothly down the throat (v. 31; see Song 7:9). "Sparkles" is literally "gives its eye". So it seems that the "eye" and "smoothness" of wine has the same power to bewitch and captivate as the seductive glances and smooth words of the adulteress (6:24–25: "smoothly" in 23:31, however, is from a different Hebrew root. More strictly it means to go "straight" down). Both fascinate and hold out promise of pleasure and enjoyment; but both *fatally* fascinate, for they each have a sting in the tail ("at the last", v. 32; cf. "in the end", 5:4). The glide of the wine is like the glide of a snake, with head back and fangs bared, ready to strike.

The effects of wine's venom are graphically depicted in verses 33–35: (1) the nightmarish stupor in which the wretched drunk can neither see straight nor think straight, but his fevered brain and confused mind lose all touch with reality and become prey to fantasies (v. 33); (2) the giddy head, heaving stomach and unsteady legs, so that even when he is clinging to a lampost or lying sprawled out on his bed he feels like he is on a boat tossing at sea in the middle of a storm (v. 34; cf. Ps. 107:27). The second line of this verse is better translated "like one who clings to [or, "lies on"] the top of the rigging" (NEB); and (3) his incapacity to feel pain (v. 35). The reference here is probably to the blows he receives in the course of . his drunken brawls (20:1). He is anaesthetized and beyond feeling. He is even less sensitive to the pain he causes. Verse 29 sums up his wretched state: he is the man who has sorrow and trouble, squabbling and strife, cuts and bruises, and bleary eyes. Moreover, as if that were not enough, 23:21 adds that poverty is in store. Such, then, is the sting in the tail. But the deepest sting of all is found at the end of verse 35: "When shall I awake? I will seek another drink". The passage describes more than a night's drinking and a morning's hangover. It describes the increasingly degenerative effects, physical and mental, of the habitual drinker and the alcoholic.

In 23:19 the "way" to which the sage's son should direct his mind is the way of wisdom, whose path calls for a clear head and a steady step. There is an implied contrast with the way of the drunkard, whose fuddled mind is on his next drink as he staggers along the path of folly. Here, as is so very often the case, wisdom is a matter of watching the company we keep (v. 20). The wretch who drinks alone in the morning most likely began hard drinking with his friends in the evening.

(ii)

According to the old story in Genesis 9:20–27, Noah became the first viticulturist, and promptly became gloriously drunk, thereby exposing himself to shame, and fathering a division between his sons. From that point onwards there runs throughout the Old Testament a strong note of condemnation for drinking wine to excess. Besides the wise, the prophets also castigated drunkards. Their condemnation was particularly directed at the leaders of the people (see Isaiah 5:11–12; 28:7; 56:11–12; Hos. 4:11; 7:5; Amos 6:6; cf. Prov. 31:4–5). On the other hand, wine is also spoken about in the Old Testament as among the good things of life, given by God to cheer the heart (Gen. 27:2; Judg. 9:13; Ps. 104:15; Eccles. 10:19). Notice too that wine and its more potent spiced variety can happily serve as symbols for instruction in wisdom (9:2, 5). Strong as their warnings are, Israel's sages were on the side of moderation rather than abstention. The Book of Ecclesiasticus nicely sums up their view-point (31:25–30):

> Do not aim to be valiant over wine,
> for wine has destroyed many.
> Fire and water prove the temper of steel,
> so wine tests hearts in the strife of the proud.
> Wine is like life to men,

if you drink it in moderation.
What is life to a man who is without wine?
It has been created to make men glad.
Wine drunk in season and temperately
is rejoicing of heart and gladness of soul.
Wine drunk to excess is bitterness of soul,
with provocation and stumbling.
Drunkenness increases the anger of a fool to his injury,
reducing his strength and adding wounds.

The New Testament maintains the same condemnatory note towards over-indulgence. Here too it is those who are leaders in the Church who must take special care (1 Tim. 3:3; Titus 1:7), although any drunkard must be expelled from the Church (1 Cor. 5:11–13). Drunkenness goes together with spiritual blindness (Luke 21:34; Rom. 13:11–14), and disqualifies the person from inheriting God's kingdom (1 Cor. 6:10; Gal. 5:21). Again, however, there is the other side. Jesus provides a generous supply of wine at the wedding in Cana of Galilee (John 2:1–10), lays himself open to the charge that he is "a glutton and a drunkard" (Matt. 11:18–19), and uses new wine as the symbol of his teaching (Mark 2:22), while Paul recommends drinking wine to Timothy for its medicinal value (1 Tim. 5:23). All in all, then, the Bible is frank in its recognition of the positive values of wine as well as insistent about its dangers. The Christian has to make up his own mind and be persuaded in his own conscience, between moderation and total abstention (cf. Rom. 14:13–23), bearing in mind that the line between use and abuse is very fine and is easily and imperceptibly crossed.

THE GREEDY

Proverbs

    27:20 Sheol and Abaddon are never satisfied,
          and never satisfied are the eyes of man.
    28:25 A greedy man stirs up strife,
          but he who trusts in the Lord will be enriched.

23:6   Do not eat the bread of a man who is stingy;
     do not desire his delicacies;
23:7   for he is like one who is inwardly reckoning.
     "Eat and drink!" he says to you;
     but his heart is not with you.
23:8   You will vomit up the morsels which you have eaten,
     and waste your pleasant words.
11:24 One man gives freely, yet grows all the richer;
     another withholds what he should give,
       and only suffers want.
11:25 A liberal man will be enriched,
     and one who waters will himself be watered.

In these proverbs two character traits of the greedy man are highlighted: his insatiable desires, and his Scrooge-like meanness.

(i)

"Abaddon", meaning "destruction", is a poetic word for Sheol (27:20; see 15:11; Job 26:6; 31:12; Ps. 88:11). The imagery here is again of Sheol as a monster that can never swallow down enough humans to satisfy its appetite (see the comment on 1:12 and the passages referred to there). Such, says this proverb, are the "eyes of man"; greedy and covetous of all that they see, but never satisfied (cf. Eccles. 2:10; 4:8). The likening of man's "eyes" to Sheol may also imply that his insatiable desires are as unruly as the underworld; and just as ruthless, both to themselves and to others. This generalization—it speaks about human nature, not simply the inordinately greedy—is less sweeping and much nearer to the bone than we might care to admit. It is easy for we who are Christians to read it as a comment on our materialistic society without pausing to reflect how far it is a comment on ourselves.

It is often remarked that the tenth commandment "You shall not covet" (Exod. 20:17) is the only one to condemn a sinful attitude of mind rather than a sinful act. If that is so, seldom will it remain a sin of thought. Sinful thoughts have a way of bearing fruit in sinful acts. Certainly, for Israel's wise, covetousness or greed was not a private vice but a public menace. As 28:25 bluntly puts it, "A greedy man stirs up strife". He is socially disruptive and destructive. His obsession to get all he can have, as well as much he can never have, is as inflammable as the anger of the hothead (29:22) or the arrogance of the scoffer (22:10). He is a grasper and a schemer; out to get whatever he has his eye on; and, in full flight, unconcerned about how he gets it and ready to fight tooth and nail for it. What he would like but cannot have he must be content to despise.

James asks the pointed question—not the kind of question we should expect him to be asking good Christian folk!— "What causes wars, and what causes fightings among you? Is it not your passions that are at war in your members? You desire and do not have; so you kill. And you covet and cannot obtain; so you fight and wage war" (Jas. 4:1–2). There are few quarrels or wars on this globe where greed is not to be found somewhere near the root of them—whether greed for money, position, power or prestige. In addition, 28:25 hints at the paradox that the gain of greed is loss (cf. 11:24); for it is alone the "great gain in godliness with contentment" (1 Tim. 6:6) which truly enriches.

(ii)

The advice in 23:6–8 strikes a lighter note. Here is a sketch of one of the miser's rare dinner-parties. He gives all the appearances of being a generous host. "Eat and drink", says he heartily; and his guests tuck in to warm dishes and warm conversation. But his heart is not in it. He is like a child watching how big a bite you take of his chocolate bar and wondering what he will have left. He is doing his sums ("reckoning", v. 7) to see how much it is going to cost him. But the miser's meanness and deceit poisons his dishes; and when his guests see through him, as they surely will, they will "vomit" with disgust and rue every friendly word they wasted on him. A mean man spends his whole life doing his sums and works out the cost to himself of everything. The words of Eliot's Prufrock would make a splendid epitaph for him: "I have measured out my life with coffee spoons". His every gesture of generosity or friendship is therefore hollow, and crumbles in the ashes of his calculations.

The paradox highlighted in 11:24 rings true: the tight-fisted man ends up the poorer and the open-handed man the richer (cf. 11:25). The saying has in mind meanness and generosity with money, and looks towards the poor in society. Speaking about Christian giving, Paul puts it this way: "he who sows sparingly will also reap sparingly, and he who sows bountifully will also reap bountifully" (2 Cor. 9:6). The underlying principle is applicable to life and human relationships in general: as we sometimes say, we get out only what we put in.

THE SEDUCTRESS

Proverbs

> 23:26 My son, give me your heart,
>   and let your eyes observe my ways.
> 23:27 For a harlot is a deep pit;
>   an adventuress is a narrow well.
> 23:28 She lies in wait like a robber
>   and increases the faithless among men.
> 22:14 The mouth of a loose woman is a deep pit;
>   he with whom the Lord is angry will fall into it.
> 30:20 This is the way of an adulteress:
>   she eats, and wipes her mouth,
>   and says, "I have done no wrong."

Chapter 23:26–28 resume the tone and a central theme of the first section of the book (see 5:1–23; 6:20–35; 7:1–27). It is a little surprising that this *femme fatale* who looms so large there rears her head so rarely in the later sections. Perhaps the sage felt that the earlier warnings against her were sufficiently lengthy and strong, and that no more was needed than the odd reminder.

It is worth noticing that verse 27 appears to lump together the common prostitute and the adulteress as equally perilous, in contrast to 6:26 (see the comment on this verse, and on 5:3). Pits were dug to trap wild animals (2 Sam. 23:20; cf. Jer. 18:22). So here again is the imagery of the seductress as a huntress waiting to trap her prey (see 6:26; 7:21–23). "Mouth" in 22:14 reminds us that seductive speech is her prime bait (see the comment on 5:3). The depth and narrowness of the pit or well ensures that her victim will be well and truly caught (cf. Jer. 38:6–13). There may also be an allusion here to Sheol (see 2:18–19; 5:5; 7:27). In 1:12, "Sheol" is paralleled by "Pit", a common poetic synonym for it; see Psalm 28:1; Isaiah 14:15; 38:18; Ezekiel 32:18. The word "pit" here in 22:14 is different in the Hebrew from the word used in all these other passages. However, it comes from the same Hebrew root as the verb "sinks down" (*ie* to Sheol) in 2:18. In 23:28 the imagery changes from the hunter to the robber to remind us that the man who falls into her clutches will be stripped of everything he has and even of his very life (see 5:10–11; 6:32–35; 7:23).

If 23:28 suggests that the seductress increases the number of the faithless, 22:14 suggests that the faithless stand most in danger of falling into her pit. In the terrible consequences this will bring upon them, they will experience God's punishment for their faithlessness.

For her part the adulteress has only one thing to say about her deadly activity: "I have done no wrong" (30:20). To her, her behaviour is as natural as eating a meal. This says as much about her ruthlessness as her moral paralysis; for if the moral issue is no longer clear to her hardened conscience, she is not blind to the damage she is causing.

THE MISCHIEF-MAKER

Proverbs

24:8   He who plans to do evil
     will be called a mischief-maker.

12:20 Deceit is in the heart of those who devise evil,
      but those who plan good have joy.
12:5 The thoughts of the righteous are just;
      the counsels of the wicked are treacherous.
16:30 He who winks his eyes plans perverse things,
      he who compresses his lips brings evil to pass.
18:1 He who is estranged seeks pretexts
      to break out against all sound judgment.
28:5 Evil men do not understand justice,
      but those who seek the Lord understand it completely.

21:8 The way of the guilty is crooked,
      but the conduct of the pure is right.
13:5 A righteous man hates falsehood,
      but a wicked man acts shamefully and disgracefully.
21:29 A wicked man puts on a bold face,
      but an upright man considers his ways.
13:2 From the fruit of his mouth a good man eats good,
      but the desire of the treacherous is for violence.
21:10 The soul of the wicked desires evil;
      his neighbour finds no mercy in his eyes.
16:29 A man of violence entices his neighbour
      and leads him in a way that is not good.
11:9 With his mouth the godless man would destroy his
      neighbour,
      but by knowledge the righteous are delivered.
29:27 An unjust man is an abomination to the righteous,
      but he whose way is straight is an abomination
      to the wicked.
29:10 Bloodthirsty men hate one who is blameless,
      and the wicked seek his life.
11:30 The fruit of the righteous is a tree of life,
      but lawlessness takes away lives.
29:7 A righteous man knows the rights of the poor;
      a wicked man does not understand such knowledge.
12:10 A righteous man has regard for the life of his beast,
      but the mercy of the wicked is cruel.

15:28 The mind of the righteous ponders how to answer,
      but the mouth of the wicked pours out evil things.

16:27 A worthless man plots evil,
        and his speech is like a scorching fire.
12:6　The words of the wicked lie in wait for blood,
        but the mouth of the upright delivers men.
10:11 The mouth of the righteous is a fountain of life,
        but the mouth of the wicked conceals violence.
10:6　Blessings are on the head of the righteous,
        but the mouth of the wicked conceals violence.
10:32 The lips of the righteous know what is acceptable,
        but the mouth of the wicked, what is perverse.
10:20 The tongue of the righteous is choice silver;
        the mind of the wicked is of little worth.

Besides the seductress, the character who loomed largest in
chapters 1–9 was the evil man with his perverted speech and his
wicked ways (1:8–19; 2:12–15; 4:14–19; 6:12–15, 16–19). We
meet him once again in these proverbs.

(i)

The "nickname" given to him in 24:8 is literally the "master of
schemes" (cf. NIV "schemer"). "Schemes" is the same word
translated "discretion" in 1:4, where it refers to that desirable
ability to plan a course of action with purpose and foresight.
Unlike the simple in 1:4, however, the mischief-maker needs no
lessons in this regard. He is an adept planner, although he
perversely directs his ability towards evil ends. His is not
impulsive, thoughtless or careless evil, but evil that is carefully
planned, coldly calculated and skilfully executed. His skill at
wrong-doing is suggested by the expression, "devise evil"
(12:20; cf. 6:14), and the word "counsels" (12:5). "Counsels" is
the word for the "skill" acquired by the wise in 1:5, while
"devises" is closely related to the Hebrew word for the skilled
workman or craftsman (Isa. 40:19; Jer. 10:9; cf. Ezek. 21:31).
The mischief-maker devotes the same kind of skills as the wise
and the same kind of expertise as the craftsman to his wicked
activities. His sly wink and pursed lips (16:30) are either means
of slandering his neighbour by insinuation (cf. 6:13–14), or

outward signs that he has successfully hatched mischief—it shows on his face.

His opposite is the man who "devises good" (see 14:22, and the topic, *Loyalty and Faithfulness*); or, as here in 12:20, "those who plan good". In this saying, "good" is actually a translation of Hebrew *shalom,* a word which we normally think of as meaning "peace" (cf. NIV, "those who promote peace"). However, we have already seen that *shalom* comprises the ideas of well-being, wholeness, and harmony (see the comment on 3:17). The New English Bible nicely catches the sense by translating, "those who seek the common good". The upright man contributes to the wholeness and welfare of the community, while the evil man is bent on destroying it. The one is the friend of society; the other its inveterate enemy. That, in a nutshell, is the way in which the mischief-maker is characterized and contrasted with the upright in these proverbs. If the RSV's rendering of 18:1 is correct (the Hebrew text is difficult), the saying is a comment on his alienation from the common life of the community and his hostility towards it—the one reinforcing and being reinforced by the other.

But there is another side to the contrast between them. This is underlined particularly by their contrast in terms of *the righteous* and *the wicked.* While these terms indicate the man who stands either in a right or a wrong relationship to society as we have just described, they also suggest that their stance towards society is rooted in a right or wrong relationship to God. The society whose *shalom* the righteous promotes and the wicked destroys, is God's society, the community of God's covenant people. So the evil of the wicked goes hand in hand with his rejection of the fear of the Lord, while the righteous fears the Lord and turns from evil. This religious foundation to their activities is made explicit in 28:5, where the wicked are contrasted with "those who seek the Lord" in humble obedience. The wicked's lack of discernment of justice, his disregard for how God has willed that men and women should live together in a just and harmonious society, is as much due to spiritual as to moral blindness. Hence in 11:9 the wicked is called the "godless" (or "impious") man. For the most part, however, this religious dimension is at best only implicit, and the sayings concern themselves with its *social outworking* (cf. Ps. 15:2–5; Isa. 33:15).

(ii)

The twisted (21:8), shameful (13:5), brazen (21:29) way of the evil man is the way of "violence" (13:2). This is a rather broad word. It embraces any kind of hostile and harmful act against another person, or any violation of his rights, as well as actual physical violence. His neighbour (21:10; 16:29; 11:9), the upright (29:27; 29:10) and the poor (29:7) are all targets for his malevolence; and even his work animals feel its backlash (12:10; cf. Deut. 25:4). The wicked are thirsty for blood (29:10). This recalls the robbers and killers of 1:8–19. The "blameless" may be their innocent victims (cf. 1:11); or, more probably, those who oppose their activities and seek to bring them to justice. The second line of this verse is difficult. The Hebrew reads, "and the upright seek his life", which can hardly be right. The RSV emends "upright" to "wicked" (a small change in the Hebrew). Alternatively, some such meaning as "values" needs to be wrested from "seek" (cf. NEB, "but the upright set much store by his life"). The text in the second line of 11:30 poses a similar problem. Here the Hebrew reads: "he who takes lives is a wise man". The Authorized Version and the New International Version understand "takes" in the sense of "wins" ("he that winneth souls is wise"; *ie* the wise man attracts others to his wisdom). Following the *Septuagint*, the RSV emends "wise" to "lawlessness" (this is the same word it renders "violence" elsewhere, cf. NEB), again a minor change in the Hebrew letters.

The violence done by the *words* of the mischief-maker is particularly stressed (11:9). His mouth is like a spring of contaminated water (15:28), and his speech consumes and destroys like a "scorching fire" (16:27; cf. Jas. 3:5–6). "Plots evil" is better rendered "digs up mischief" (which NEB paraphrases "repeats evil gossip"). He works assiduously at destroying lives and reputations by spreading gossip and slander (12:6;

11:9), although he is adept at cloaking his malice and hostility from his victims ("conceals violence", 10:11; 10:6). This side to his activities is sharpened and developed in a good number of other proverbs (see the next section, *The Liar, the Flatterer, and the Whisperer*). It would not be going too far to say that it was the violence and destruction worked by the *words* of the mischief-maker which most impressed the sages and filled them with horror. The considered (15:28), vitalizing (10:11, on the metaphor of the "fountain of life", see the comment on 3:18), choice speech of the wise, is also developed in a number of proverbs we shall be looking at later (see the topic, *Wise Ways with Words*).

THE LIAR, THE FLATTERER, AND THE WHISPERER

Proverbs

12:22 Lying lips are an abomination to the Lord,
      but those who act faithfully are his delight.
12:19 Truthful lips endure for ever,
      but a lying tongue is but for a moment.
26:28 A lying tongue hates its victims,
      and a flattering mouth works ruin.

29:5 A man who flatters his neighbour
      spreads a net for his feet.
26:23 Like the glaze covering an earthen vessel
      are smooth lips with an evil heart.

18:8 The words of a whisperer are like delicious morsels;
      they go down into the inner parts of the body.
26:22 The words of a whisperer are like delicious morsels,
      they go down into the inner parts of the body.
16:28 A perverse man spreads strife,
      and a whisperer separates close friends.
26:20 For lack of wood the fire goes out;
      and where there is no whisperer, quarrelling ceases.

11:13 He who goes about as a talebearer reveals secrets,
      but he who is trustworthy in spirit keeps a thing hidden.
20:19 He who goes about gossiping reveals secrets;
      therefore do not associate with one who speaks foolishly.
11:12 He who belittles his neighbour lacks sense,
      but a man of understanding remains silent.
10:18 He who conceals hatred has lying lips,
      and he who utters slander is a fool.
25:23 The north wind brings forth rain;
      and a backbiting tongue, angry looks.
17:4 An evildoer listens to wicked lips;
      and a liar gives heed to a mischievous tongue.

These three characters share two things in common: they are mischief-makers, and they make mischief with their tongues:

(a) *The Liar*. Pride of place must be given to the liar, for he is the parent of the flatterer and the whisperer—and also of the false witness, as we shall see later. Israel's sages are unremitting in their condemnation of lying, of all shapes and forms. Three things are said of it here: (1) it is abhorrent to God (12:22; cf. 6:16–17); (2) it harbours and fosters hatred (26:28; cf. 10:18; 26:24–26: the first line here is difficult, however; the New English Bible hazards "A lying tongue makes innocence seem guilty"); and (3) it is short-lived; "but for a moment" (12:19). As the saying has it, "A lie has no legs". The lie told to save face, to get oneself out of trouble, or to gain some small advantage, as well as the web of deceit spun by the practised and fluent liar, have no substance in reality, and sooner or later the liar will be found out. Truth must out, for it alone "endures".

The lying tongue is contrasted with "acting faithfully" (12:22) and "speaking truth" (12:19). The words "faithfully" (or "faithfulness", Hebrew *emunah*) and "truth[ful]" (*emeth*), come from the same root. The word *emeth* can also be found translated "faithfulness", especially when it has in view the whole of a person's conduct (*eg* 3:3; 1 Kings 2:4; Isa. 38:3). Both words have the basic meaning of what is firm, solid, reliable. This underlines two important aspects of "truthfulness" in the Old Testament: *first* "truth" is not only something to be told, but also something to be done; *second* the "truthful" man is not so much the man who gets his facts right and tells things as they are, as the man who is honest, trustworthy and dependable, in both word and deed (see the topic, *Loyalty and Faithfulness*). To be "true" to other people and not merely to the facts is what is most important. The person who is sensitive to the facts and insensitive to people, and who takes pride in "being blunt", wins no plaudits from the wise; for he can do just as much damage as the liar.

(b) *The Flatterer.* This fellow is literally the man "who makes smooth [his words]" (29:5). This is from the same root used earlier of the "smooth words" of the seductress (see the comment on 5:3). The flatterer's words are in the same debased currency of deceit and duplicity as hers. Hence in 26:28, a "flattering mouth" stands happily in parallelism with "a lying tongue". In 26:23 "smooth lips" follows the reading of the *Septuagint* (so NEB). The Hebrew text has "burning lips" (AV, cf. NIV). If the Hebrew is right, it presumably means *warm* protestations of friendship. A comparison between smoothness and the glaze coating on a piece of pottery, however, makes much better sense. In that case the reference may be to flattery or, more generally, to any kind of speech which lacks honesty and candour and cloaks malicious intent.

Although flattery need not always be guileful, typically in Proverbs the flatterer is the sycophant who fawns his way through life, worming his way into favour with other people in order to manipulate them for his own advantage and to his own ends. But while his words, be they guileful or guileless, may be good for a man's ego, they are decidedly bad for his feet (29:5). Disraeli once remarked to Matthew Arnold, "Everyone likes flattery; and when you come to Royalty you should lay it on with a trowel". There is truth in that, and the flatterer knows it. It is always nice to be told what wonderful people we are, even if we know the person is exaggerating—just a little, of course! There may be little harm in that in itself. But the trouble is that we may soon begin to believe it and think that we really are such wonderful people. Flattery creates and inflates pride. That is its "snare" and its "ruin".

(c) *The Whisperer.* We know this unsavoury character better under other names: slanderer, gossip, tattler, talebearer and the like. At his worst, the whisperer trades in slander. He thinks nothing about inventing and spreading lies about another person out of sheer spite. So the whisperer and the "perverse man"—the man who turns truth upside down and inside out (see the comment on 2:12–15)—are close companions (16:28). More often than not, however, the whisperer is in the more "respectable" (!) business of gossip. Naturally *he* would never dream of telling a lie. So he trades in innuendoes, half-truths, and facts distorted and exaggerated beyond recognition, and spreads them for no better reason than that it makes him feel knowledgeable and important (cf. 11:12). But whether as slanderer, talebearer or gossip, the whisperer is in the business of poisoning relationships (16:28), creating strife (26:20), betraying friends and neighbours (11:13), and also assassination—the ruining of reputations and lives (cf. 11:9; Lev. 19:16).

There is a sad comment on human nature in 18:8. There are two related thoughts here. *First,* there seems to be nothing people find more tasty than a juicy piece of gossip—and they seem always ready to believe the worst. *Second,* once digested, the whisperer's words are never forgotten. They remain indelibly imprinted on the mind. So while the hearer might keep it to himself, the very fact that he heard means the damage has been done; for thereafter his attitude to and relationship with the whisperer's victim will never be quite the same. To listen to the whisperer is every bit as bad as being one (17:4; cf. 20:19). The Rabbis called gossiping or slander "a third tongue", explaining: "it slays three persons: the speaker, the spoken to, and the spoken of". And as a golden rule on avoiding being slain by this tongue as speaker or as spoken to, their advice cannot be bettered: "Let the honour of your neighbour be as dear to you as your own" (see the topic, *A Good Name*).

THE RIGHTEOUS AND THE WICKED (The Proverbs)

Proverbs

10:3 The Lord does not let the righteous go hungry,
but he thwarts the craving of the wicked.

10:9 He who walks in integrity walks securely,
but he who perverts his ways will be found out.

10:16 The wage of the righteous leads to life,
the gain of the wicked to sin.

10:24 What the wicked dreads will come upon him,
but the desire of the righteous will be granted.

10:25 When the tempest passes, the wicked is no more,
but the righteous is established for ever.

10:28 The hope of the righteous ends in gladness,
but the expectation of the wicked comes to naught.

10:29 The Lord is a stronghold to him whose way is upright,
but destruction to evildoers.

10:30 The righteous will never be removed,
but the wicked will not dwell in the land.

10:31 The mouth of the righteous brings forth wisdom,
but the perverse tongue will be cut off.

11:3 The integrity of the upright guides them,
but the crookedness of the treacherous destroys them.

11:5 The righteousness of the blameless keeps his way straight,
but the wicked falls by his own wickedness.

11:6 The righteousness of the upright delivers them,
but the treacherous are taken captive by their lust.

11:7 When the wicked dies, his hope perishes,
and the expectation of the godless comes to naught.

11:8 The righteous is delivered from trouble,
and the wicked gets into it instead.

11:18 A wicked man earns deceptive wages,
but one who sows righteousness gets a sure reward.

11:19 He who is steadfast in righteousness will live,
but he who pursues evil will die.

11:20 Men of perverse mind are an abomination to the Lord,
but those of blameless ways are his delight.

11:21 Be assured, an evil man will not go unpunished,
but those who are righteous will be delivered.

11:23 The desire of the righteous ends only in good;
        the expectation of the wicked in wrath.
11:31 If the righteous is requited on earth,
        how much more the wicked and the sinner!
12:2 A good man obtains favour from the Lord,
        but a man of evil devices he condemns.
12:3 A man is not established by wickedness,
        but the root of the righteous will never be moved.
12:7 The wicked are overthrown and are no more,
        but the house of the righteous will stand.
12:12 The strong tower of the wicked comes to ruin,
        but the root of the righteous stands firm.
12:13 An evil man is ensnared by the transgression of his lips,
        but the righteous escapes from trouble.
12:21 No ill befalls the righteous,
        but the wicked are filled with trouble.
12:26 A righteous man turns away from evil,
        but the way of the wicked leads them astray.
12:28 In the path of righteousness is life,
        but the way of error leads to death.
13:6 Righteousness guards him whose way is upright,
        but sin overthrows the wicked.
13:9 The light of the righteous rejoices,
        but the lamp of the wicked will be put out.
13:21 Misfortune pursues sinners,
        but prosperity rewards the righteous.
13:22 A good man leaves an inheritance to his
            children's children,
        but the sinner's wealth is laid up for the righteous.
13:25 The righteous has enough to satisfy his appetite,
        but the belly of the wicked suffers want.
14:9 God scorns the wicked,
        but the upright enjoy his favour.
14:11 The house of the wicked will be destroyed,
        but the tent of the upright will flourish.
14:14 A perverse man will be filled with the fruit of his ways,
        and a good man with the fruit of his deeds.
14:19 The evil bow down before the good,
        the wicked at the gates of the righteous.
14:32 The wicked is overthrown through his evil-doing,

but the righteous finds refuge through his integrity.

15:6 In the house of the righteous there is much treasure,
but trouble befalls the income of the wicked.

15:9 The way of the wicked is an abomination to the Lord,
but he loves him who pursues righteousness.

15:26 The thoughts of the wicked are an abomination to the Lord,
the words of the pure are pleasing to him.

16:4 The Lord has made everything for its purpose,
even the wicked for the day of trouble.

16:17 The highway of the upright turns aside from evil;
he who guards his way preserves his life.

17:20 A man of crooked mind does not prosper,
and one with a perverse tongue falls into calamity.

18:10 The name of the Lord is a strong tower;
the righteous man runs into it and is safe.

21:7 The violence of the wicked will sweep them away,
because they refuse to do what is just.

21:12 The righteous observes the house of the wicked;
the wicked are cast down to ruin.

21:15 When justice is done, it is a joy to the righteous,
but dismay to evildoers.

21:18 The wicked is a ransom for the righteous,
and the faithless for the upright.

22:5 Thorns and snares are in the way of the perverse;
he who guards himself will keep far from them.

22:8 He who sows injustice will reap calamity,
and the rod of his fury will fail.

24:1 Be not envious of evil men,
nor desire to be with them;

24:2 for their minds devise violence,
and their lips talk of mischief.

24:15 Lie not in wait as a wicked man
against the dwelling of the righteous;
do not violence to his home;

24:16 for a righteous man falls seven times, and rises again;
but the wicked are overthrown by calamity.

24:19 Fret not yourself because of evildoers,
and be not envious of the wicked;

24:20 for the evil man has no future;
the lamp of the wicked will be put out.

25:26 Like a muddied spring or a polluted fountain,
      is a righteous man who gives way before the wicked.
26:27 He who digs a pit will fall into it,
      and a stone will come back upon him who starts it rolling.
28:1 The wicked flee when no one pursues,
      but the righteous are bold as a lion.
28:10 He who misleads the upright into an evil way
      will fall into his own pit;
      but the blameless will have a goodly inheritance.
28:18 He who walks in integrity will be delivered,
      but he who is perverse in his ways will fall into a pit.
29:6 An evil man is ensnared in his transgression,
      but a righteous man sings and rejoices.

THE RIGHTEOUS AND THE WICKED (Comment)

By far the largest number of sayings on any single topic deals with the righteous and the wicked. We have already noticed the close connection between these character types and the theme of the "two ways" (see the comment on 2:20–22 and 4:10–19). Indeed, the two ways are explicitly called the "path[s] of the righteous" (2:20; 4:18), and the "path [way] of the wicked" (4:14, 19), and it is in these terms that we meet the theme in Psalm 1. We also find various other terms describing the paths and those who walk in them: for example, "the way of evil" walked by "men of perverted speech" (2:12), and "paths of uprightness" walked by "good men", by "men of integrity" (4:11; 2:20–21). The theme of the two ways is also found running through these sayings on the righteous and the wicked (10:9; 10:29; 12:26; 12:28; 13:6; 14:14; 15:9; 16:17; 22:5; 28:10; 28:18). We saw earlier that this theme served primarily as a teaching aid, which helped the teacher to sum up the thrust of his teaching in a way his pupils would have no difficulty understanding, by highlighting the contrast between two different *life styles* and two different *destinations* of travellers walking through life. We have already considered the life styles of the righteous and the wicked under the topic *The Mischief-*

Maker. The present proverbs are now concerned with their contrasting destinations or fates.

(i)

All these many proverbs are variations on a single theme: the righteous prosper, and the wicked suffer—and this in just about every conceivable way.

The harvest of righteousness (cf. 11:18) as outlined here runs along much the same lines as what were presented in chapters 1–9 as the benefits of heeding the teacher's instruction or acquiring wisdom. We will recall that in that section of the book too it was the moral and religious aspects of wisdom which were most in view. So the righteous man walks securely through life with unfaltering and unswerving step (10:9; see the comment on 3:5–8, 21–26); for his uprightness is a guide (11:3; 11:5; cf. 2:9; 6:22) and a guard (13:6; 16:17; 14:32; see the comment on 2:9–22) against the pitfalls and snares which lurk by the way to impede his steps and trip him up (22:5). Indeed, God himself is his protection (10:29; 18:10; see the comment on 2:6–8). So his life is firmly rooted in and erected on a solid foundation (10:25; 10:30; 12:3; 12:7; 12:12), well able to weather the storms which threaten to demolish it. He wins God's smile (11:20; 12:2; 15:9; 15:26); enjoys prosperity (13:21; 13:22; 15:6) and has never a bare cupboard (10:3; 13:25); while his every hope comes to fruition (10:24; 11:23). In a word, he finds *fullness of life* (10:16; 11:19; 12:21; 12:28; cf. 3:16, 18). Little wonder, then, that he finds much to sing and rejoice over (29:6; 13:9).

On the other hand, the wicked man has little to sing about. He is in fact of all men most miserable. True, his wicked ways may bring him wealth (which he will invest in further wickedness, 10:16), but he earns deceptive wages (11:18)—wages which are without real substance, benefit or endurance (cf. 13:22; 15:6; 17:20). His darkened, perverse path through life is impeded at every step (22:5) with misfortune snapping at his heels (13:21; 11:8; 12:21); his foot gets trapped in a snare (11:6; 12:13; 29:6); his hopes and expectations are frustrated at every turn (10:3; 10:28; 11:23); he wins God's condemnation (11:21;

12:2; 14:9; 15:9; 15:26), and he will find that the wealth on which he relies for security offers no protection, for God will destroy him (10:29).

(ii)

Israel's sages had a strong conviction that they lived in an orderly world in which wise and right conduct was rewarded, and foolish and wicked conduct was punished. Sometimes they speak of this link between acts and their consequences as part of the natural order of the world: a man reaps what he sows. So "a perverse man will be filled with the fruit of his ways, and a good man with the fruit of his deeds" (14:14; see the comment on 1:24–33). That is the idea expressed in the saying about the pit and the stone in 26:27. But since this is God's world, at other times they speak of God seeing to it that the righteous and the wicked reap their just deserts (*eg*, 10:3; 10:29). This conviction of the moral orderliness of the world meets us in proverb after proverb throughout the book, but it is in the sayings on the fates of the righteous and the wicked that it is expressed most vigorously.

According to these proverbs, then, this is a very good world for the righteous to live in, but a very bad world for the wicked. It is not, however, the kind of world we live in. In our world the righteous do not always prosper, and the wicked do not always suffer. And there is no reason to suppose that Israel's sages inhabited a different world from ours. Of course, they were not totally unaware that their tidy scheme did not fit in with folks' experience. They did acknowledge that the wicked sometimes prospered and that the righteous sometimes experienced misfortune, but this did not unduly trouble them. A little patience was all that was required. When the wicked prosper, they are not to be envied; for their prosperity is quite insubstantial and sooner or later their lamp will be extinguished (24:19–20): when the righteous suffer misfortune, they are not to despair; for they will always rise up again (24:16). There is a strong suspicion that here Israel's sages have confused their belief about what *ought* to be the case with what actually *is* the case. It is to the wisdom books of Job and Ecclesiastes we must turn to find the maturer reflection of Israel's wise on the enigmas of the suffering of the righteous and the prosperity of the wicked (see the comment on 2:20–22).

Nevertheless, we must not forget that these proverbs are connected with the theme of the two ways and have a didactic purpose. We noticed earlier that besides contrasting "life styles" and "destinations" of travellers through life, the theme of the two ways also served to emphasize that a *choice of direction* has to be made. So if these proverbs on the righteous and the wicked are concerned to assert a moral orderliness, it is to strengthen our resolve to "turn away from evil" (12:26) and to "pursue righteousness" (15:9; see the comment on 4:20–27).

II. WISDOM IN VARIOUS SETTINGS

A. THE HOME

PARENTAL DISCIPLINE

Proverbs

22:6 Train up a child in the way he should go,
and when he is old he will not depart from it.

29:15 The rod and reproof give wisdom,
but a child left to himself brings shame to his mother.

20:30 Blows that wound cleanse away evil;
strokes make clean the innermost parts.

22:15 Folly is bound up in the heart of a child,
but the rod of discipline drives it far from him.

19:18 Discipline your son while there is hope;
do not set your heart on his destruction.

29:17 Discipline your son, and he will give you rest;
he will give delight to your heart.

13:24 He who spares the rod hates his son,
but he who loves him is diligent to discipline him.

23:13 Do not withhold discipline from a child;
if you beat him with a rod, he will not die.

23:14 If you beat him with the rod
you will save his life from Sheol.

(i)

"Train up a child in the way he should go" (22:6) is the solemn duty laid upon parents. The Hebrew in the second half of this line is ambiguous. It reads simply, "according to his [the child's] way". This could mean that the training must be tailored to fit the needs and aptitudes of the individual child. The wise parent will always keep that in mind. But doubtless the RSV is correct in taking "his way" as the way a child *ought* to go, namely the *right* way, the way of wisdom and uprightness (4:11).

The key to training is "discipline". We must be careful not to understand this word too narrowly as we read these proverbs. Discipline is first and foremost a matter of *instructing* a child (see the comment on 1:2) and only thereafter of *punishing* him for his wrong-doings. Punishment which is not subject to the higher ends of instruction is at best arbitrary, and at worst abuses the child. Contrary to what many seem to think, the counsel Proverbs has to give on parental discipline has more to do with a listening ear (see the comment on 4:1–9) than an upturned backside! Nevertheless, Israel's sages shared the view of their Egyptian counterparts that—as they dryly put it— "Boys have ears on their backsides"; and in this group of proverbs it is the corrective side of discipline that is prominent.

Two means of disciplinary correction are commended: the "rod" and "reproof" (29:15); or, as we might say, a sound thrashing and a good telling-off. It is perhaps worth noting that the Hebrew word for "reproof" is also the word for reasoned argument such as would be put forward by a lawyer in the courtroom (cf. Job 13:6; 23:4). Too often we parents are inclined to raise our voice to our children when we should be trying to quietly reason with them. It is a mark of the wise that they readily accept reproof (9:8; 12:1). That is enough to set them straight. But, the sages are convinced, for the child who has yet to learn wisdom it is not enough: the word of reproof needs to be reinforced and driven home by the sting of the rod.

The advice given here, "Spare the rod and spoil the child", has been the guiding principle for many generations of parents and teachers. There is no doubt that Israel's sages set great store by it. That is made plain by 20:30. Of late, however, it has come under heavy fire by many who question both its wisdom and its humaneness. They have a point. For there is no question that some children have been nothing short of brutalized and their lives made a misery by stupid parents and teachers hiding behind the letter, if not the spirit, of these proverbs. Of course, because corporal punishment can be easily abused and can be counter-productive does not mean that there can be no place for its sensible and proper use; but it ought to give pause for thought. We might take the view that within a stable and wholesome family relationship it does a child no harm and can maybe do him some good. But we might also wonder whether it is ever really necessary and whether there are not better and more effective means to the same end. In any case, the lesson of these proverbs is how important it is for parents to discipline their children and not how this should be done. How they set about it is a test of the wisdom of the individual parent.

(ii)

A kind but firm hand is called for by the nature of the task of child training. Three aspects are touched on here:

(a) *It is a difficult task.* Its difficulty arises from the fact that "folly is bound up in the heart of a child" (22:15). Folly here is that 'little devil' which makes its presence felt in even the sweetest little angel. And a stubborn little devil it is too! It likes to get its own way and does not take kindly to being told what to do. So simply to try to drum in wisdom (29:15) is like trying to put together a jigsaw and finding the edges do not match. Folly has also got to be drummed out of him (22:15).

(b) *It is an important task.* The folly tethered to a child is not the sort lapped up and delighted in by the fool (cf. 26:11; 15:21)—at least, not yet. It is closer to the folly of the "simple", who are bent on following the dictates of their whims and inclinations without giving it too much thought. But the trouble with little devils is that they have a habit of growing up into big ones if they do not learn any better. And the time to learn is "while there is hope" (19:18)—that is, during the formative years of childhood when folly can be nipped in the bud before it blooms into the full-flowered folly of the hardened fool, when even the most severe and painful discipline will not budge him from it (cf. 17:10).

(c) *It is a serious task.* The sages firmly believe that there is more at stake here than merely the "spoiled child" of proverbial lore. To leave a child to himself, either out of sheer neglect or out of deference to the popular cult of "free expression" is, they believe, to bring shame and sleepless nights upon the parents (29:15; 29:17); more importantly, it is as good as consigning the child over to destruction (19:18). The expression "he will not die" (23:13) could be an extravagant way of saying that the rod will not do him irreparable harm. But since the next verse goes on to say that "you will save his life from Sheol", the thought is most probably that firm discipline will save a child from going down the paths that lead towards death, and will instead direct him along the path of life (cf. 13:14; 15:24).

Parents who take seriously the responsibility to train their children are encouraged by 22:6 to rest in hope: "when he is old he will not depart from it". They can do no more.

HONOURING PARENTS

Proverbs

10:1 A wise son makes a glad father,
    but a foolish son is a sorrow to his mother.

15:20 A wise son makes a glad father,
    but a foolish man despises his mother.

17:21 A stupid son is a grief to a father;
    and the father of a fool has no joy.

17:25 A foolish son is a grief to his father
    and bitterness to her who bore him.

23:24 The father of the righteous will greatly rejoice;
    he who begets a wise son will be glad in him.

23:25 Let your father and mother be glad,
    let her who bore you rejoice.

23:15 My son, if your heart is wise,
    my heart too will be glad.

23:16 My soul will rejoice
   when your lips speak what is right.
27:11 Be wise, my son, and make my heart glad,
   that I may answer him who reproaches me.

13:1 A wise son hears his father's instruction,
   but a scoffer does not listen to rebuke.
15:5 A fool despises his father's instruction,
   but he who heeds admonition is prudent.
23:22 Hearken to your father who begot you,
   and do not despise your mother when she is old.
30:17 The eye that mocks a father
   and scorns to obey a mother
  will be picked out by the ravens of the valley
   and eaten by the vultures.
30:11 There are those who curse their fathers
   and do not bless their mothers.
20:20 If one curses his father or his mother,
   his lamp will be put out in utter darkness.
19:26 He who does violence to his father
   and chases away his mother
  is a son who causes shame and brings reproach.
28:24 He who robs his father or his mother
   and says, "That is no transgression,"
  is the companion of a man who destroys.
10:5 A son who gathers in summer is prudent,
   but a son who sleeps in harvest brings shame.
29:3 He who loves wisdom makes his father glad,
   but one who keeps company with harlots
    squanders his substance.
28:7 He who keeps the law is a wise son,
   but a companion of gluttons shames his father.

(i)

Despite the hopeful note struck by 22:6, many parents know
only too well that things do not always turn out that way. Sadly,
parents may carefully and lovingly bring up their children in the
ways which are right, only to find that they turn out to be
'wrong 'uns'. They are left wondering where they went wrong
with them. Were they too strict, or not strict enough? Perhaps if

they had . . . ! And instead of joy at seeing their children grow up into fine and responsible young men and women, they experience grief and bitter sorrow at seeing them as fools going about their folly. To father a fool is grievous enough. But in ancient Israel, where the son worked alongside his father and would in time step into his shoes, take over his responsibilities and carry on the family name, it was doubly grievous.

The *first* few proverbs (10:1; 15:20; 17:21; 17:25), however, are not the sad reflections of a disappointed parent. Neither are they meant to be simply observations on a hard fact of family life. Rather they are intended to impress upon the young that what they do can bring joy or sorrow to their parents. So their theme is also taken up in the form of direct appeal (23:24–25; 23:15–16; 27:11), urging upon them that to "Give your father and your mother cause for delight" (23:25, NEB) is a worthy motive and guide for their conduct. This is quite in line with the fifth commandment, "Honour your father and your mother" (Exod. 20:12). There is little that brings more joy to parents than to be honoured by their children.

(ii)

The *second* group of proverbs can be regarded as drawing out some of the content and underlining the wisdom of the fifth commandment. To honour parents is not only the duty of children; it is also the mark of the wise child. Five ways of showing honour to parents are highlighted by these proverbs:

(a) *Listen to them!* (13:1; 15:5; 23:22; 30:17). The exasperated, sometimes anguished "He just won't listen!" expresses well the problem many parents encounter as they try to teach 'home truths' to their children. Here we are given a sharp analysis of the root of the problem: some children are fools; and more, they are "scoffers"—so cocksure of themselves and the nonsense in their heads that they are not only unteachable but also contemptuous towards those who try to teach them. Doubtless they regard their parents as old fuddy-duddies who don't know what it's all about. Not that they need express their contempt in so many words: the look on their faces can say it all (30:17).

The law took a very serious view of rebellious and disobedient children who stubbornly refused to listen and learn in the home. According to Deuteronomy 21:18–21 they were to be stoned to death. This provision did not spring from an inflated sense of the wisdom and authority of parents, but from a very sober sense of the importance of the family as the basis for nourishing the lives of individuals and the life of the community, and especially as the means through which the covenant faith of Israel was to be passed down from generation to generation (Deut. 6:4–7, 20–24). To rebel against parents was to rebel against God's institution and design for order and responsibility in society. Whether any parent actually took that final step is another matter. But the point was made.

The sage makes a similar point in 30:17. Along the lines of "an eye for an eye", insolent and rebellious children will meet a violent death and will be left unburied as carrion for the birds (cf. 1 Kings 14:11; Jer. 16:4). If less horrific, the Christian young person ought to find the words of Colossians 3:20 no less compelling: "Children, obey your parents in everything, *for this pleases the Lord.*"

(b) *Don't speak ill of them!* (30:11; 20:20). In the law, the cursing of parents was also a capital offence (Exod. 21:17; Lev. 20:9). Although there the primary offence in view is actively seeking their harm by unleashing a curse against them, here it also carries the more extended sense of speaking harmfully of them, whether by reviling or defaming them. Warning is served that such harmful speaking does most harm to the speaker: he will be snuffed out like a lamp, leaving him in utter darkness, as the proverb puts it. We have already met the metaphor of the extinguished lamp used in describing the fate of the wicked (see 13:9; 24:20; Job 18:5–6; 21:17). The use of the metaphor here is not a veiled reference to the death penalty (Exod. 21:17), any more than 30:17 looks back to the provision in Deuteronomy 21:18–21. It is unlikely that these sanctions were still in force at the time of Proverbs. In both cases the thought is simply that God will take note and punish the offender.

The proper thing to do is to "bless" our parents (30:11), that is, to speak well of them. Some children are never done picking faults in their parents and criticizing them. Even if we feel our parents leave a lot to be desired, perhaps with a little more gratitude and a little less selfishness we might just find that we have more good things and less bad things to say about them.

(c) *Don't mistreat them!* (19:26; 28:24). If the RSV is right, the offence envisaged in the first line of 19:26 is 'father beating'. The meaning of the word rendered "does violence", however, is very uncertain. The Jerusalem Bible translates, "He who dispossesses his father", which makes for a closer parallelism with the next line. The warning would then be against the eviction of aged parents from the family home to fend for themselves. For a son to mistreat his parents in this way is scandalous; and the blackguard will be recognized for what he is. Arranging for an elderly parent to be cared for in a special home is not a modern parallel.

While ordinary theft would be included, the offence in 28:24 is probably the attempt to get hold of the property of parents under some pretext which could make it seem like a right thing to do. If that is the case, Mark 7:9–13 gives us an example of the kind of ploy that might be used. We sometimes hear it said of a child that he is a devil inside the house and an angel outside. One wonders! Common sense would tell us that if children have not learned to show kindness and honesty in the home they will not show these things outside it.

(d) *Pull your weight!* (10:5). Some children treat their home as a hotel that costs them nothing. They eat and sleep in it, but are nowhere to be seen when there is work to be done. Shame on them! They are a disgrace to their parents.

(e) *Watch the company you keep!* (29:3; 28:7). The friends young people make can often be a cause of friction between them and their parents. For parents there may be a lesson to be learned from Samson's parents. They strongly disapproved of his choice of a wife, but they still went to the wedding (Judg. 14). Here, however, the lesson is for young people. In short, it is a reminder that to get into bad company is not only foolish in itself; it also dishonours their parents and causes grief. Moreover, they must remember that they have the good name of their parents to consider besides their own.

NAGGING WIVES

Proverbs

19:13 A foolish son is ruin to his father,
          and a wife's quarrelling is a continual dripping of rain.
27:15 A continual dripping on a rainy day
          and a contentious woman are alike;
27:16 to restrain her is to restrain the wind
          or to grasp oil in his right hand.
21:9   It is better to live in a corner of the housetop
          than in a house shared with a contentious woman.
25:24 It is better to live in a corner of the housetop
          than in a house shared with a contentious woman.
21:19 It is better to live in a desert land
          than with a contentious and fretful woman.

The men-folk will read these proverbs with a smile, but they might not sit too well with their wives. Doubtless they would wish to cap them with a few proverbs of their own!

The picture in 19:13 and 17:15–16 is the incessant drip-drop of rain seeping through the loose wooden boards with their clay or plaster overlay which served for the roof of an ordinary house. This kind of roof needed constant attention during the rainy season if some semblance of dryness was to be kept inside, and if it was not to cave in (see Eccles. 10:18). Among the Canaanites, so an old folk tale tells us, repairing the roof in wet weather was one of the most highly prized virtues in a good son. There is nothing quite so maddening as a leaky roof—except a quarrelsome, nagging wife who never lets up! At least a leaky roof can be plugged up; but as well try to put the wind in wraps or pick up a handful of oil as try to tame the shrew!

So the best thing to be done for the sake of some peace and quiet is to get out of her way. One sage suggests trying the roof top, where the beleaguered husband can always pitch a tent (Judith 8:5) if there is no upper chamber to the house (1 Kings 17:19; 2 Kings 4:10). For good measure this proverb is repeated. Another sage, however, feels that this is still much too close for comfort. He suggests the best line of retreat is into the desert. The point both proverbs make is that any kind of discomfort and privation, however extreme, is a thousand times better than all the comforts of home so long as there is a nagging wife around.

There is more than a glint of humour in these sayings, although it scarcely redeems them from that terrible thing which is nowadays called male chauvinism!

THE GOOD WIFE—I

Proverbs

    18:22 He who finds a wife finds a good thing,
           and obtains favour from the Lord.
    12:4   A good wife is the crown of her husband,
           but she who brings shame is like rottenness in his bones.
    14:1   Wisdom builds her house,
           but folly with her own hands tears it down.
    19:14 House and wealth are inherited from fathers,
           but a prudent wife is from the Lord.

In view of the proverbs in the last section, we may well wonder whether 18:22 was coined by an optimistic and romantic young fellow on the look-out for a wife. For it is one thing to find a wife; quite another to find a good wife! Although, as is made explicit in 12:4, a *good* wife is surely meant. The first line echoes and the second line repeats the words of Lady Wisdom in 8:35: "he who finds me finds life and obtains favour from the Lord"—as if to say that finding a good wife is on a par with finding wisdom. High commendation indeed, coming from the wise!

To marry a wife is no light matter, for she will be the making or breaking of husband and home. In 12:4 the word "good" is a different word in Hebrew from the one used in 18:22. Basically it means "strength, firmness". It is the word found in the phrase "men of *valour*" (Josh. 1:14), and it often means simply an "army" (Exod. 15:4, NEB). Here it means strength of character, embracing both her capabilities as a housewife (cf. NEB) and her integrity as a woman (cf. AV). The same word is used in Ruth 3:11 to describe the heroine as "a woman of worth". Such a woman is royal indeed, who not only brings honour and dignity to her husband, but also brings out the very best in him. How different from the kind of wife who, through her shameful behaviour, makes herself worthless, brings disgrace to her husband and saps his vitality like a wasting and fatal bone disease (cf. 14:30).

With a slightly different twist the Jewish Rabbis also underlined the great influence a wife can have on her husband for good or ill in this anecdote:

> It is related of a pious man who was married to a pious woman that, being childless, they divorced one another. He went and married a wicked woman and she made him wicked. She went and married a wicked man and made him righteous. It follows that all depends upon the woman.

As it stands, 14:1 harks back to the passage in 9:1–6, where Lady Wisdom builds her house and invites the simple to enter and enjoy her fare: what Wisdom is at pains to build, Folly is at pains to demolish. On the other hand, as the RSV notes in the margin, the Hebrew text actually reads "the wisdom of woman", and some other modern versions prefer to retain this. Thus the New International Version translates the verse: "The wise woman builds her house, but with her own hands the foolish one tears hers down". In that case, the thought of the proverb is apparently that by her womanly wisdom the good wife will make the house a home for husband and children, and give it its strength and stability, whereas a bad wife will bring it tumbling down about their ears. The Rabbis caught the inner truth here in their dictum, "A man's home is his wife". One of them tells us that he always called his wife "My home".

The theme of the good wife as the husband's crown and homebuilder is developed at length in 31:10–31. With so much at stake and so much expected, it is perhaps not surprising that Israel's sages should ask the question, "A good wife who can find?" (31:10). This verse goes on to remark that she is "more precious than jewels"—and the clear implication is that she is every bit as rare. The answer given by 19:14 is that such a rare gem of a wife comes from the Lord. The lesson is sometimes drawn from this proverb that the young Christian ought to seek God's guidance in selecting a life partner so as to find the right one, the spouse of God's choice. That is surely good advice; but it is rather remote from what this proverb is actually saying. There are two thoughts here. *First,* marrying a wife is a risky business. When a man inherits house and wealth he knows exactly what is in store for him, but when he marries a wife he can never be fully sure. Only time will tell whether or not she is a good wife. *Second*, when a man finds himself blessed with a good wife, he can be sure that he has received a special gift from God (cf. 18:22). This is one case where we have to say that God's gifts are for the deserving. A good wife ill befits a bad husband.

THE GOOD WIFE—II

Proverbs

31:10 A good wife who can find?
   She is far more precious than jewels.
31:11 The heart of her husband trusts in her,
   and he will have no lack of gain.
31:12 She does him good, and not harm,
   all the days of her life.
31:13 She seeks wool and flax,
   and works with willing hands.
31:14 She is like the ships of the merchant,
   she brings her food from afar.

31:15 She rises while it is yet night
　　　 and provides food for her household
　　　 and tasks for her maidens.
31:16 She considers a field and buys it;
　　　 with the fruit of her hands
　　　　 she plants a vineyard.
31:17 She girds her loins with strength
　　　 and makes her arms strong.
31:18 She perceives that her merchandise is profitable.
　　　 Her lamp does not go out at night.
31:19 She puts her hands to the distaff,
　　　 and her hands hold the spindle.
31:20 She opens her hand to the poor,
　　　 and reaches out her hands to the needy.
31:21 She is not afraid of snow for her household,
　　　 for all her household are clothed in scarlet.
31:22 She makes herself coverings;
　　　 her clothing is fine linen and purple.
31:23 Her husband is known in the gates,
　　　 when he sits among the elders of the land.
31:24 She makes linen garments and sells them;
　　　 she delivers girdles to the merchant.
31:25 Strength and dignity are her clothing,
　　　 and she laughs at the time to come.
31:26 She opens her mouth with wisdom,
　　　 and the teaching of kindness is on her tongue.
31:27 She looks well to the ways of her household,
　　　 and does not eat the bread of idleness.
31:28 Her children rise up and call her blessed;
　　　 her husband also, and he praises her:
31:29 "Many women have done excellently,
　　　 but you surpass them all."
31:30 Charm is deceitful, and beauty is vain,
　　　 but a woman who fears the Lord is to be praised.
31:31 Give her of the fruit of her hands,
　　　 and let her works praise her in the gates.

(i)

This paean in praise of the good wife is an acrostic poem, where
each of its twenty-two verses begins with a different letter of the

Hebrew alphabet in sequence. This is a fairly common device in Hebrew poetry (*eg* Pss. 9; 10; 37; 119; Lam. 1; 2), and was probably intended to make the poems more easily memorized. The need to start each verse with a certain letter explains why the poem jumps back and forward so much.

That this good woman "does not eat the bread of idleness" (v. 27) puts it mildly! From early morning (v. 15) until late at night (v. 18) she has her skirt ends tucked into her belt—or as we would say, she has her sleeves rolled up—(v. 17), busy managing the affairs of her household (v. 27). She is up before the crack of dawn preparing the day's meals—a time-consuming task before the days of mod-cons and convenience foods—and setting her maidservants about their daily tasks (v. 15). Evidently too, she takes the trouble to shop around in the markets for the more exotic foodstuffs and delicatessen brought by foreign merchants, to add interest and spice to her dishes (v. 14).

She is also as industrious at making clothes as she is at cooking. She buys in the raw materials, wool and flax (v. 13). Wool, and linen (v. 22) manufactured from flax, were the common materials from which clothes were made (Job 31:19–20; Isa. 19:9). The law prohibited mixing them in the same garment (Deut. 22:11), perhaps because one was a natural product and the other was manufactured. She then sets to work spinning the threads (v. 19), and weaving the cloth. The "distaff" (if that is what this obscure Hebrew word means) was the stick which supported the fibres while the thread was spun and wound round the spindle. The word "willing" in verse 13 expresses the "pleasure" which she derives from her craftsmanship. Through her industry and skill both she and her family are dressed in the finest of clothes and are well-protected from the cold (vv. 21–22). Clothes made from material dyed scarlet or purple were clothes fit for kings, and thus a mark of great distinction and wealth (Judg. 8:26; 2 Sam. 1:24; Jer. 4:30; 10:9).

But this good wife is not only a very busy housewife; she is also a shrewd and enterprising business woman. As well as providing for the family wardrobe, she trades in garments with the merchants (v. 24). From the proceeds ("the fruit of her hands", v. 16), and after carefully considering the deal from all angles, she buys a field and plants a vineyard. She can hold her own in a man's world, and knows how to drive a hard bargain. Nevertheless, she is not hard-hearted with it. She is kind and open-handed towards the poor and needy (v. 20). Moreover, despite her busy life, she does not neglect her duty to teach her children (see the comment on 4:1–9); and her neighbours find in her a listening ear and a wise counsellor (v. 26).

Given such a woman, it is little wonder that husband and children sing her praises (v. 28), and that her husband has such complete confidence in her: his wealth and his reputation are safe in her hands (vv. 11–12; cf. v. 23). Praise is no more than she deserves (v. 31). And the secret of this good wife's industry, business acumen, reliability and kindness? According to verse 30, it is that she "fears the Lord".

(ii)

This passage gives us an insight into the place of women in the Israelite family. Notice, however, that she is not an ordinary housewife. She is very decidedly "upper class". She manages a large household and has maidservants to help her; she and her family wear the best of clothes; she has money to invest, and her husband enjoys a position of prominence in the community. So while there are "ordinary" points in the portrait which should commend themselves to any housewife—above all that she "fears the Lord"—as a whole it cannot be read as a kind of blueprint of the ideal Israelite housewife, either for men to measure their wives against or for their wives to try to live up to. Far less, of course, can it be read as a blueprint for the ideal housewife in our own Western society. From our modern viewpoint we are liable to be struck by the complete lack of any mention of relationships between the good wife and her husband, and also by the way that she is viewed solely in terms of enhancing her husband's honour and managing the household's affairs.

TROUBLESOME FATHERS

Proverbs

> 11:29 He who troubles his household will inherit wind,
> and the fool will be servant to the wise.
> 27:8   Like a bird that strays from its nest,
> is a man who strays from his home.
> 20:7   A righteous man who walks in his integrity—
> blessed are his sons after him!

In the proverbs we have looked at so far the sages have had some strong things to say about children and wives who give trouble to the man of the house. However, beyond needing a reminder not to spare the rod, it almost seems to be taken for granted that he will be a model father and husband. He may like to think of himself as that; but his wife and children know differently; and they are likely to feel that the sages' proverbs have been unfairly biased against them. There is truth in that. These are men's proverbs, coined by fathers and husbands. So they tend to see things from their point of view. At a deeper level, however, they reflect the viewpoint that, all things being equal, the greatest threat to the stability of the family is the undermining of the father's authority. If the father's position in the family was undermined, so was his position in the community—and with it the standing of the whole family. At the same time, the sages also recognized that the man of the house could cause as much trouble for his wife and children, and wreak as much havoc in the home as they could. That is the theme touched on in the three proverbs we have here.

The *first* may be taken as either (1) a rather general warning to the householder against behaving in ways which bring distress to the folk of the family and poison relationships, or (2) a specific warning against careless and negligent handling of the family's property and assets. The Hebrew words translated "troubles" and "household" are vague enough to permit either. The rest of the saying seems however to fit in better with the latter. The 'troubler' who squanders his resources will end up with nothing of value left ("wide", cf. Eccles. 1:14) and will—in fact or in effect—end up as the slave of the man who manages his household wisely. Here the lesson is that the man who does not care well for his family and home will wake up one day and find them gone. We have seen this happen—literally or metaphorically.

The word "strays" in 27:8 (the *second* proverb) is a distant relative of the name of the region to which Cain was banished, the land of *Nod* (*ie* "Wandering", Gen. 4:16). There he would be "a fugitive and a wanderer" (Gen. 4:12); and the passage speaks of the perils to which such a man, cut off from kith and kin and the protection of the community, is exposed. Whether as a fugitive or as a traveller of some other description, this saying may be a comment on his unhappy lot: exposed to danger, like a bird that has left its nest (cf. Isa. 16:2), and restless for home. It would therefore be an expression of the sentiment: "there's no place like home". But the proverb could also be taken in a different way. Home is where a man belongs; and the "strayer" may be not an honest, if unhappy traveller, but an irresponsible gadabout. In that case the saying reinforces the point made by 11:29. A man ought to look well to his own home and not leave his charges to fend for themselves, like deserted fledglings.

The *third* and last proverb caps the other two: it is the man who does right by his family and by the community at large who leaves the best kind of inheritance his children can ever receive.

OLD AGE

Proverbs

17:6 Grandchildren are the crown of the aged,
    and the glory of sons is their fathers.
20:29 The glory of young men is their strength,
    but the beauty of old men is their grey hair.
16:31 A hoary head is a crown of glory;
    it is gained in a righteous life.

In 17:6 we have a fine picture of the solidity and harmony of family life spanning three generations. Here there are no "generation gaps" of misunderstanding or antipathy. Instead each generation finds enrichment in and derives honour and dignity from the other. To have children was regarded by the Israelites as a mark of divine blessing and was reckoned among the things which gave a man weight and influence in the community (Pss. 127:3–5; 128:3–4; 144:12–15). To have grandchildren running about the house was to be doubly blessed (Ps. 128:5–6). Not only were they one of the chief joys of old age; they were also an assurance that the family name would live on for a long time to come. Grandchildren were therefore the fitting adornment and fulfilment of old age. So the story of the worthy Job climaxes with the words: "[Job] saw his sons, and his sons' sons, four generations. And Job died, an old man, and full of days" (Job 42:16–17). The second line adds the complementary thought that the children's dignity and honour is conferred on them by their father. This is reflected in the common form of Hebrew names like "Elkanah ben [*ie* son of] Jeroham" (1 Sam. 1:1). The thought that a foolish son can bring shame upon his father is often stressed in Proverbs, as we have seen; that a foolish father can bring shame upon his sons is no more than hinted at, but it is equally true (see the topic, *A Good Name*).

In 20:29 the adornment of the young and the old is their "strength" and "grey hair" respectively. By "strength" is meant not only strength of arm, but also the power and capacity to experience and enjoy to the full all that life has to offer. The opposite, the weakness and lack of vitality that comes with age, is well-expressed by the octogenarian Barzillai, who declines David's invitation to live at his court in Jerusalem and explains: "Can I discern what is pleasant and what is not? Can your servant taste what he eats or what he drinks? Can I still listen to the voice of singing men and singing women?" (2 Sam. 19:35). Similarly, in Ecclesiastes 12:1–7 we have a graphic and realistic description of the increasing weakness of old age before finally "the silver cord is snapped". But what the increasing years lose in vigour and strength, they (ought to) gain in experience and wisdom. Says Job in 12:12, "Wisdom is with the aged, and understanding in length of days" (cf. Job 15:10). We can find a fine illustration of the reckless and headstrong counsel of young men in contrast with the sober and wise counsel of old men in I Kings 12. There King Rehoboam followed the advice of the young men, and the result was disastrous. This story also illustrates the fact that old men are not always honoured for their age and wisdom, even in a society in which the affairs of the family and the community were firmly in their hands. As an observation on the place of the elderly in our own society, the proverb hardly rings true. As an observation on the resource of experience, that the elderly have to contribute to the development of youth, there is food for thought in it. At the same time, grey hairs are not a guarantee of wisdom, nor is wisdom denied to youth. Speaking as if he were Solomon, the sage of Ecclesiastes reflects: "Better is a poor and wise youth than an old and foolish king, who will no longer take advice" (Eccles. 4:13).

The saying in 16:31 follows the same line of thought as all the sayings on the fate of the righteous and the wicked. Grey hair is the mark and the reward of a righteous life. The wicked will be cut off before they reach old age. No account, of course, is taken of the fact that many wicked men are to be found sporting grey hair.

HOUSEHOLD SERVANTS

Proverbs

> 29:19 By mere words a servant is not disciplined,
> for though he understands, he will not give heed.
> 29:21 He who pampers his servant from childhood,
> will in the end find him his heir.
> 30:10 Do not slander a servant to his master,
> lest he curse you, and you be held guilty.

27:18 He who tends a fig tree will eat its fruit,
         and he who guards his master will be honoured.
17:2 A slave who deals wisely will rule over a son who acts
         shamefully,
         and will share the inheritance as one of the brothers.

The household slave or servant was to be found in many of the more prosperous Israelite homes (cf. 31:15; 1 Sam. 25:42; 2 Sam 9:10). The first couple of proverbs have some words of advice for the master. A servant is likely to be very stubborn and rebellious and so he needs very firm handling. If you simply scold him, he will look at you with dumb insolence and pay not the slightest bit of attention. So it is better to save your breath and wield your trusty rod instead (29:19). The law in Exodus 21:20–21 reflects just how severely some servants were beaten. The second saying (29:21) makes much the same point. It has in mind the slave who is born in the house (Gen. 17:23; Exod. 21:4), and warns the master against mollycoddling him when he is a small child. The sense of the second line is unclear. The New English Bible renders, "he will prove ungrateful"; and the New International Version, "he will bring grief in the end". Clearly, the servant has enough troubles as it is without anyone adding to them (30:10).

Balancing this harsh line taken towards household servants, in 27:18 and 17:2 there are more hopeful words of counsel and encouragement for the servant. His lot need not be all blood, sweat and tears. If he carries out his duties faithfully, and attends well to the interests of his master, in due time he will reap the rewards (27:18). Indeed, despite his lowly status, his wise and loyal service will stand him in better stead than privilege of birth matched with worthlessness of character (17:2). Though a servant could become the heir when the master had no sons of his own (cf. Gen. 15:2–3), the law makes no provision for a slave disinheriting a son. Presumably it could and sometimes did happen as a happy acknowledgment that character and ability always count for more in the end than status and privilege.

B. THE COMMUNITY

A GOOD NAME

Proverbs

22:1   A good name is to be chosen rather than great riches,
       and favour is better than silver or gold.
10:7   The memory of the righteous is a blessing,
       but the name of the wicked will rot.
13:15 Good sense wins favour,
       but the way of the faithless is their ruin.
12:8   A man is commended according to his good sense,
       but one of perverse mind is despised.
11:27 He who diligently seeks good seeks favour,
       but evil comes to him who searches for it.
21:21 He who pursues righteousness and kindness
       will find life and honour.
18:3   When wickedness comes, contempt comes also;
       and with dishonour comes disgrace.
11:16 A gracious woman gets honour,
       and violent men get riches.
11:22 Like a gold ring in a swine's snout
       is a beautiful woman without discretion.
27:21 The crucible is for silver, and the furnace is for gold,
       and a man is judged by his praise.

(i)

Although seldom mentioned, the invaluable asset of a good name (22:1) has an important place in the thought of Israel's sages and underlies many of their sayings. In 22:1 the Hebrew is simply "a name", the word "good" being supplied by the translators to make the meaning clearer. The word is used several times in the Old Testament with the meaning "reputation". So most infamously, the builders of the tower of Babel seek to make a "name" for themselves (Gen. 11:4); while, on a happier note and by way of direct contrast, God promises to make Abraham's "name" great (Gen. 12:2; see also 2 Sam. 7:9; 8:13). Men with a bad reputation are simply called "nameless" (Job 30:8, NIV).

Behind the saying in 22:1 (see also Eccles. 7:1) lies the ancient Hebrew thought that a name was not merely a label, but ideally the outward expression of the inner nature and character of its bearer. So, for example, when Jacob's name was changed to Israel, it was matched by a change in his character (Gen. 32:28; cf. Gen. 27:36). The man was in his name, as it were. That is very important here. For the good name which surpasses the value of riches is not one in name alone —which might be undeserved—but one which corresponds to the actual character and worth of its bearer and which is therefore fully deserved. Notice that more was at stake than that a man should be well spoken about during his lifetime, important as that was. A man's name was also seen as that "immortal part" of him which survived his death (2 Sam. 14:7; 18:18; Ruth 4:10; Job 18:17). Let a man leave behind a good name, and he would be remembered and his memory blessed long after he was gone; let him leave behind a bad name (*ie* be "nameless") and it rotted away into oblivion, and he with it (10:7). Perhaps more to the point: his family still had to live with it! It has not been unknown for a family to change their name because of the shame the father and husband have brought upon it.

The theme of a good name is taken up by later sages. Thus in Ecclesiasticus we are encouraged (41:12–13):

> Have regard for your name, since it will remain for you
>   longer than a thousand great stores of gold.
> The days of a good life are numbered,
>   but a good name endures for ever.

And we are warned (6:1):

> A bad name incurs shame and reproach.

Again, in the Jewish *Sayings of the Fathers,* we are told (4:17):

> There are three crowns, the crown of the Torah, the crown of the priesthood, and the crown of kingship, but the crown of a good name excels them all.

(ii)

Typically in Proverbs, however, the notion of a good reputation lies hidden behind the words "favour" and "honour".The *first* has in view men's (and God's! 3:4, 34) acceptance and approval; the *second* their respect and esteem—and, consequently, the "weight" or influence the man in question carries in the affairs of the community (see the comment on 3:16). Job in his happier days provides a good example of the man who has won favour and is held in honour (see Job 29). Here again we should notice that both words also involve the thought of the inner worth of the individual balancing the favour and honour he obtains. This comes out nicely in 11:16. "Gracious" is the same word rendered "favour" in 13:15. This is a woman whose charm and attractiveness of bearing, and integrity of character, make her deserving of the approval and honour she receives (see ch. 31, and the topic, *The Good Wife*)—quite the opposite of the lady in 11:22, whose beauty is only skin deep and is ill-matched by her lack of good taste and moral discernment. People will see the snout behind the ring. The force of the comparison to men of violence is probably that they obtain wealth, but preclude themselves from the honour that ought to go with it (see 3:16). As outer beauty ought to be an index of inner beauty, a man's wealth ought to be an index of his value in his community; that ill-gotten gain can never be (see the topic, *Wisdom and Wealth*). Favour and honour rightly belong to those who bring good sense to bear in the practical affairs of life (13:15; 12:8), who actively contribute to the good and well-being of their fellows (11:27), and who pursue all that righteousness and kindness (*chesed;* see the topic, *Loyalty and Faithfulness*) entails (21:21)—that is, to the wise and the righteous. Their opposites, faithless men of twisted minds and evil ways, who have nothing positive to contribute but who insidiously chip away at the fabric of the community, wreaking havoc and destruction, will obtain "contempt" and "disgrace" (18:3). "Disgrace" comes from a root meaning "to be light". Such people, then, are "lightweights"; chaff blown with the winds (cf. Ps. 1:4); and their fellows will acknowledge them for what they are—they will be 'nameless'.

(iii)

It is clear that the sages have a great deal of confidence in the good sense of the community to bestow honour on those deserving honour, and contempt on those deserving contempt. This lies behind the saying in 27:21. Just as the value of silver and gold is tested in the crucible, so the worth of a man's character is tested by his reputation. A man's reputation is a wonderful character reference.

That the opinion of men can be wrong, and that some men's honour is dishonour, and their dishonour honour, are things which need to be said to get a proper balance. There are times when the approval of conscience and the approval of God lead a man to beat a lonely track among his fellows, that wins for him their derision and contempt. Jeremiah was one such man; Jesus was another. There is a cross for Jesus' disciples to bear along the same track (see Luke 6:22–23, 26). But it is one thing to be "nameless" ("cast out your name as evil", Luke 6:22) on account of the name of Christ; another thing on our own account (cf. 1 Pet. 4:14–15). We must never forget there is a difference. The New Testament gives us no encouragement to be thoughtless or careless about our reputations. Several times it echoes the note in Proverbs 3:4 that the ways of true wisdom win the approval of God *and* the approval of men (Luke 2:52; Acts 2:47; Rom. 14:18; 2 Cor. 8:21). A good reputation in the community at large is singled out as one of the qualifications for leadership in the Church (1 Tim. 3:2, 7). There is something far wrong with our Christianity if no-one who knows us outside our Church has a good word to say about us.

FRIENDS AND NEIGHBOURS

Proverbs

18:24 There are friends who pretend to be friends,
        but there is a friend who sticks closer than a brother.
17:17 A friend loves at all times,
        and a brother is born for adversity.

27:10 Your friend, and your father's friend, do not forsake;
      and do not go to your brother's house
        in the day of your calamity.
     Better is a neighbour who is near
      than a brother who is far away.

27:9 Oil and perfume make the heart glad,
      but the soul is torn by trouble.

27:6 Faithful are the wounds of a friend;
      profuse are the kisses of an enemy.

27:17 Iron sharpens iron,
      and one man sharpens another.

26:18 Like a madman who throws firebrands,
      arrows, and death,
26:19 is the man who deceives his neighbour
      and says, "I am only joking!"

25:17 Let your foot be seldom in your neighbour's house,
      lest he become weary of you and hate you.

27:14 He who blesses his neighbour with a loud voice,
      rising early in the morning,
      will be counted as cursing.

17:9 He who forgives an offence seeks love,
      but he who repeats a matter alienates a friend.

25:8 What your eyes have seen
     do not hastily bring into court;
     for what will you do in the end,
      when your neighbour puts you to shame?

25:9 Argue your case with your neighbour himself,
      and do not disclose another's secret;
25:10 lest he who hears you bring shame upon you,
      and your ill repute have no end.

(i)

The Authorized Version translates the first line of 18:24, "A man that hath friends must shew himself friendly". This oft-quoted dictum expresses a fine sentiment which is always worth bearing in mind. But although the Hebrew here is rather obscure, it is much more likely that the proverb is drawing a contrast between two different kinds of friends. But are the first those who give the appearance of being friendly (RSV), or who are good only for small talk (NEB), or who are so unreliable that they may prove a man's undoing (NIV, JB)? At any rate, they would seem to be the kind Jack revels in:

> In every mess I finds a friend,
>> In every port a wife.

No doubt quite sociable; but very superficial! In contrast to such friends, there is the one for whom the bond of friendship is closer than kinship, and who "sticks" with his friend through thick and thin. "Sticks" is the same word used in Ruth 1:14 of Ruth "clinging" to her mother-in-law, Naomi. Ecclesiasticus puts the contrast this way: "There is a friend who is a table companion, but will not stand by you in your day of trouble" (6:10). Just as it is in times of trouble that a brother proves himself, so it is then that you can tell who your real friends are (17:17).

There appears to be three separate sayings strung together in 27:10. The *first* applies and presses home the point that a real friend "loves at all times" by emphasizing the need to keep "friendship in constant repair", especially with friends of long standing and proven worth: "Do not forget the friend who fought your battles" (Ecclesiasticus 37:6, JB). None of us has friends like that enough and to spare. It is always easier to lose an old friend than to gain a new one. The *second* reads very strangely. Where should a man go if not to his brother's house (cf. 17:17) when he is in trouble? It is just possible that the sense is "don't pester your brother with all your problems" (cf. 25:17). Most commentators, however, think that something has gone awry with the text. The New English Bible omits the line altogether. The *third* saying reminds us that in many a crisis it will often be our next-door neighbour and not our brother who is on hand and best able to help (see the comment on 3:27–28).

As 27:9 stands in the RSV, it has nothing to do with friends. The second line, however, adopts the *Septuagint* reading in place of the difficult Hebrew, "but the pleasantness of his friend from the counsel of the soul". This might mean, "but friendship is sweeter than one's own counsel" (NEB OT edit. ftn.). But friendship is not all oil and perfume, as 27:6 underlines. There are unpleasant things about us which our best friends ought to tell us. We may not like to hear them; but their well-meant and well-directed truths are "wounds" which make us more healthy people, and sooner or later we will thank them for being so direct (cf. 28:23). That is what real friends are for; and if someone fawns over us and has only nice things to say about us . . . beware the kisses of a Judas!

An incisive comment is made in 27:17 on the value of mixing with other people. A man's character and wits do not develop in a cocoon, but by interaction with others: good conversation, the exchange of views, healthy disagreements and the like are necessary to sharpen the mind and shape the character. The darker side to this is that "bad company corrupts good character" (1 Cor. 15:33, NIV; cf. Prov. 13:20).

(ii)

Dr. Johnson's wise advice, "A man, Sir, should keep his friendship in constant repair", is the theme underlying the second group of sayings. Friendships between companions, colleagues or neighbours, do not grow of their own accord but have to be carefully nurtured and tended; and they are sooner broken than mended. Five pieces of advice on tending friendship and good neighbourliness are given here:

(a) *Know when a joke is not a joke!* (26:18–19). This saying might well have been included among those on the fool, for the kind of practical joking warned against here is right up his street—"it is like sport to a fool to do wrong" (10:23). He recklessly throws around words like flaming arrows, and when his neighbour is pierced he thinks that his lame "I am only joking" excuses him. He has graduated from teasing and ragging to downright mischief-making, and he cannot tell the difference.

(b) *Don't make a pest of yourself!* (25:17). This proverb warns against taking advantage of our neighbour's kindness and hospitality, whether selfishly or tactlessly. We all know the kind of neighbour who comes to the door every other day to borrow some sugar, and wedges her foot in the door; or the kind who always comes round to borrow your tools and expects you to do the job for him as well. The Egyptian *Instruction of Ani* gives a similar warning against living on a neighbour's doorstep and living on his kindness: "Do not go freely to your neighbour's house, but enter it only when you are invited".

(c) *Don't be inconsiderate!* (27:14). In a more modern idiom, the point this saying seems to be making is that the fellow who blasts his record player or his television at unearthly hours will have some decidedly unkind things said about him by his neighbours! Alternatively, the point may be that this man is insincere. He pretends to be very friendly, but his "Hail fellow, well met" is too overdone to be true. He is probably up to some mischief; at the very least he is trying to worm something out of you (cf. 27:6).

(d) *Don't tell tales!* (17:9). The New English Bible interprets this verse as dealing with "harping on" to your friend about his shortcomings and faults—a reminder that to be a friend along the lines of 27:6 needs great wisdom and tact. The RSV may be right, however, in understanding it to refer to telling hurtful tales about your friend behind his back. Both, in any case, are sure ways to lose a friend. Friendship thrives on the soil of forgiveness and love; and they bear no grudges and tell no tales (cf. 1 Cor. 13).

(e) *Don't betray confidences!* (25:8–10). It is not clear whether these verses warn against impetuous litigation against a neighbour in a court of law, or against pursuing your side of the quarrel with him in public by harmful gossip and breach of confidences. The verses underline that the one who tries to score over his neighbour and undermine his good name in this way will himself end up with a bad name as a man who is disloyal and untrustworthy. The right and wise course is to keep a quarrel private and to settle it in private (cf. Matt. 18:15–17).

ENEMIES AND REVENGE

Proverbs

20:22 Do not say, "I will repay evil";
     wait for the Lord, and he will help you.
17:13 If a man returns evil for good,
     evil will not depart from his house.

24:17 Do not rejoice when your enemy falls,
     and let not your heart be glad when he stumbles;
24:18 lest the Lord see it, and be displeased,
     and turn away his anger from him.
25:21 If your enemy is hungry, give him bread to eat;
     and if he is thirsty, give him water to drink;
25:22 for you will heap coals of fire on his head,
     and the Lord will reward you.
16:7 When a man's ways please the Lord,
     he makes even his enemies to be at peace with him.

While a man can always choose his friends, he cannot always choose his enemies. Nor can he always avoid having them. What he can avoid is showing the same animosity towards them as they show towards him, and that is what the sage is concerned with here.

(i)

The Old Testament's *lex talionis,* "life for life, eye for eye, tooth for tooth" (Exod. 21:23–24), has a harsh ring to it in our ears. However, its design was to curb the kind of unrestrained vengeance boasted by Lamech (Gen. 4:24), which was all too common in the ancient world. The principle neither demands nor recommends an eye for an eye, but insists, *no more* than an eye. Nevertheless, 20:22 shows us a better way for dealing with personal wrongs: "Do not say, 'I will repay evil'". Vengeance belongs to God and must be left to him (Deut. 32:35; Rom. 12:17–21; 1 Thess. 5:15; Heb. 10:30). Man's part is to wait and hope for God's help, and not to raise his hand in vengeance. His "wild justice" does not work the justice of God. The theme of quiet and steady waiting on God's help in the face of the malice of enemies is elaborated in many of the Psalms (see Pss. 25:3; 27:14; 37:34; 62:5). In the Sermon on the Mount, Jesus reinforces the point, adds that his disciples should "turn the other cheek", and caps it by telling them to "Love your enemies" (Matt. 5:38–48). It is well to note that vengeance in the Old Testament was not properly a matter of giving vent to personal vindictiveness, but was a matter of restoring the harmony and balance to the community which the offence had disrupted—of restoring what, we have seen, the Old Testament calls *shalom,* "peace". So when the Lord, the God of vengeance, shines forth (Ps. 94:1) to help us against our enemies, he may do so in ways which will surprise us—for he is also the God of peace (cf. 16:7).

We have a fine illustration of the stupidity and perversity of the man in 17:13 in the figure of Nabal, who, as his wife tells David, was well named "Fool" (1 Sam. 25:21–22, 25; cf. Pss. 35:12; 109:4–5). To return evil for good is not only to treat a friend as an enemy; it is, says the sage, to be your own enemy and the enemy of those nearest and dearest to you. David found out the truth in this after his scurrilous treatment of Uriah (2 Sam. 12:7–12; cf. especially v. 11).

(ii)

In 24:17–18 warning is given against gloating when our enemy comes unstuck. While we may not raise a hand against someone who wrongs us, if we are being honest with ourselves most of us would admit to lacking more than the patience of Job (see Job 31:29): "It serves him right," we are apt to say with a smug look on our face, "and I can't say I'm sorry!" At first sight the next verse rather spoils the fine sentiment of the first. It seems to say that we must not gloat because it will only bring our enemy relief. More probably, however, it simply means that gloating over his misfortune is as bad as his emnity towards us and as displeasing to God. Does the sage intend that we should go further and show sympathy and compassion to our enemy in his plight, as shown by the Psalmist in Psalm 35:11–14? At any rate, the next passage (Prov. 25:21–22) embraces that thought.

It encourages showing kindness and consideration towards our enemies in very practical ways, especially when we have the advantage. But what are we to make of verse 22? Here again the first impression is that it rather tarnishes the shine of verse 21. In the Psalms we also hear the prayer of a man beset by enemies: "Let burning coals fall upon them! Let them be cast into pits, no more to rise!" (Ps. 140:10). Is that the thought expressed here as well? If so, the meaning is that by heaping kindness on our enemies we stoke the fire of their punishment, and win for ourselves a more handsome reward. On the other hand, there was a ritual practice in Egypt in which a man put a brazier of burning charcoal on his head as a public sign of his shame and remorse for his wrong-doing. That might be the explanation of the coals of fire in 25:22. The point of the saying would then be that by meeting hostility with kindness, our enemy will be thoroughly ashamed of himself, and we will turn him into a friend. The *Instruction of Amenemopet* gives the same piece of advice: "Fill his belly with bread of yours, so that he shall be satisfied and ashamed". That is how the apostle Paul understands the saying. After quoting it, he goes on to write: "Do not be overcome by evil, but overcome evil with good" (Rom. 12:20–21). This passage in Romans (see vv. 14–21) also provides apt comment on 16:7. The ways of the man approved by God are the ways of the peacemaker (see Gen. 26:26–30; Ps. 34:14; Matt. 5:9; Jas. 3:17–18). In the end they command also the approval of men.

Though they do not say it in so many words, there is little between the practical counsels of Israel's sages on the treatment of enemies and Jesus' command to "love your enemies". What "was said" in days past (Matt. 5:43) was not said by a wise man.

HATRED AND STRIFE

Proverbs

> 26:24 He who hates, dissembles with his lips
> and harbours deceit in his heart;

26:25 when he speaks graciously, believe him not,
    for there are seven abominations in his heart;
26:26 though his hatred be covered with guile,
    his wickedness will be exposed in the assembly.
10:12 Hatred stirs up strife,
    but love covers all offences.

15:17 Better is a dinner of herbs where love is
    than a fatted ox and hatred with it.
17:1 Better is a dry morsel with quiet
    than a house full of feasting with strife.

26:21 As charcoal to hot embers and wood to fire,
    so is a quarrelsome man for kindling strife.
17:19 He who loves transgression loves strife;
    he who makes his door high seeks destruction.
26:17 He who meddles in a quarrel not his own
    is like one who takes a passing dog by the ears.
17:14 The beginning of strife is like letting out water;
    so quit before the quarrel breaks out.
18:19 A brother helped is like a strong city,
    but quarrelling is like the bars of a castle.

(i)

In 27:6 the rebukes of a faithful friend were contrasted with the treacherous kisses of an enemy (see the topic, *Friends and Neighbours*). The word "enemy" in this verse is literally "hater". So here now in 26:24–26 we have a sketch of this, the worst kind of enemy, and a warning not to be fooled by him. This enemy is always found close to home. It is someone you regard as a very good friend or colleague, and as the last person who might wish you harm. But behind a veneer of friendly words "seven abominations" lurk; while he smiles to your face he will stab you in the back. "Seven abominations" may look back to 6:16–19; but more likely the thought is that hatred is the spawning ground for any number of wicked thoughts and actions. Verse 26 adds that sooner or later his duplicity and treachery will be exposed for all to see. Unfortunately this seldom happens before the damage has been done, for that is what finally gives him away. Probably many of us have had some bitter experience of this friend proved enemy. So very easily can friendships turn sour when offence is given and is not forgiven (10:12; cf. 17:9, *Friends and Neighbours*); instead the offended party bears a grudge and allows his resentment to smoulder on until finally, and almost inevitably, it flares up into hatred. Then 'getting even' is all that counts (see the topic, *Enemies and Revenge*). Indeed the offended friend, neighbour, or colleague turned spiteful enemy, is the most common type around. It is also the sort of enemy all of us stand in danger of becoming if we have not learned to forgive and forget.

(ii)

In 15:17 two dinner parties are contrasted. In the one a sumptuous spread is provided. Nothing but the best here. The "fatted ox" is royal fare (1 Kings 4:23), and a sign of prosperity and luxury (Amos 6:4; cf. Luke 15:23). But there are bitter resentments, rivalries and hatred smouldering away underneath the pleasantries being passed across the table. So instead of this meal being an occasion for expressing and strengthening the bonds of friendship, it is a grand exercise in deception. The other meal is a poor show by comparison: a dish of vegetables; simple, everyday fare. Nothing to titillate the taste-buds here. But love is the host at this table, and so there is everything to cheer the spirit. The sage has no doubt at which table he would prefer to eat.

The theme of the two dinner parties is taken a step further in 17:1. Here now the contrast is between the strife which hatred fosters (cf. 10:12) and the quiet harmony which love engenders. "Feasting with strife" is literally "sacrifices of strife". In the case of some Old Testament sacrifices, the meat was not burnt on the altar but was eaten by the worshipper's family and friends as a fellowship meal. So once again what ought to have been an occasion for festivity and fellowship has become an occasion for conflict and strife (cf. 1 Sam. 1:3–8). We might notice that the very strong warning in the New Testament about partaking unworthily of the Lord's Supper or Holy Communion is linked with, among other things, the existence of divisions and dissensions within the Church (1 Cor. 11:17–34).

(iii)

The sayings on the dinner parties show just how much Israel's sages prized peace and harmony in men's relationships with one another. They had a keen eye for the kinds of behaviour and the types of people that disrupted the peace and sowed discord, and they were quick to condemn them. The man whose heart is filled with hatred and spite is only one among the many characters in Proverbs who are adept at stirring up strife. Among his fellows are, for example, the fool (18:6; 20:3), the hot-head (15:18; 29:22), the scoffer (22:10; 29:8), the drunkard (23:29–35), the greedy (28:25), the mischief-maker (24:8) and the whisperer (26:20).

The last group of proverbs contains some further observations and reflections on the theme of strife.

The quarrelsome man in 26:21 may be the whisperer of 26:20, or he may simply be the fellow who is always spoiling for a quarrel and loves to see other people at loggerheads with one another. At any rate, the meddler in 26:17 is just that sort of fellow. He thrives on strife and division, and he is always poking his nose into other folk's quarrels and pouring fuel on the flames of their disputes. It serves him right if he gets his nose bitten!

Israel's sages had no patience with the man who needlessly involved himself in quarrels not his own, but they were realistic enough to know that disputes could not always be avoided (cf. "for no reason", in 3:30). We have already seen them advising that such disputes should be kept private and settled in private; 25:8–10, *Friends and Neighbours*). Nevertheless, 17:14 makes the point that we should do our utmost to avoid becoming embroiled in a quarrel in the first place. This does not mean that we should turn our backs and walk away from it, but rather that we should seek to "make it up", to be reconciled. And the time to do this is before the quarrel really gets underway and becomes impossible to stop – it is always wise to repair a crack before the dam bursts. The Hebrew text in 18:19 is very obscure. The New International Version reading is preferable: "An offended brother is more unyielding than a fortified city, and disputes are like the barred gates of a citadel". The closer the relationship, the greater the alienation when a quarrel breaks out, and the more difficult reconciliation becomes. The barriers standing in its way are formidable. That of course lends greater weight and wisdom to the advice: "quit before the quarrel breaks out".

LOYALTY AND FAITHFULNESS

Proverbs

19:22 What is desired in a man is loyalty,
   and a poor man is better than a liar.
20:6 Many a man proclaims his own loyalty,
   but a faithful man who can find?
25:19 Trust in a faithless man in time of trouble
   is like a bad tooth or a foot that slips.
14:22 Do they not err that devise evil?
   Those who devise good meet loyalty and faithfulness.
11:17 A man who is kind benefits himself,
   but a cruel man hurts himself.

Here we meet once again the two great words which treat all men as friend and neighbour: "loyalty" (*chesed*) and "faithfulness" (see the comment on 3:3 and 3:27–29).

The first line of 19:22 is difficult. The Hebrew reads "the desire of a man is his loyalty". This is eased by the RSV to give better sense (cf. NIV). The New English Bible however assumes "loyalty" is a mistake for "disgrace", and renders: "Greed is a disgrace to a man". If the *Septuagint's* reading is followed, the line could be rendered, "A man's produce is his loyalty". The sense of the proverb might therefore be that even the poorest of men who produces loyalty makes a far richer contribution to the life of the community than any liar, however wealthy. No community can flourish healthily either where people are deceiving one another or where their relationships are governed by hard economics.

When loyalty is put to the test, observes 20:6, there is a discrepancy between promise and performance. When the chips are down and actions and not words are looked for, loyalty and faithfulness become much rarer commodities than was supposed. The next proverb (25:19) likens the reliance placed on the man who disappoints and betrays that trust, to a decayed tooth or a lame foot: utterly useless, and as apt to cause pain and to cripple. That was the bitter experience of Job (see Job 6:14–23).

These sayings provide further comment on the theme of fair and foul-weather friends (see the topic, *Friends and Neighbours*). But they go further than that. The word "faithless" is the same rendered "treacherous" in other passages. In them, the treacherous man is not merely a bad friend; he is also a public enemy (see 2:22; 11:3; 11:6; 13:2). Hence here loyalty and faithfulness stand opposed to lying, treachery, evil scheming and cruelty ("kind[ness]" in 11:17 is another shade of meaning to this word, *chesed*). Apt commentary on this contrast is provided by the prophet Hosea when he hurls this terrible charge at the people (Hos. 4:1–2):

> There is no *faithfulness* or *kindness* [*chesed*],
>   and no knowledge of God in the land;
> there is swearing, lying, killing, stealing
>   and committing adultery;
> they break all bounds and murder follows murder.

The negatives of verse 1 and the positives of verse 2 belong together. For whenever men allow their relations and dealings with one another to be dictated by self-interest, and place no value on "faithfulness" and "kindness", they are turning what ought to be a caring community into a bloody jungle in which the strongest survive—but to the detriment of themselves

(11:17) and at the cost of their humanity. They are also, as Hosea makes abundantly clear, inviting the judgment of God upon their community.

THE RICH AND THE POOR:
A FACT OF LIFE

Proverbs

22:2   The rich and the poor meet together;
            the Lord is the maker of them all.
29:13   The poor man and the oppressor meet together;
            the Lord gives light to the eyes of both.

The first proverb is apt to remind us of the lines:

The rich man in his castle,
   The poor man at his gate,
God made them, high or lowly,
   And order'd their estate.

It is unlikely that the sage is being quite so obtuse as that. Rather, he is saying that within the world God has created, and over which he holds sway, the rich and the poor (and the poor and their oppressors, 29:13; cf. Matt. 5:45) are to be found side by side—without thereby implying that responsibility for this state of affairs lies with God and has the mark of his handiwork or the seal of his approval. But it must be admitted that 22:2 does strike a rather conservative note; and one, indeed, which sets the key for all the proverbs on this subject. Some folk are rich and others poor. Some can afford all the luxuries of life; others have to struggle to make ends meet; while many are destitute. That is *a fact of life*. Israel's sages accepted the fact; they did not try to change it. They were neither political economists nor social reformers. So they did not try to work out in theory or try to implement in practice measures designed to give everyone a fairer share of the cake, or to eradicate poverty from the community altogether. The prophet was the real radical in ancient Israel. And even when the sage touches on the theme of social justice for the poor, he lacks a prophet's fiery passion and his deep sense of outrage. We must not expect too much from him!

ADVANTAGES OF WEALTH AND DISADVANTAGES OF POVERTY

Proverbs

10:15 A rich man's wealth is his strong city;
      the poverty of the poor is their ruin.
18:11 A rich man's wealth is his strong city,
      and like a high wall protecting him.
13:8 The ransom of a man's life is his wealth,
      but a poor man has no means of redemption.
19:4 Wealth brings many new friends,
      but a poor man is deserted by his friend.
14:20 The poor is disliked even by his neighbour,
      but the rich has many friends.
19:7 All a poor man's brothers hate him;
      how much more do his friends go far from him!
    He pursues them with words,
      but does not have them.
22:7 The rich rules over the poor,
      and the borrower is the slave of the lender.
18:23 The poor use entreaties,
      but the rich answer roughly.

The conservative attitude of Israel's sages is finely illustrated in these proverbs, which quite dispassionately contrast the social advantages of wealth with the disadvantages of poverty. They were quite sure that there was much to be said for being rich, but little, if anything, for being poor; and they were not afraid to say so. Four observations are made:

(a) *Wealth gives a man security* (10:15; 18:11). The rich can not only provide well for themselves and meet all their financial commitments; they are also amply protected against any sudden change of fortune. They are insured to the hilt and have money in the bank for a rainy day. The poor man is not so fortunate. His is a very vulnerable and precarious kind of existence. He may manage well enough from day to day. But let an unexpected bill drop through his letter-box and the result can be disastrous. In 18:11 the marginal reading should be followed, "and like a high wall *in his imagination*". This could imply that the rich are actually deluding themselves (cf. 11:28). But probably it means no more than that the rich find the thought of their security comforting.

As rendered in the RSV, 13:8 is a case in point. The rich man can buy his way out of trouble when his life is threatened by robbers, kidnappers, blackmailers and the like. Since the poor man has nothing to bargain with, he is completely at their mercy. On the other hand, who would take the trouble to rob a poor man? It is the rich who are the target for such nefarious activities. So this seems a rather dubious advantage. In fact that appears to be the point of the proverb. In the second line the Hebrew actually reads, "but a poor man does not heed rebuke", and the New English Bible is probably right in taking this to mean that he is "immune from threats". So this is a case where the poor man comes off best. He at least cannot be robbed. But the irony of this should not escape us!

(b) *Wealth brings a man friends* (19:4; 14:20; 19:7). We might well be tempted to wonder whether wealth's new-found friends are friends worth having. But these proverbs are not a sarcastic dig at spongers and sycophants. They simply make the sharp observation that, human nature being what it is, no-one wants to befriend a poor man. He tries the patience of his neighbours, and even becomes too much of a burden to his own kith and kin. Friendship with him is just too demanding. Folk have enough troubles of their own to be getting on with, without taking on board a poor man's troubles as well. In the last two lines of 19:7, the RSV makes the best it can of an impossible Hebrew text. The New English Bible follows the lead of the *Septuagint* and produces a separate proverb on a different topic: "Practice in evil makes the perfect scoundrel; a man who talks too much meets his deserts".

(c) *Wealth brings a man power* (22:7). Political and economic power are concentrated in the hands of the rich. They manage the affairs of the community, control the prices in the markets, pay the wages and lend the money. They pull the strings, and the poor man is the puppet who has to dance.

(d) *Wealth lets a man say what he likes* (18:23). The poor man must watch what he says, especially when he is looking for charity. Ingratiating speech is called for, and is what he carefully cultivates. But since the rich man is dealing the cards and he holds all the aces, he does not need to watch his p's and q's. He can even be downright rude and brush the poor aside, and get away with it. Ecclesiasticus makes the witty observation: "A rich man does wrong, and adds insult to injury; a poor man is wronged, and must apologize into the bargain" (13:3, NEB).

So then, the rich have these social advantages over the poor. This is presented in a non-committal way. It is simply the way that things are. Of course, to what advantage the rich put their advantages is another matter. That will be the proof of their wisdom or the mark of their folly. But at least in key areas of social life the rich have the choice of acting wisely or foolishly. That is the point. They have elbow room – freedom of movement and decision. In these areas the poor have none. That is why the proverbs on the subject are meant to catch the ear of the rich rather than the poor.

FOLLY AND POVERTY

Proverbs

13:18   Poverty and disgrace come to him who ignores instruction,
        but he who heeds reproof is honoured.
10:4   A slack hand causes poverty,
        but the hand of the diligent makes rich.
12:11   He who tills his land will have plenty of bread,
        but he who follows worthless pursuits has no sense.

28:19 He who tills his land will have plenty of bread,
   but he who follows worthless pursuits will have
    plenty of poverty.
21:17 He who loves pleasure will be a poor man;
   he who loves wine and oil will not be rich.
21:20 Precious treasure remains in a wise man's dwelling,
   but a foolish man devours it.
13:23 The fallow ground of the poor yields much food,
   but it is swept away through injustice.

A constant note sounded in chapters 1–9 is that honour and riches go hand in hand with wisdom, and belong to its bounty (cf. 3:16; 8:18, 21). This note is echoed in 13:18 together with its opposite: poverty and disgrace go hand in hand with folly. It is this counter-note that strikes up the theme of these proverbs.

The idler who fights shy of a hard day's work (10:4), and the fool who fritters his time and energy on frivolities (12:11; 28:19), or in high living and sensuous self-indulgence (21:17), will end up paupers. They can have no complaints for they have only themselves to blame. They are short in wisdom and will always be short of money (21:20). The word "disgrace" (13:18) indicates the lack of respect sensible folk have for them, and their worthlessness to the community. They are "lightweights"; with nothing sensible to say and nothing valuable to contribute towards the common good (see the comment on 18:3, *A Good Name*).

The truth of these proverbs is self-evident. But Israel's sages were not so naive—as some Christians have been—to think that poor people are mostly poor through their own fault, through their lack of industry, thrift and foresight. The poor farmer in 13:23 has put his back into working his rather meagre plot of land, and has reaped a good harvest of grain; but only to have it extorted from him by greedy, unscrupulous men. The poor people of this world are far more often the victims of the greed and folly of others than of their own folly, and the sages will have something further to say about that.

WISDOM AND WEALTH—I

Proverbs

13:11 Wealth hastily gotten will dwindle,
    but he who gathers little by little will increase it.
27:23 Know well the condition of your flocks,
    and give attention to your herds;
27:24 for riches do not last for ever;
    and does a crown endure to all generations?
27:25 When the grass is gone, and the new growth appears,
    and the herbage of the mountains is gathered,
27:26 the lambs will provide your clothing,
    and the goats the price of a field;
27:27 there will be enough goats' milk for your food,
    for the food of your household
    and maintenance for your maidens.
20:21 An inheritance gotten hastily in the beginning
    will in the end not be blessed.
28:22 A miserly man hastens after wealth,
    and does not know that want will come upon him.
28:20 A faithful man will abound with blessings,
    but he who hastens to be rich will not go unpunished.
20:17 Bread gained by deceit is sweet to a man,
    but afterward his mouth will be full of gravel.
21:6 The getting of treasures by a lying tongue
    is a fleeting vapour and a snare of death.
10:2 Treasures gained by wickedness do not profit,
    but righteousness delivers from death.
11:4 Riches do not profit in the day of wrath,
    but righteousness delivers from death.

While Israel's sages were sure that wealth was a fruit of wisdom, they were equally sure that not all wealth was wisdom's fruit. Wealth married to wisdom made a happy couple, but wealth divorced from wisdom made an unhappy bachelor—indeed, an ill-begotten and ill-fated one. So how a man acquires his wealth has to be weighed on the scales of wisdom's balance to assess its real value: asset or liability.

(i)

The best and most enduring kind of wealth is the kind that is built up gradually through the honest sweat of the brow (13:11; cf. 10:4; 12:11; 28:19). There is wisdom and sure reward in sheer industry. This is brought out with a homely touch in 27:23–27. This passage recommends the values and virtues of pastoral life as the best basis for the family economy.

In 13:11, wealth gained by honest, hard work is contrasted with the kind that is achieved overnight. The reference here is probably to 'a killing' made through speculative investments in trade and commerce. "Hastily gotten" might imply that the speculator uses dishonest and underhand methods, or at any rate that they are suspect. It could be that this is a proverb from a sage whose heart is in the soil, voicing his suspicions about what goes on in the city markets. But if there is a grain of prejudice in it, there is also more than a grain of good sense. The money markets have always been notoriously fickle paymasters. The proverb is widely applicable in situations where we might observe, "easy come, easy go".

Much the same point is probably being made in 27:23–27, although this sage is a shepherd and not a farmer at heart. The smallholder who is tempted to sell up and go and make his fortune by investing the proceeds in the markets would be well advised to think again. Even if he strikes gold, his money will run out in time. He would do better to pay attention to his sheep and goats. They are assets which do not dwindle but increase each spring when the lambs are born, and they will provide for all his household's needs. There is little of the entrepreneur in the sage. But he gives good advice on the prudence of weighing up the financial risks of any new venture and avoiding recklessness.

"Haste" is also the key word in the next three proverbs (20:21; 28:22; 28:20). Proverb 20:21 probably has in mind laying hands on an inheritance before the proper time, especially by fraudulent or violent means. Though from a different angle, sons are warned against this kind of thing in 19:26 and 28:24 (see the topic, *Honouring Parents*). The story of the Prodigal Son in

Luke 15 would be a case in point, and a fine illustration of the truth in the second line of the verse.

(ii)

In 28:20 and 28:22 we have a contrast between the miserly and the faithful man. We will have something to say about the faithful man shortly (see the topic, *Care for the Poor*). "Miserly" is literally "one of evil eye". This man is more than tight-fisted. He is the fellow who is out to get rich quick and is not fussy about how he does it or who suffers in the process: "deceit" (20:17), "lying" (21:6), plain "wickedness" (10:2)—anything at all for a "fast buck". This fellow is found anywhere money is to be had, from the company boardroom to the used-car lot, from the halls of government to the back streets. He may pat his bulging wallet and savour its sweet taste, but sooner or later, says the sage, it will give him indigestion (20:17). Ill-gotten gain is a "fleeting vapour" (21:6), without substance. In Ecclesiasticus 40:13, a less gentle·metaphor expresses the same thought: "The wealth of the unjust will dry up like a torrent, and crash like a loud clap of thunder in a rain". It is also a lethal "snare" (21:6), quite profitless in the "day of wrath" (10:2; 11:4)—that is, the day when God brings such offenders to book, and punishes them. So ill-gotten gain is not only weighed in the balances of wisdom; it is also weighed in the balances of God—and found wanting: its gain is a *dead(ly) loss!*

WISDOM AND WEALTH—II

Proverbs

23:4   Do not toil to acquire wealth;
       be wise enough to desist.
23:5   When your eyes light upon it, it is gone;
       for suddenly it takes to itself wings,
       flying like an eagle toward heaven.
11:28 He who trusts in his riches will wither,
       but the righteous will flourish like a green leaf.

22:1   A good name is to be chosen rather than great riches,
       and favour is better than silver or gold.
16:8   Better is a little with righteousness
       than great revenues with injustice.
19:1   Better is a poor man who walks in his integrity
       than a man who is perverse in speech, and is a fool.
28:6   Better is a poor man who walks in his integrity
       than a rich man who is perverse in his ways.
15:16 Better is a little with the fear of the Lord
       than great treasure and trouble with it.
10:22 The blessing of the Lord makes rich,
       and he adds no sorrow with it.
28:11 A rich man is wise in his own eyes,
       but a poor man who has understanding will find him out.
30:7   Two things I ask of thee;
       deny them not to me before I die:
30:8   Remove far from me falsehood and lying;
       give me neither poverty nor riches;
       feed me with the food that is needful for me,
30:9   lest I be full, and deny thee,
       and say, "Who is the Lord?"
    or lest I be poor, and steal,
       and profane the name of my God.

But we do not need to take a dishonest penny to be found wanting. There is another respect in which wealth is weighed on the balances of wisdom: how *we* weigh it on our own scale of values.

(a) If wisdom is more precious than gold or silver and of the highest value to men, then it is wisdom and not money which counts most in life. To be wise rather than rich ought therefore to be a man's first priority and prime occupation in life.

The problem with money is that it just does not last. It has a habit of sprouting wings and taking flight (23:4–5), or, as Jesus puts it, of becoming moth-eaten and rust-riddled—if a thief does not get to it first (Matt. 6:19). So the man who gives his life to making money is a foolish man, and is giving his life to a lost cause. The more he wins, the more he loses. And if not before, then at the end of the day he will discover, as an old Italian proverb has it, "the last coat a man wears has no pockets in it".

As we have seen, the sages readily admitted that money does lend a certain security in life. It can cushion many of life's blows. But they were also convinced that to root your life in money and to place your trust in it was a stupid thing to do. It is in fact, says 11:28, to "wither" away (but see RSV ftn.). Few things shrivel up a man's character quite so thoroughly as letting his money do the thinking and the talking for him. By contrast, the man who roots his life in righteousness and whose trust is rightly placed (cf. 3:5) abounds with the sap of life, and flourishes (see Ps. 1:3).

(b) For the sages of Proverbs, the flourishing of the righteous man included material prosperity. The series of "better" sayings, however, makes two main points: (1) while wealth properly acquired is a "good" thing, (2) there are much "better" things in life than it. Three of these better things are singled out: *a good name* (22:1), *uprightness* (16:8; 19:1; 28:6), and *the fear of the Lord* (15:16). The real danger of wealth underlined here is that it can distort our sense of values and priorities and make us blind to and lose out on the "better" things which really matter and which truly enrich (cf. 10:22).

(c) Notice that these "better" sayings assume that wisdom does not necessarily bring wealth in its train. This thought is rather exceptional in Proverbs, where wealth is part of the *wholeness* of wisdom (cf. 3:13–18; 8:17–21), although it is truer to life. From the viewpoint of Israel's sages, then, a saying like 28:6 could well have been capped by, "Best is a rich man who walks in his integrity". The bald statement in 28:11, however, seems to suggest that he is a rare species, for "a rich man is wise in his own eyes".

In 30:7–9 we have the prayer of a man who is keenly alert to the danger that wealth can breed moral and spiritual blindness. He knows how hard it is for a camel to go through the eye of a needle (Matt. 19:24). But he is also quite sure that poverty is not a step towards godliness. It is as likely to turn him into a thief as wealth is to turn him into a scoffer. His ideal is the 'golden mean': neither poverty nor riches, an ideal that springs from his clear perception of the better things of life. The Jerusalem Bible has a telling rendering in the last line of verse 8: "grant me only my share of bread to eat". If individuals and nations were thus contented, two-thirds of the world's population would not be living in poverty. And that brings us to our next topic.

CARE FOR THE POOR—I

Proverbs

17:5   He who mocks the poor insults his Maker;
      he who is glad at calamity will not go unpunished.
14:21 He who despises his neighbour is a sinner,
      but happy is he who is kind to the poor.
14:31 He who oppresses a poor man insults his Maker,
      but he who is kind to the needy honours him.
22:16 He who oppresses the poor to increase his own wealth,
      or gives to the rich, will only come to want.
30:14 There are those whose teeth are swords,
        whose teeth are knives,
    to devour the poor from off the earth,
      the needy from among men.
28:3   A poor man who oppresses the poor
    is a beating rain that leaves no food.
22:22 Do not rob the poor, because he is poor,
      or crush the afflicted at the gate;
22:23 for the Lord will plead their cause
      and despoil of life those who despoil them.
15:25 The Lord tears down the house of the proud,
      but maintains the widow's boundaries.
22:28 Remove not the ancient landmark
      which your fathers have set.
23:10 Do not remove an ancient landmark
      or enter the fields of the fatherless;
23:11 for their Redeemer is strong;
      he will plead their cause against you.

The saying in 14:31 sums up what Israel's sages have to say about caring for the poor. In a word: do not oppress them, but be kind to them. The proverbs in the present section are concerned with the oppression of the poor.

(i)

The first three proverbs form a little family of sayings. They trace the course to oppression from "mock" (17:5), through "despise" (14:21) to "oppress" (14:31). In 14:21 we can safely assume that it is a poor neighbour who is primarily in view. The New English Bible's "a hungry man" assumes a slight correction to the Hebrew text. What starts out in a seemingly harmless way (poking fun at the plight of the poor) soon grows into a fixed attitude (regarding them with utter contempt), which then bursts into the full flower of deeds (oppressing them). But notice that the same verdict is applied to the bud as to the flower—and it is a remarkable verdict: God takes it as a personal insult! And notice too that this verdict is grounded in the fact that God has created mankind, the poor included. All forms of oppression and discrimination against others, whether by reason of their social status, colour, religion, political views or the like, are a denial of God, the creator of all mankind, and fall under the same verdict.

In 30:14 perpetrators of injustice and oppression against the poor are likened to cannibals. The prophet Micah uses this imagery, but is much more graphic when he condemns the leading citizens and rulers of the people:

> [You] who tear the skin from off my people,
>   and their flesh from off their bones;
> who eat the flesh of my people,
>   and flay their skin from off them,
> and break their bones in pieces,
>   and chop them up like meat in a kettle,
>   like flesh in a cauldron.
>
> (Mic. 3:2–3; see Pss. 14:4; 57:4)

The metaphor in 28:3 is more modest: the oppressor of the poor is like a violent rainstorm which flattens and destroys the grain, resulting in a lack of bread. Evidently too the oppressor here is of more modest means than his powerful and carnivorous counterparts. He himself is numbered among the poor. Many commentators think that this must be a mistake in the text and that the word "poor" should be corrected to one meaning a powerful tyrant (so, NEB), a sense which can be achieved by only a slight change to the Hebrew. In a film documentary on India, the late James Cameron recounts the story of a villager who fell into the clutches of a money-lender, lost house and home and went to the city. There he fared well, and began to save up some money. After a time he returned back to his village—and set himself up in business as a money-lender! Is this the kind of oppression—oppression compounded by betrayal—that is being hinted at here? People like that, and there have been and are many of them in this world, are the worst kind of tyrants.

(ii)

To "crush the afflicted at the gate" (22:22) means to deprive them of justice. In ancient Israel the law court was convened at the city gate (see Ruth 4:1–12). The Old Testament is insistent in its demand that justice be done to the poor, and repeatedly warns against denying them their rights. It also makes it absolutely clear that this is a matter about which God is specially concerned (see Exod. 22:22–24; Deut. 10:17–18; Isa. 1:23; 10:1–2; 25:4; Jer. 5:28; Amos 2:6; 4:1; 5:12; Mic. 3:11). The poor, together with the widow (15:25) and the orphan (23:10), with whom the poor are often linked (see Ps. 82:3–4; Isa. 10:2), belonged to the periphery of society. They were socially weak and powerless, and were unable to assert their own rights. Therefore, then as now, they were an easy and a very tempting target (the Book of Amos in particular shows just how tempting) for the sharp practices and blatant injustices of their more powerful and influential neighbours. But these two verses warn that if justice is corrupted and the law court becomes a weapon against the poor and needy, God will be quick to leap to their defence (Exod. 22:22–24) and he will mete out (poetic) justice.

The "landmarks" (22:28; 23:10; cf. 15:25) were stone pillars or cairns erected to mark out the boundaries between properties and to mark legal ownership. To remove these stones was regarded as a very serious offence (cf. Deut. 19:14; 27:17; Job 24:2), since it meant illegally depriving a family of their plot of land. The prophets roundly condemned greedy landowners who were forming large estates at the expense of their poorer neighbours through sharp practices:

> They covet fields, and seize them;
>   and houses, and take them away;
> they oppress a man and his house,
>   a man and his inheritance.

(Mic. 2:2)

> Woe to those who join house to house,
>   who add field to field,
> until there is no more room,
>   and you are made to dwell alone
>   in the midst of the land.

(Isa. 5:8; cf. 1 Kings 21)

The use of landmarks was common throughout the ancient Near East, and tampering with them was everywhere condemned. Thus in the *Instruction of Amenemopet,* the sage similarly warns:

> Do not carry off the landmark at the boundaries of the
>   arable land,
> Nor disturb the position of the measuring-cord;
> Be not greedy after a cubit of land,
> Nor encroach upon the boundaries of a widow ...
> One satisfies god with the will of the Lord,
> Who determines the boundaries of the arable land.

In Israel, the family plot was normally passed down from father to son as an inheritance. Besides being the victims of unscrupulous men, in hard times families might be forced to sell off part of their property or might lose the whole of it through defaulting on their debts. In these circumstances, it was the duty of the nearest kinsman to buy back the property and restore it to the family (cf. Lev. 25:25). He is the "redeemer" (Hebrew, *goel*). The family redeemer, however, was helpless to restore property which had been alienated from his kinsfolk by extortion and oppression. But God is not helpless, says 23:11: he is the kinsman and the redeemer of the needy and the oppressed, and he will take up their cause and restore them to their land.

CARE FOR THE POOR—II

Proverbs

22:9　He who has a bountiful eye will be blessed,
　　　　for he shares his bread with the poor.
19:17　He who is kind to the poor lends to the Lord,
　　　　and he will repay him for his deed.
28:27　He who gives to the poor will not want,
　　　　but he who hides his eyes will get many a curse.
21:13　He who closes his ear to the cry of the poor
　　　　will himself cry out and not be heard.

If the "faithful man" is the opposite of the "miserly man" ("one of evil eye") in the way he acquires his pay-cheque (cf. 28:20, 22; *Wisdom and Wealth—I*), when it comes to spending it his opposite number is the "bounteous man" (22:9, literally, "one of good eye"). Faithful men know not only how to acquire wealth wisely, they know how to spend it wisely as well. Some of the qualities of the faithful man emerged in our comments on 3:3, 3:27–29 and the topic *Loyalty and Faithfulness*. He is the man who knows the real meaning of the word "community", and who places "faithfulness" and "kindness" above self-interest, so that he keeps faith with God (Isa. 26:2), keeps faith with his neighbour (3:27–29), and keeps faith with the poor: "he shares his bread with the poor" (22:9). In doing so the bounteous man puts God in his debt (19:17)! Jesus takes the thought still further and says that, "as you did it to one of the least of these my brethren, you did it to me" (Matt. 25:40). And notice that we do not need to have "teeth like swords" (30:14) to fall under the judgment of Jesus' next words (Matt. 25:41–46)—a "blind eye" (28:27) and a "deaf ear" (21:13) will do! The hard-hearted and tight-fisted man who turns a blind eye to the poor, says the sage, "will get many a curse". The sage in Ecclesiasticus elaborates (4:5–6):

> Do not avert your eye from the needy,
> nor give a man occasion to curse you;
> for if in bitterness of soul
> he calls down a curse upon you,
> his Creator will hear his prayer.

And the man who turns a deaf ear today might well find himself on the receiving end tomorrow. Jesus states the general principle: "the measure you give will be the measure you get back" (Luke 6:38).

In his book *Rich Christians in an Age of Hunger,* Ronald Sider says strikingly: "World poverty is a hundred million mothers weeping . . . because they cannot feed their children". In the face of this, Christians ought to ponder together the implications of the Old Testament's demand for social justice on their behalf, as well as how best, as individuals and as a Church, to give practical expression to the counsel of the wise and of Jesus: be kind to the poor and share your bread with them. Christians ought also to ponder the story of the Good Samaritan (Luke 10), and Jesus' sobering words in Matthew 25:31–46 and Luke 16:19–26. Here are a couple of sayings by the Rabbis which are also worth thinking about:

> Whoever practises charity and justice is as though he filled the world with loving-kindness.

> Superior is he who lends money to the poor than the giver of alms; but best of all is he who invests money with a poor man in partnership.

UNDERWRITING DEBTS

Proverbs

17:18 A man without sense gives a pledge,
         and becomes surety in the presence of his neighbour.
11:15 He who gives surety for a stranger will smart for it,
         but he who hates suretyship is secure.
22:26 Be not one of those who give pledges,
         who become surety for debts.
22:27 If you have nothing with which to pay,
         why should your bed be taken from under you?
  6:1 My son, if you have become surety for your neighbour,
         have given your pledge for a stranger;
  6:2 if you are snared in the utterance of your lips,
         caught in the words of your mouth;
  6:3 then do this, my son, and save yourself,
         for you have come into your neighbour's power:
         go, hasten, and importune your neighbour.
  6:4 Give your eyes no sleep
         and your eyelids no slumber;
  6:5 save yourself like a gazelle from the hunter,
         like a bird from the hand of the fowler.
27:13 Take a man's garment when he has
            given surety for a stranger,
         and hold him in pledge when he
            gives surety for foreigners.
20:16 Take a man's garment when he has
            given surety for a stranger,
         and hold him in pledge when he
            gives surety for foreigners.

(i)

The theme of these sayings is the inadvisability of acting as
guarantor ("surety") assuming legal responsibility for another man's debts. The practice of "suretyship" was a common
means of securing loans in Israel and elsewhere in the ancient
Near East. The sages may have specifically in mind the complex
credit arrangements made by merchants and traders in the

market place, although their sayings would equally apply to underwriting debts incurred by a friend or neighbour who had fallen on hard times.

The advice Israel's sages give is that it is wise to have nothing to do with the practice, particularly when you do not know the debtor very well ("stranger", 11:15; 6:1—unless this simply means "another", see NIV). So 17:18 declares bluntly that to stand surety is a mark of sheer stupidity; while 6:1–5 urges that if a pledge has already been given, no time should be lost and no effort spared in seeking to be released from it. The Hebrew in the last line of 6:3 is more vigorous than the RSV translates it: "go, swallow your pride, and besiege your neighbour". The phrase, "give a pledge", is literally "strike hands" (6:1; 17:18; 22:26; differently, 27:13), and refers to the custom of sealing an agreement by a handshake. Evidently the sages had seen enough debtors default, and enough well-intentioned but imprudent guarantors come to grief for underwriting their debts and recklessly committing themselves beyond their means, to convince them that this was the wisest course. With a hint of humour 22:27 warns what can happen to the unwise guarantor. But as well as being reduced to penury, slavery also threatened him if he was unable to pay off the defaulter's debts (cf. 2 Kings 4:1–7; Neh. 5:1–8).

The last saying (20:16; 27:13) can be taken in two ways: (1) as an ironical warning that the guarantor need expect no mercy at the hands of the creditor: he will be held to his pledge and the creditor will have his pound of flesh; or (2) as advising the creditor to take the extra precaution of taking security from the guarantor when he is underwriting the debts of a foreigner, since foreigners were a bad risk. A garment was often offered as security for a loan (Exod. 22:25–27; Deut. 24:10–13; cf. Amos 2:8).

(ii)

If we may read between the lines, the warning sounded in these sayings is primarily against *rash* and *ill-considered* pledges, which are made on the spur of the moment in a fit of generosity and which may later cost dearly. There may nevertheless be times when standing surety for a friend or neighbour is the wise and kind thing to do. That, at least, is the view taken by the sage of Ecclesiasticus, although he also warns against its dangers (29:14–15, 18, 20):

> A good man will be surety for his neighbour,
> but a man who has lost his sense of shame will fail him.
> Do not forget all the kindness of your surety,
> for he has given his life for you . . . .
> Being surety has ruined many men who were prosperous,
> and has shaken them like a wave of the sea;
> it has driven men of power into exile,
> and they have wandered among foreign nations . . . .
> Assist your neighbour according to your ability,
> but take heed to yourself lest you fall.

In the Book of Hebrews the language of suretyship is applied to Jesus, "the surety of a better covenant" (7:22). The thought is that Jesus has underwritten and made himself answerable for the fulfilment of the covenant, not only from the side of God but also from the side of his people, acting as their representative—his people, a bad risk if ever there was one; but he, an unfailing surety.

GIFTS AND BRIBES

Proverbs

15:27   He who is greedy for unjust gain
        makes trouble for his household,
      but he who hates bribes will live.
17:8   A bribe is like a magic stone
        in the eyes of him who gives it;
      wherever he turns he prospers.
19:6   Many seek the favour of a generous man,
      and every one is a friend to a man who gives gifts.

18:16 A man's gift makes room for him
and brings him before great men.
21:14 A gift in secret averts anger;
and a bribe in the bosom, strong wrath.
25:14 Like clouds and wind without rain
is a man who boasts of a gift he does not give.

In 15:27 we have an unequivocal condemnation of bribery. The implication is that these are bribes given or received by the grasper who is out to make a quick profit at another's expense, perhaps in a business enterprise, or by perverting the course of justice (cf. 17:23). The next proverb reads strangely coming after such a forthright condemnation. A bribe is a like a "magic wand", as we would say: wave it, and (hey presto!) "wherever he turns he prospers" (17:8). The man with a bribe or gift in his hand can win friends and influence people (19:6), pave his way to social advancement (18:16), and extricate himself from difficult situations (21:14). In short, gifts and bribes are a wonderful social lubricant. They ease a man's way through life and bring him success.

There is therefore, it seems, some ambiguity about whether Israel's sages think a bribe is a bad thing or a good thing. We might think that this ambiguity is removed by a distinction between "bribes" and "gifts". But while two separate Hebrew words are used in the proverbs, they are equated in 21:14, and the word regularly translated "gift" is in fact the word "bribes" in 15:27. Two points, however, should be noted. *First,* as observations on the giving and receiving of bribes, these proverbs ring true. That is the way things are. The sage is not necessarily recommending the practice. *Second,* in ancient Israelite society, as in many eastern societies today, the giving of a gift when seeking the favour of a superior or patron was an accepted social custom. The distinction between a gift and a bribe is not always easy to draw at the best of times; but it is much harder to draw in some societies than in others. Further, where the line has to be drawn need not necessarily be the same for all societies. While motive doubtlessly counts the most, and

the openness or secrecy with which the gift is conveyed is a sure
sign on which side of the line it stands, where there is any doubt
the words of 1 Thessalonians 5:22 offer sound counsel to the
Christian: "Abstain from all appearance of evil" (AV).

RIGHTEOUSNESS AND WICKEDNESS IN HIGH PLACES

Proverbs

11:11 By the blessing of the upright a city is exalted,
        but it is overthrown by the mouth of the wicked.
11:10 When it goes well with the righteous, the city rejoices;
        and when the wicked perish there are shouts of gladness.
29:16 When the wicked are in authority, transgression increases;
        but the righteous will look upon their downfall.
28:28 When the wicked rise, men hide themselves,
        but when they perish, the righteous increase.
28:12 When the righteous triumph, there is great glory;
        but when the wicked rise, men hide themselves.
29:2 When the righteous are in authority, the people rejoice;
        but when the wicked rule, the people groan.
14:34 Righteousness exalts a nation,
        but sin is a reproach to any people.

(i)

We have already noticed (see the topic, *The Mischief-Maker*)
that the righteous man's words and actions contribute to the
wholeness and well-being of the community, while the wicked
man's work contributes to its destruction. It is the social
outworking of righteousness and wickedness for the good or ill
of the body politic which is now spelled out in these proverbs.
This is summed up in 11:11. The "blessing" of the upright may
be the blessing conferred on them by God, which spills over, as
it were, to benefit the whole community ("city"), or the blessing
conferred by the upright upon their fellow citizens through
their good words and deeds. Perhaps both are meant. The result
is that the city is exalted or "built up" (NEB)—a quite capital

city! By contrast, the evil and malicious words of wicked men strike at its foundations and raze the whole city to the ground.

Four companion proverbs point in particular to the importance of a community having the right kind of leadership (29:16; 28:28; 28:12; 29:2). Their theme is the contrasting consequences for society when either wicked or righteous men hold the reins of power and influence. When the wicked are in power and control the affairs of state, violence and injustice are actively encouraged and flourish unchecked (29:16), and the people groan under an intolerable burden of oppression (29:2) and make themselves scarce for fear of life and limb (28:28; 28:12). When righteous men rise to power and the wicked perish, the people—especially the poor—have great cause for rejoicing, for righteousness and justice will abound.

(ii)

The broadest view is taken in 14:34: righteousness is the path to a nation's exaltation; sin is the sure path to its reproach. This picks up a theme which is of central importance in the thought of the Old Testament in general, and in the message of the Hebrew prophets in particular. The principle is perhaps presented most clearly in Deuteronomy 28 in its contrasting series of blessings and curses: "If you [Israel] obey the voice of the Lord your God . . . all these blessings shall come upon you . . ."(vv. 1–14); "but if you will not obey the voice of the Lord your God . . . all these curses shall come upon you . . ."(vv. 15–68). The story of the people of Israel as it is presented by the Old Testament is largely an illustration and an outworking of this theme. That the curses in this chapter far outweigh the blessings reflects the fact that Israel and its leaders more often chose to disobey than to obey the voice of God, until they were finally carried off into exile as a punishment for their sins. But although the story of Israel illustrates the theme, the Old Testament sees the principle working itself out in communities and nations in general, from the cities of Sodom and Gomorrah (Gen. 19) to the mighty Babylonian Empire (Dan. 5).

In his book, *Christianity and History,* Herbert Butterfield writes on the theme of "Judgment in History":

Judgment in history falls heaviest on those who come to think themselves gods, who fly in the face of Providence and history, who put their trust in man-made systems and worship the work of their own hands, and who say that the strength of their own right arm gave them the victory . . . If men put their faith in science and make it the be-all and end-all of life, as though it were not to be subdued to any higher ethical end, there is something in the very composition of the universe that will make it execute judgment on itself, if only in the shape of the atomic bomb.

If these words are not to become prophetic for our own nation, what Professor Butterfield has to say on learning the lesson from the rise and fall of past nations and empires needs to be taken to heart:

There is a sense in which all that we may say on this subject and all the moral verdicts that we may pass on human history are only valid in their application as self-judgments—only useful in so far as we bring them home to ourselves.

C. THE MARKET

A GOOD BARGAIN, HOARDING GRAIN, AND FALSE WEIGHTS

Proverbs

20:14 "It is bad, it is bad," says the buyer;
      but when he goes away, then he boasts.
11:26 The people curse him who holds back grain,
      but a blessing is on the head of him who sells it.

20:10 Diverse weights and diverse measures
      are both alike an abomination to the Lord.
20:23 Diverse weights are an abomination to the Lord,
      and false scales are not good.

11:1   A false balance is an abomination to the Lord,
       but a just weight is his delight.

16:11   A just balance and scales are the Lord's;
       all the weights in the bag are his work.

(i)

Haggling over prices was and still is the way goods are bought and sold in the Eastern bazaars. In 20:14 we have a humorous thumb-nail sketch of a sharp customer. He complains that he is being sold inferior quality goods so as to knock the price down, and then he goes away and brags about how clever he was. The saying is in the form of a simple observation of a fact of life. This happens. Perhaps we are meant to reflect that dishonesty can be found on either side of the counter. Perhaps we are simply meant to smile.

In 11:26 it is the seller who is up to his tricks. The allusion here is probably to the practice of stockpiling grain in order to push up the price and make a larger profit. The speculator is left in no doubt about what his customers will think of him: they will "curse" him. But the shopkeeper who has the interests of his customers and not only his own profits at heart will win their "blessing".

(ii)

The law, the prophets and the wise, join voices to condemn dishonest trade practices involving the use of false weights and measures and false balances (cf. Lev. 19:36; Deut. 25:13–16; Ezek. 45:10–12; Amos 8:5; Mic. 6:11). The scales or balances were simple affairs of a kind that are still in use: a beam with a pan suspended by a cord at each end, either held by the hand or standing on a central support. They were easily manipulated to give short weight. The Hebrew for "diverse weights and diverse measures" (20:10) is "stone and a stone, ephah and an ephah". Weights were usually made of stone and inscribed to indicate their value. They were kept together in a bag (cf. 16:11). The basic unit of weight in daily use was the "shekel" (about 11 grammes, 2 Kings 7:1; Ezek 4:10). The ephah was a dry measure of capacity used for cereals (Judg. 6:19), equivalent to the capacity of a vessel large enough to contain a man (cf. Zech. 5:6–11), and reckoned as one tenth of a "donkey load" (*ie* a "homer"; cf. Isa. 5:10). So the dishonest merchant would have two sets of weights and measures, the one falling below the standard (the "accurate" weight, 11:1, see NIV) for selling, and the other in excess of the standard, for buying. We might notice that although we hear of the "royal shekel" (2 Sam. 14:26) and the "shekel of the temple" (Exod. 30:13), and these may represent the standard for tax purposes and the like, the actual standard weights used by traders varied from region to region and city to city (see Gen. 23:16). That made it all the easier for the unscrupulous to falsify the weights.

The first three of the four sayings underline that such commercial malpractice is abhorrent to God. The last saying, however, goes further and says that accurate scales and weights belong to God and are the work of his hand. He has, as it were, laid down how much weight there should be in a shekel, or capacity in an ephah, and he takes the trouble to see if the merchant's weights and measures matches his. So these proverbs press home the lesson that God's searching scrutiny falls upon the shop counter, and he looks for scrupulous honesty. The lesson is applicable to all our commercial and business transactions.

The Jewish Rabbis also stressed the need for scrupulous honesty in the matter of weights and measures and laid down strict rules to prevent even unintentional distortion. Thus, for example, they laid down that, "The shopkeeper must wipe his measures twice a week, his weights once a week, and his scales after every weighing". And again, commenting on Leviticus 19:35: "Ye shall do no unrighteousness in judgment, in meteyard, in weight, or in measure—'In meteyard' refers to the measurement of land, that he may not measure for one in summer and for another in winter [in summer the measuring line contracts]; 'in weight', he may not keep his weights in salt [it makes them heavier]; 'in measure', he may not make the liquid produce a foam". We may not care much for the legalistic trappings of such Rabbinical dictums, but we must admire their attention to details. According to an old saying, "Honesty in little things is not a little thing"; and another, "Honesty is exact to the penny". It is the "little things", the "pennies" which we easily overlook that God looks over.

D. THE LAW COURT

FALSE WITNESSES

Proverbs

12:17 He who speaks the truth gives honest evidence,
      but a false witness utters deceit.
14:5 A faithful witness does not lie,
      but a false witness breathes out lies.
14:25 A truthful witness saves lives,
      but one who utters lies is a betrayer.
25:18 A man who bears false witness against his neighbour
      is like a war club, or a sword, or a sharp arrow.
24:28 Be not a witness against your neighbour without cause,
      and do not deceive with your lips.
24:29 Do not say, "I will do to him as he has done to me;
      I will pay the man back for what he has done."
19:28 A worthless witness mocks at justice,
      and the mouth of the wicked devours iniquity.
19:5 A false witness will not go unpunished,
      and he who utters lies will not escape.
19:9 A false witness will not go unpunished,
      and he who utters lies will perish.
21:28 A false witness will perish,
      but the word of a man who hears will endure.
29:24 The partner of a thief hates his own life;
      he hears the curse, but discloses nothing.

In the towns and cities throughout Israel, the courts met at the city gates. The judges were drawn from the elders—the family heads and leading citizens in the community (Deut. 21:19; 22:15). They tried both criminal and civil cases, although this is a distinction which is never clearly drawn in the Old Testament. A good example of these courts at work can be found in Ruth 4:1–12; a less happy one in 1 Kings 21:8–14.

The carriage or miscarriage of justice depends in large measure on the truthfulness of the witnesses (12:17; 14:5). So a witness takes the stand under solemn oath "to tell the truth, the whole truth and nothing but the truth". Perjury is the sin specifically condemned by the ninth commandment: "You shall not bear false witness against your neighbour" (Exod. 20:16). It is the worst form of lying, for it makes a mockery of (19:28) and defeats the ends of justice (14:25).

The situation envisaged in these proverbs is the giving of false testimony against an innocent man and not on behalf of a guilty man—for example, by providing the guilty with a false alibi. In ancient Israel a large variety of offences carried the death penalty, and it was presumably often carried out. Hence the perjurer's lies are truly lethal weapons (25:18), which can not only destroy an innocent man's good name and leave him battered and bruised, but can literally kill him (14:25). The fate of Naboth illustrates this well. At the instigation of Queen Jezebel, he was arraigned on a trumped up charge and, on the strength of the word of two characters hired to testify against him, he was convicted and stoned to death (1 Kings 21:8–14). When the death penalty was carried out, the law required the witnesses to "cast the first stone" (Deut. 17:7; cf. John 8:7) as a public acknowledgment of their responsibility for his conviction and execution.

In 24:28 the expression "without cause" is ambiguous. It might mean to make an accusation *without grounds;* or it could mean to act as a witness *without necessity, ie* when there is no legal obligation to do so. In the latter case, while the man who does this may be a scoundrel, he is not necessarily a perjurer. The second line shows, however, that such a person thinks nothing of perjuring himself. Whichever the case may be, the next verse exposes the motive behind it: the desire for revenge. Here then, we have a further warning against seeking revenge (see the topic, *Enemies and Revenge*), with now the added thought that the man who speaks against his neighbour out of spite may quickly find himself telling lies.

The word "mocks" in 19:28 comes from the same root as the word "scoffer". This is the scoffer at his most cynical and dangerous. Like a malicious, and not the genial, Mr. Bumble, he thinks that if the law supposes bearing false witness is wrong, then "the law is an ass—an idiot"; and he finds the harm he causes a tasty bite (cf. 19:28). But the justice he mocks will have the last laugh. The false witness will not escape punishment (19:5; 19:9; 21:28). Applying the *lex talionis,* the law provided that the false accuser had to suffer the same punishment which would have befallen the accused had he been convicted by his testimony (Deut. 19:16–21). It is more likely, however, that these proverbs mean that the perjurer will be punished by God than through the due processes of the law. If the second line of 21:28 is saying that the truthful witness will live—as the first line would lead us to expect it was saying—then it is an odd way of saying it, and even odder in the Hebrew ("a man who hears will speak for ever", cf. AV). The meaning is very obscure and the versions go their own ways to try to get sense out of it (cf. NEB, NIV).

A more specific case of perjury is singled out in 29:24. The circumstances appear to be that the judges have publicly adjured anyone with knowledge of an offence to step forward and bear testimony (see Lev. 5:1). An accomplice to the theft hears the solemn charge, but keeps silent since he will only implicate himself. As a result he adds perjury to theft and brings down a curse on his own head (cf. Judg. 17:2).

CORRUPT JUDGES

Proverbs

> 17:15 He who justifies the wicked
> and he who condemns the righteous
> are both alike an abomination to the Lord.

24:23 Partiality in judging is not good.
24:24 He who says to the wicked, "You are innocent,"
      will be cursed by peoples, abhorred by nations;
24:25 but those who rebuke the wicked will have delight,
      and a good blessing will be upon them.
18:5 It is not good to be partial to a wicked man,
      or to deprive a righteous man of justice.
17:23 A wicked man accepts a bribe from the bosom
      to pervert the ways of justice.
28:21 To show partiality is not good;
      but for a piece of bread a man will do wrong.
17:26 To impose a fine on a righteous man is not good;
      to flog noble men is wrong.

To be accused by false witnesses is bad enough, but misfortunate indeed is the man whose case, like Naboth's (1 Kings 21:8–14), is also being heard by corrupt judges. For it was their responsibility to cross-examine the witnesses and probe their testimony to see where the truth lay (cf. Deut. 19:18), and so to reach the right verdict.

The corrupt judge diverts the wheels of justice from their tracks (17:23) by *justifying the wicked* and *condemning the righteous* (17:15). In the context of the courtroom, declaring a man to be wicked or righteous is not to pass an observation on the kind of fellow he is, but rather to pass a verdict as to whether he is guilty or innocent of the charge brought against him. So to justify the wicked simply means to declare the man in the wrong to be in the right—*ie* to pronounce the guilty innocent; while to condemn the righteous means to declare the man in the right to be in the wrong—*ie* to pronounce the innocent guilty (cf. 24:24–25; Exod. 23:7; Isa. 5:23; see also Deut. 25:1 for the right way round!). This language forms the background to Paul's exposition of "justification by faith" in the early chapters of Romans. There the great truth is that God is just *and* justifies the ungodly (Rom. 3:26; 4:5)—which is here what a judge ought never to do! But such is the paradox of divine grace; and the very daring of the thought warns against pressing the legal language too far, as theologians have often been tempted to do.

Put otherwise, the corrupt judge shows favouritism to the guilty and robs the innocent of his rights (18:5). "To be partial" is literally "to raise the face". The expression harks back to the monarch lifting the face of a prostrate subject begging for mercy or for some other bounty as an indication that he has won favour (cf. Mal. 1:8). Although few of us will be in the position to show partiality from the bench, James 2:1–4 shows how all of us can show it in the pew simply by being snobs and, in effect, making ourselves judges. The first Book of Timothy 5:21 also has a word for Church leaders.

The "wicked man" in 17:23 is the corrupt judge. References in the books of the prophets show that bribery of court officials was just as prevalent in ancient Israel as it is in some parts of the world today (Isa. 1:23; Amos 5:12; Mic. 3:11; cf. 1 Sam. 8:3). Those on the wrong side of the law have always found it a sound investment to have a judge or two in their pockets. The "bosom" refers to the fold in a garment at the breast, where money could be concealed and slipped out surreptitiously. The greed and degeneration that goes with taking bribes to pervert justice is underlined in 28:21: "a piece of bread", *ie* a small sum, will in time be considered reward enough (see Amos 2:6; cf. Ezek. 13:19).

The first line of 17:26 is clear enough: an innocent man ought not to be fined. But what does the second line mean? Since nobility in *rank* is no guarantee of nobility in *character,* does it mean that a noble man ought never to be flogged (cf. Deut. 25:1–3) because of his rank, or that a man of noble character (*ie* "innocent") should not be flogged. If the second is intended, then the line says more or less the same thing as the first. But in that case, "noble" would be an odd word to use, for it ordinarily points to a man's rank and not his character. The first is the more natural way of taking the line, even if it smacks to us of partiality. But it is a difficult line. The New International Version translates: "or to flog officials for their integrity"; which, if right, would appear to mean that officials who refuse to be corrupted by the 'system' should not be victimized.

THE LOT

Proverbs

18:17 He who states his case first seems right,
        until the other comes and examines him.
18:18 The lot puts an end to disputes
        and decides between powerful contenders.
16:33 The lot is cast into the lap,
        but the decision is wholly from the Lord.

The first proverb warns against reaching premature judgments. Its setting is the law court. The first to present his case is the man who brought the action against another. When he says his piece, he seems quite clearly to be in the right. The matter, however, often takes on a different complexion when the defendant gets a chance to have his say; and only then can a fair and balanced judgment be made. As a general principle that there are two sides to every argument, the proverb has wide applicability. It is an obvious enough point, but one that is easily forgotten.

There were times when, after a full hearing and a careful scrutiny of the case, the judges were still unable to arrive at a decision. In these circumstances the "lot" came into play. We hear of the lot being used in a variety of situations—for example, the division of the land among the tribes (Josh. 18:10); the choice of Saul as king (1 Sam. 10:20–21); and the selection of the goat to be driven into the wilderness on the Day of Atonement (Lev. 16:8). This is in fact the only place where we hear of its use in the settlement of disputes. What was actually involved in casting lots is unknown. They may have been small stones with markings on them which were thrown on the ground, rather like tossing a coin; or they may have been drawn from a container, rather like drawing straws. Flipping a coin may be a splendid way of deciding which cricket team goes in to bat first, but we would deem it a very unsatisfactory way of deciding whether a man was guilty or innocent. But what we call "chance", the Hebrews called, if not in so many words, "the providence of God". As they saw it, men may toss the coin, but God determines whether it comes up heads or tails: "the decision [literally "judgment"] is wholly from the Lord" (16:33).

The lot was used by the early apostles to add one to their numbers (see Acts 1:26), but thereafter seems to have been discarded, made obsolete with the coming of the Holy Spirit to guide the Church into God's truth. We need to be very wary of using any mechanical means of ascertaining God's will and seeking his guidance.

E. THE PALACE

THE MEASURE OF A KING—I

Proverbs

28:15 Like a roaring lion or a charging bear
      is a wicked ruler over a poor people.
28:16 A ruler who lacks understanding is a cruel oppressor;
      but he who hates unjust gain will prolong his days.

16:10 Inspired decisions are on the lips of a king;
      his mouth does not sin in judgment.
20:8 A king who sits on the throne of judgment
      winnows all evil with his eyes.
20:26 A wise king winnows the wicked,
      and drives the wheel over them.
29:14 If a king judges the poor with equity
      his throne will be established for ever.
29:4 By justice a king gives stability to the land,
      but one who exacts gifts ruins it.
20:28 Loyalty and faithfulness preserve the king,
      and his throne is upheld by righteousness.

Set against the all-to-familiar portrait of ancient oriental despots and modern tinpot dictators (28:15–16), the sayings here and in the next section sketch in bold outline a portrait of the good and wise ruler. Although the portrait is largely an idealistic one, the maxims are designed to catch the ear of the king and to remind him that these are the ideals which he should try to measure up to and rule by.

(i)

For Israel's sages, the marks of kingly wisdom were, above all, the perceptiveness and the integrity with which the king upheld the cause of justice. In 1 Kings 3:16–28 Solomon settles a dispute between two prostitutes, "and all Israel heard of the judgment which the king had rendered; and they stood in awe of the king, because they perceived that the wisdom of God was in him, to render justice" (v. 28). And in Proverb 8:15 the good Lady Wisdom declares, "By me kings reign, and rulers decree what is just". So the wise king in Proverbs is first and foremost a *just king*.

The "throne of judgment" (20:8) most probably refers to a special seat which the king took when cases were brought before him. In Solomon's palace there was a special "Hall of Judgment" built for that purpose (1 Kings 7:7). Although cases would normally be heard by the elders in the local courts, it appears that every Israelite had the right to bring his grievance directly to the king, and his was also the final court of appeal (cf. 2 Sam. 14:4–11; 1 Kings 3:16–28; 2 Kings 8:1–6).

The judgments pronounced by the king are "inspired decisions" (16:10). The Hebrew word used here is interesting. It is actually the word "divination". The art of divination was widely practised in the ancient world (Num. 22:7; 1 Sam. 6:2; Ezek. 21:21), but was forbidden to God's people in any form (Deut. 18:10). The same word is also used to describe the oracles of the false prophets, who laid claim to have "divined" the word of God (Jer. 14:14; Ezek. 13:6–7). In fact, only in this proverb does the word carry a good sense. But what does it mean? It could mean that the king's judgments rest on divinely-given wisdom (8:15; 1 Kings 3:28); or it could refer to the 'uncanny' perceptiveness of the wise king which made it seem *as if* his decisions were oracles from the mouth of God (cf. 2 Sam. 16:23). Either way, the result is the same: "he cannot err when he passes sentence" (NEB, 16:10). The New International Version eliminates this note of the king's infallible judgments by translating, "his mouth should not betray justice" (16:10). That is no doubt the lesson the king is meant to learn here; but it is not the most natural translation of the Hebrew. Certainly, the wise were not so naive as to believe that kings could do no wrong; but they did believe that truth would always "out" under the patient and probing eye of a wise king (see the comment on 25:2, *The Measure of a King—II*), so enabling him to reach the right verdict.

(ii)

The king's oversight of justice was a double-sided task.

(a) He had to see to it that wrong-doers were brought to book and punished. Here, as we should expect, the wise king will have the discernment to see through the wily schemes concocted by miscreants to cloak their evil and pull the wool over his eyes. He will separate truth from falsehood as surely as a winnower separates the chaff from the wheat (20:8); and he will not be slack to punish them as 'crushingly' as the wheel of a cart crushes the sheaves when it is driven back and forth across the threshing floor (20:26; cf. Isa. 28:27-28, Amos 1:3). No soft measures here!

(b) But more importantly, he had to see to it that the rights of the poor and needy were protected from the sharp practices and flagrant injustices of the rich and powerful (29:14). This, indeed, is the quality which the Old Testament looks for most in a ruler. So during the coronation ceremony of each new king the prayer was offered:

> Give the king thy justice, O God,
>   and thy righteousness to the royal son!
> May he judge thy people with righteousness,
>   and thy poor with justice!
> May he defend the cause of the poor of the people,
>   give deliverance to the needy,
>   and crush the oppressor!
>
> (Ps. 72:1-2, 4)

It was also the quality which Israel's kings all too often lacked. Ahab is a particularly glaring example of a king who not only turned a blind eye to social injustice, but who actively encouraged it by his own example (1 Kings 21:1–16). Some of the hardest words of the prophets are reserved for the king and his fellow political leaders for using their power to further their own ends at the expense of the poor and needy, who should have been the object of their especial care and concern (see Isa. 3:13–15; Jer. 22:13–19; Ezek. 34:1–10; Mic. 3:1–4, 9–12).

(iii)

The ideal of the just king is seen from the particular angle of Israel's faith in 20:28. This saying looks back to the covenant God made with David and his house in 2 Samuel 7:11–16. This special bond between God and king is upheld by God's "loyalty (or "steadfast love", *chesed*) and faithfulness" (2 Sam. 7:15; Ps. 89:24—see the comment on Prov. 3:3), depicted here as standing guard over the king's throne. But these too are qualities which the king ought to display towards his subjects (cf. 3:3; Isa. 16:5) so that all the people can stand in the good and blessing vouchsafed to the king. David himself summed up the implications of God's covenant with him, for king and people, in his "last words":

> The God of Israel has spoken,
>   the Rock of Israel has said to me:
> When one rules justly over men,
>   ruling in the fear of God,
> he dawns on them like the morning light,
>   like the sun shining forth upon a cloudless morning,
>   like rain that makes grass to sprout from the earth.
> Yea, does not my house stand so with God?
>   For he has made with me an everlasting covenant,
>   ordered in all things and secure.
>   (2 Sam. 23:3–5; cf. 2 Sam. 8:15)

The lesson for the king to learn is that the selfish and unjust use of power undermines his throne and brings ruin to his people. Only the power which devotes itself to building up a more just society, and to righting the wrongs done to the powerless, can in the end prevail and provide the foundation for a stable throne and a stable society (29:4; 29:14). The political instability that plagues many nations and costs countless lives in modern times shows how far this lesson is from being learned. But it is a lesson which readily translates to more modest forms of leadership, inside as well as outside the Church.

THE MEASURE OF A KING—II

Proverbs

25:2 It is the glory of God to conceal things,
   but the glory of kings is to search things out.
25:3 As the heavens for height, and the earth for depth,
   so the mind of kings is unsearchable.
25:4 Take away the dross from the silver,
   and the smith has material for a vessel;
25:5 take away the wicked from the presence of the king,
   and his throne will be established in righteousness.
16:12 It is an abomination to kings to do evil,
   for his throne is established by righteousness
17:7 Fine speech is not becoming to a fool,
   still less is false speech to a prince.
29:12 If a ruler listens to falsehood,
   all his officials will be wicked.
21:1 The king's heart is a stream of water
    in the hand of the Lord;
   he turns it wherever he will.

(i)

Despite the rather esoteric language in which they are cast, the maxims in 25:2–3 make two very down-to-earth points:

(a) The wise king will keep his ear to the ground (v. 2). It is one thing for God to be enveloped in things mysterious which no man can fathom out (Deut. 29:29; Job 26:14; Isa. 45:15); but it is a poor king who does not know (not what God has concealed, but) what is going on around him. In 2 Samuel 14:20 the wise woman from Tekoa compliments David and says

"Your majesty is as wise as the angel of God and knows all that goes on in the land" (NEB). The king has a duty to be well on top of the affairs of state, to keep a close eye on how his ministers are carrying out their duties, and to keep himself well-informed about the circumstances of the common people. Especially, he has a duty to carry out a very careful and complete investigation into any matter which calls for his attention, in order to get to the bottom of it and sort out the facts from the fiction before taking any action. For well-intentioned but ill-informed and ill-judged actions can do every bit as much damage as ones taken with ill-intent and without regard to the truth.

(b) The wise king will play his cards close to his chest (25:3). Here "earth" probably stands for the "underworld" (cf. NEB ftn.; see also Job 11:8). The point the comparison makes is not as much the profundity of a king's thoughts as the unpredictability of his actions. The king who does not give too much away will win greater respect from his subjects. He will keep them on their toes and make them tread lightly in his presence without presuming upon him—after all, a king is a king!

There is nothing further from the thought of these maxims than the 'big brother is watching you' tactic of using spying, secrecy and fear as pillars of power. Rather they underline that the government which wins public confidence and respect ("glory", 25:2) is the one which, although it knows when to keep its own counsel, shows itself committed to taking actions and decisions on the basis of a careful consideration of all the available evidence and relevant facts, and with the interests of truth and the people uppermost; not on partisan interests, narrow political ideology or short-term political expediency.

(ii)

A further mark of the wise king is that he will take care to surround himself with officials and counsellors of like integrity. That is the point made in 25:4–5. In verse 4 the RSV has supplied the words "material for" to make better sense of an obscure Hebrew text. The TEV smoothes it out by translating "and the artist can produce a thing of beauty", and that is perhaps better. A process of refining, then, is just as necessary to bring out the best in kings as to bring out the best in the silversmith. So the king must take steps to root out wicked officials if he is to lay a solid foundation for a good and just rule.

The first line of 16:12 is better translated with the New International Version, "Kings detest wrong-doing" (cf. NEB), for it is primarily the wrong-doing of others that is meant. The proverb therefore links up with the thought of 25:4–5. But that does not let the king out of the refining process; for 29:12 gives warning that here, as so often, example is decisive. A wicked king will get the officials he deserves.

(iii)

The theme of the last proverb (21:1) is God's control of the decisions and actions of the king. The wise king will not behave as if he were an autocrat, following the dictates of his own pleasure, and responsible to none but himself. Rather he will readily submit himself to God's control so that God can direct him to serve his own purposes as easily as a farmer can direct water to where it is most needed by channelling it through his irrigation canals. That is part of what it means for the king to be God's "servant" (Pss. 78:70; 89:3, 50). It is what God always expects of his servants. At the same time, however, this proverb also makes the point that the autocratic king is not the master he thinks he is; for in the providence of God even kings find themselves God's unwitting servants – witness Cyrus (Isa. 44:28), Nebuchadnezzar (Jer. 25:9) and Herod (Acts 4:27–28).

WHAT KING LEMUEL'S MOTHER TAUGHT HIM

Proverbs

31:1   The words of Lemuel, king of Massa, which his mother taught him:

31:2   What, my son? What, son of my womb?
       What, son of my vows?

31:3   Give not your strength to women,
          your ways to those who destroy kings.
31:4   It is not for kings, O Lemuel,
          it is not for kings to drink wine,
          or for rulers to desire strong drink;
31:5   lest they drink and forget what has been decreed,
          and pervert the rights of all the afflicted.
31:6   Give strong drink to him who is perishing,
          and wine to those in bitter distress;
31:7   let them drink and forget their poverty,
          and remember their misery no more.
31:8   Open your mouth for the dumb,
          for the rights of all who are left desolate.
31:9   Open your mouth, judge righteously,
          maintain the rights of the poor and needy.

The ideal of the wise and just king was widely cherished among the peoples of the ancient Near East, so that there is little that is specifically Israelite about the proverbs we have been looking at. In his famous law code, King Hammurabi tells us that he was called by the supreme gods "to promote the welfare of the people . . . to cause justice to prevail in the land, to destroy the wicked and the evil"; and he boasts: "I always governed them in peace; I sheltered them in my wisdom; in order that the strong might not oppress the weak, that justice might be dealt the orphan and the widow". Again, in the Egyptian *Instruction for King Merikare,* the king is told, "Do justice whilst thou endurest upon earth . . . do not oppress the widow, supplant no man in the property of his father . . . be on thy guard against punishing wrongfully".

The present passage is another case in point. Here we have a piece of non-Israelite wisdom literature preserved in the Book of Proverbs, which emphasizes even more directly the main theme of the proverbs dealing with the duty of the king.

Nothing is known about King Lemuel or his mother outside this passage. Massa (see also 30:1), however, is known as the name of a tribe or region in North Arabia (Gen. 25:14)—an area renowned for its wisdom (1 Kings 4:30; Jer. 49:7). On the other hand, *massa* is also a common noun in Hebrew meaning "oracle" (literally "burden"). So rather than indicating where Lemuel came from (RSV, NEB), it may describe what is being said as a "weighty word" (cf. NIV, TEV).

Whether we should think of Lemuel as a young king being given some words of motherly advice, or as a dissolute king being severely scolded by her, is difficult to say. At all events, there is no mistaking this mother's strong concern for her son. This comes out very clearly in verse 2 with its three-fold repetition of "What". The New English Bible takes the exclamation to mean, "What shall I say to you". It might equally well imply, "What on earth are you doing", especially if the tone is reproachful. She appeals to his finer feelings of respect for his mother and to the fact that he was born as an answer to her prayers—much like Samuel (1 Sam. 1:11). Here the name Lemuel may be significant, for it probably means "Devoted-To-God".

In 31:3–4 we have two of the favourite themes of Proverbs: sexual promiscuity and drunkenness. Notice that the Queen Mother no more intends that her son should be teetotal than that he should be celibate. Her point is that a king of all people must avoid over-indulgence on both counts; for the one (probably a large harem is meant) distracts the attention and saps the strength, while the other erodes the will and fuddles the mind. And a king in these states is neither physically nor morally fit to attend to his duties, and to see that justice is being done (v.5; cf. the later Solomon, 1 Kings 11:1–6). In particular, the king must champion the cause of the "dumb", that is, of those who lack the 'muscle' to make their voice heard in defence of their legal rights: the destitute, the poor and the needy (vv. 8–9). To do this the king has to have strength of character and a clear head, and has always to be vigilant.

Taken at face value, verses 6–7 rather cynically approve drowning one's sorrows in a wine glass, and seeking relief from misery in a drunken stupor. Some commentators think that it is the use of wine as a medicine or restorative that is being commended. While the wise did recognize its medicinal value, it is hard to believe that the verses are speaking about a little wine for the stomach's sake. Perhaps significantly, the verb "give" is plural; so that the instruction is not being specifically addressed to Lemuel. This rather suggests that the verses are no more than an observation on a common use of alcohol; as much as to say, 'it is one thing for the wretched to seek oblivion in a glass', but kings cannot afford to become oblivious to their wretchedness'.

THE WISE COURTIER

Proverbs

16:15 In the light of a king's face there is life,
   and his favour is like the clouds that
    bring the spring rain.
19:12 A king's wrath is like the growling of a lion,
   but his favour is like dew upon the grass.
20:2 The dread wrath of a king is like the growling of a lion;
   he who provokes him to anger forfeits his life.
16:14 A king's wrath is a messenger of death,
   and a wise man will appease it.
14:35 A servant who deals wisely has the king's favour,
   but his wrath falls on one who acts shamefully.
22:29 Do you see a man skilful in his work?
   he will stand before kings;
   he will not stand before obscure men.
25:15 With patience a ruler may be persuaded,
   and a soft tongue will break a bone.
16:13 Righteous lips are the delight of a king,
   and he loves him who speaks what is right.
22:11 He who loves purity of heart,
   and whose speech is gracious,
    will have the king as his friend.
24:21 My son, fear the Lord and the king,
   and do not disobey either of them;
24:22 for disaster from them will rise suddenly,
   and who knows the ruin that will come from them both?

23:1   When you sit down to eat with a ruler,
      observe carefully what is before you;
23:2   and put a knife to your throat
      if you are a man given to appetite.
23:3   Do not desire his delicacies,
      for they are deceptive food.
25:6   Do not put yourself forward in the king's presence
      or stand in the place of the great;
25:7   for it is better to be told, "Come up here,"
      than to be put lower in the presence of the prince.

The words of warning and advice in these proverbs are now for the ear of young men about to embark upon a career in one of the branches of the king's service.

(i)

The first few proverbs warn the young men about an occupational hazard. They will find that the king's service can be just as dangerous as it can be rewarding. They can rise to high office, or just as soon fall from office. All depends on the disposition of the king towards them. And the king's pleasure can not only make or break their careers; he also holds over his servants the power of life and death.

The first proverb (16:15) dwells on the happier prospect. The spring rain (the "latter rain" of the AV) fell around March–April and ripened the crops just before they were harvested. So the clouds which harbingered the rain held out the promise of a good harvest (Zech. 10:1), whereas the failure of the rain spelled disaster for the farmer. In the same way, a friendly look from the king gave promise of a prosperous life and a successful career to the favoured courtier.

On the other hand, woe betide them if they put a foot wrong and make the king angry with them. They may as well provoke a lion; for a king's wrath is just as terrifying and just as much a harbinger of death as the growl of a lion (19:12; 20:2). The wise courtier will be on the look-out for the first tell-tale sign of the king's displeasure and will immediately take steps to pacify him (16:14).

The theme of these proverbs is well illustrated in the stories about Joseph (Gen. 39–50), Daniel and his companions (Dan. 1–6) and Esther, and also in the gruesome fate which befell Adonijah, Joab and Shimei (1 Kings 2).

(ii)

The other proverbs give some practical advice on how to win the king's favour and avoid arousing his anger. For the most part it is the kind of advice any father might give his son when he leaves school to begin work—even if it is only in the local supermarket.

(a) Although to some extent a courtier is at the mercy of the king's whims, he can expect approval and promotion only if he merits it. The official who carries out his duties efficiently and judiciously will go places, but the incompetent bungler who brings the administration into disrepute had better watch out (14:35; 22:29).

(b) When he is called upon to advise the king, he must speak tactfully. The king will take advice and can be made to change his mind. But for the courtier to get all worked up and to try to browbeat the king round to his way of thinking is counter-productive, not to say unhealthy. What is required is calm and gentle, but persistent persuasion; for that will eventually wear down even the hardest resistence to his advice (25:15).

(c) The next proverb (16:13) stresses now the need for truthful rather than tactful speech. It reinforces the theme of 25:4–5, 16:12 and 29:12 (see the topic, *The Measure of a King—II*), but now from the angle of the official. What the (wise and just) king wants to hear from his officials is not what they think he would like to hear, but the truth.

The integrity demanded by 16:13 and the gentleness demanded by 25:15 appear to be combined in 22:11. Here, however, the Hebrew text is difficult. The New English Bible reads, "The Lord loves a sincere man; but you will make a king your friend with your fine phrases". It would then imply that flattery and eloquence are a more sure route to advancement than sincerity and truth. If the New English Bible's rendering is the right one, then as an observation on the facts of life the saying has a greater ring of truth to it than 16:13; but as a piece of advice it leaves something to be desired for the man who takes the first line seriously.

(d) The courtier must fear and obey the king as he would God. To give anything less than the utmost respect and implicit obedience is to court disaster (24:21–22). If, as this saying suggests, his loyalty to the king is on a par with his loyalty to God, it is clear that he could easily find himself on the horns of a dilemma. What does he do in a situation where these loyalties clash? None of the proverbs actually contemplate this situation arising, although the possibility is real enough. And not only for courtiers in ancient Israel. The Christian today may find that his career prospects depend upon him engaging in dubious practices at the instruction of his superiors. The stories in the Book of Daniel to which we have just referred, largely revolve around this issue of conflicting loyalties. There the great principle is, as the apostles of the early Church later put it, "Obedience to God comes before obedience to men" (Acts 5:29, JB).

(e) However able, tactful, honest and obedient he may be, a courtier may still come to grief if he does not watch his table manners (23:1–3). Faced with a sumptuous spread, the temptation is for him to grab for the 'goodies' and make a glutton of himself. The expression "put a knife to your throat" could mean that to act the glutton is suicidal, an act of hara-kiri; or it could be a colourful way of saying, "curb your appetite". Why the king's titbits are called "deceptive food" (literally, "bread of lies") is not clear. Perhaps it means that it is likely that he has some sinister motive behind his hospitality. The Arabs have a saying: "The dainties of a king burn the lips". So, courtiers beware! More probably, however, it simply means that the king's hospitality can prove to be a courtier's undoing. The king will take note of the glutton, and will quite reasonably assume that this man is just as barbaric in carrying out his duties.

(f) When the king's ministers and the nobility are assembled at court on some formal occasion, the courtier must know his place (25:6–7). If he tries to hob-nob with his betters, he risks a reprimand and loss of face in front of everyone who matters. That will do no end of damage to his career prospects. The best strategy is for him to join in the company of his inferiors, for then he may have the satisfaction of a public acknowledgment of his worth to the king when he is called on to join more exalted company.

This maxim probably underlies Jesus' story about the wedding feast in Luke 14:7–11. Jesus caps it with a proverbial saying to draw out the broader lesson (v. 11) "For every one who exalts himself will be humbled, and he who humbles himself will be exalted". Worth remembering the next time we assume airs and graces of superiority!

F. THE SCHOOL OF WISDOM

HEAR THE WORDS OF THE WISE

Proverbs

22:17 Incline your ear, and hear the words of the wise,
    and apply your mind to my knowledge;
22:18 for it will be pleasant if you keep them within you,
    if all of them are ready on your lips.
22:19 That your trust may be in the Lord,
    I have made them known to you today, even to you.
22:20 Have I not written for you thirty sayings
    of admonition and knowledge,
22:21 to show you what is right and true,
    that you may give a true answer to those who sent you?

This passage and the sayings brought together in the next section take us back once more (cf. chs. 1–9) to the school of wisdom and to the feet of the wisdom teacher.

This passage is the introduction to the third section of the book (22:17–24:22). Like chapters 1–9, it takes the form of a series of lessons addressed by a father to his son (23:15, 19, 22,

26; 24:13, 21—see the comment on 1:8–19, *The School Lesson*). Its title was probably "The words of the wise" (v.17), which was later incorporated into verse 17 by mistake. The first line should then read with the *Septuagint*, "Incline your ear and hear my words". As we have already said, this section of Proverbs is an adaptation of the Egyptian *Instruction of Amenemopet*. Notice the similarity between our passage and the way in which the Egyptian sage begins his lessons:

> Give thy ears, hear what is said,
> Give thy heart to understand them.
> To put them in thy heart is worth-while.

Notice too, the striking parallel between "that you may give a true answer to those who sent you" (v.21), and "to direct a report to one who has sent him", which is given as one of the purposes of the Egyptian text in its general introduction (see the quotation from it given in the comment on 1:1–6, *Pondering Proverbs*). There are also close parallels in content—some of which we have already noted. Here are two examples:

> Make no friendship with a man given to anger,
>   nor go with a wrathful man,
> lest you learn his ways
>   and entangle yourself in a snare.
>
> (22:24–25)

> Do not associate to thyself the heated man,
> Nor visit him for conversation ...
> Lest a terror carry thee off.
>
> (*Amenemopet*)

> Do not toil to acquire wealth;
>   be wise enough to desist.
> When your eyes light upon it, it is gone;
>   for suddenly it takes to itself wings,
>   flying like an eagle toward heaven.
>
> (23:4–5)

Cast not thy heart in pursuit of riches,
for there is no ignoring Fate and Fortune...
They have made for themselves wings like geese
And are flown away to the heavens.

(*Amenemopet*)

(Note the reference to "thirty sayings" in verse 20). Interestingly enough, the *Instruction of Amenemopet* is divided into thirty brief chapters. Although only about a third of the sayings actually correspond, it does seem that the Israelite sages who adapted it have kept the same number. The text is laid out into thirty sayings by the TEV, although there is some disagreement among commentators over the precise number and the division of some of the sayings.

As we have seen, the *Instruction of Amenemopet* was designed to educate government officials and civil servants for successful careers in the service of the state. However, in the course of its adaptation and reworking by Israel's sages, it was severed from its moorings in professional training and was made to serve their wider educational goals. The clearest mark of this change of direction is verse 19, which ties this section in with the first (cf. 1:7; 3:5–8).

THE TEACHING OF THE WISE

Proverbs

20:12 The hearing ear and the seeing eye,
    the Lord has made them both.
15:31 He whose ear heeds wholesome admonition
    will abide among the wise.
18:15 An intelligent mind acquires knowledge,
    and the ear of the wise seeks knowledge.
23:12 Apply your mind to instruction
    and your ear to words of knowledge.
19:20 Listen to advice and accept instruction,
    that you may gain wisdom for the future.

29:1   He who is often reproved, yet stiffens his neck
   will suddenly be broken beyond healing.

15:10 There is severe discipline for him who forsakes the way;
   he who hates reproof will die.

12:1   Whoever loves discipline loves knowledge,
   but he who hates reproof is stupid.

19:8   He who gets wisdom loves himself;
   he who keeps understanding will prosper.

15:32 He who ignores instruction despises himself,
   but he who heeds admonition gains understanding.

19:27 Cease, my son, to hear instruction
   only to stray from the words of knowledge.

16:16 To get wisdom is better than gold;
   to get understanding is to be chosen rather than silver.

23:23 Buy truth, and do not sell it;
   buy wisdom, instruction, and understanding.

24:13 My son, eat honey, for it is good,
   and the drippings of the honeycomb
   are sweet to your taste.

24:14 Know that wisdom is such to your soul;
   if you find it, there will be a future,
   and your hope will not be cut off.

24:3   By wisdom a house is built,
   and by understanding it is established;

24:4   by knowledge the rooms are filled
   with all precious and pleasant riches.

13:14 The teaching of the wise is a fountain of life,
   that one may avoid the snares of death.

15:24 The wise man's path leads upward to life,
   that he may avoid Sheol beneath.

19:16 He who keeps the commandment keeps his life;
   he who despises the word will die.

10:17 He who heeds instruction is on the path to life,
   but he who rejects reproof goes astray.

13:13 He who despises the word brings destruction on himself,
   but he who respects the commandment will be rewarded.

21:16 A man who wanders from the way of understanding
   will rest in the assembly of the dead.

15:33 The fear of the Lord is instruction in wisdom,
    and humility goes before honour.
16:20 He who gives heed to the word will prosper,
    and happy is he who trusts in the Lord.
14:27 The fear of the Lord is a fountain of life,
    that one may avoid the snares of death.
19:23 The fear of the Lord leads to life;
    and he who has it rests satisfied;
    he will not be visited by harm.
14:26 In the fear of the Lord one has strong confidence,
    and his children will have a refuge.
10:27 The fear of the Lord prolongs life,
    but the years of the wicked will be short.
14:2 He who walks in uprightness fears the Lord,
    but he who is devious in his ways despises him.
29:25 The fear of man lays a snare,
    but he who trusts in the Lord is safe.
28:14 Blessed is the man who fears the Lord always;
    but he who hardens his heart will fall into calamity.
23:17 Let not your heart envy sinners,
    but continue in the fear of the Lord all the day.
23:18 Surely there is a future,
    and your hope will not be cut off.

These proverbs have a familiar ring to them. They centre around four themes which were prominent in the teacher's instruction as presented in the first section of the book (chs. 1–9):

(a) *A listening ear.* The first group emphasize the importance of paying close attention to what the teacher has to say. They echo the customary introduction to the school lesson: "Hear, my son, your father's instruction" (1:8 *etc*). The observant eye (cf. "I saw and considered it; I looked and received instruction", 24:32) and, above all, the hearing ear, are the means by which wisdom is learned—and they are, says 20:12, the handiwork of God. The sense may be that the wisdom which comes through seeing and hearing is thoroughly reliable; or that the eyes and the ears ought to be directed towards learning wisdom, since that is what God made them for. Besides lending his ears, the wisdom seeker must also apply his mind to what the teacher says (18:15; 23:12; see the comment on 2:1–5). This is nicely brought out in Solomon's prayer for wisdom, when he asks God to give him a "hearing heart" (RSV, "understanding mind", 1 Kings 3:9). In Egyptian wisdom literature the wise man is sometimes simply called "the hearing heart". The student with a "hearing heart" is his own best friend (19:8); for in the end (19:20) he will join the company of the wise (15:31), and will enjoy life's "good" (literally, "will find good [things]," 19:8).

The importance of a listening ear is reinforced by warnings about the fate in store for the fool who has a diseased ear which the severest discipline fails to cure (15:10) but which succeeds only in hardening an already rebellious, stiffened neck (29:1). While effecting to despise all reproof and correction (12:1), he is in effect despising himself (15:32). His "hardened neck" will become so brittle that when calamity comes it will be shattered—beyond all hope of a cure (29:1; cf. 6:15). In Jeremiah 19:10–15, the prophet applies the metaphor to the rebellious people and shatters a pottery vessel before them to press home the point.

(b) *The value of wisdom.* The first two sayings in the second group return to the theme of the inestimable value of wisdom, for which no price is too high to pay (16:16; 23:23). The next two reinforce its value by stressing (1) its sweetness and health-giving properties (24:13–14; cf. 16:24 and contrast 5:3), and (2) its practicality (24:3–4). This last saying could be meant either literally or metaphorically of health and harmony in family relationships. In the *first* case, a commentary is provided by the sayings on *Wisdom and Wealth;* in the *second,* the commentary is provided by those brought together under the general topic heading, *The Home.*

(c) *The two ways.* The next group picks up the theme of the two ways and their contrasting destinations: the one destination "life", and the other "death" (see the comment on 4:10–19). On the metaphor of a "fountain of life" (13:14) see the comment on 3:18. It reinforces for us once again that the "path to life" (10:17) in Proverbs is not the route to mere existence, but to life at its fullest and best. Here, then, the sage's teaching is presented as the source of life's vitality and growth, of its fullness and happiness, of its wholeness and fruitfulness for those who have ears to hear (10:17; 13:13). Those who have no ears to hear, but who "despise" (19:16; 13:13) instruction like a scoffer or who "reject" (10:17) it like a fool, walk in the path of death. Notice in 13:14 (also 14:27) the lively picture of death as a hunter setting traps to ensnare the unwary and the uninstructed and bring them down to Sheol (15:24; 21:16). But once again we may remind ourselves that this route is presented not simply as a short-cut to the grave but primarily as a weakening and deadening of life's vitality and an impoverishment of the things which make a person well and truly alive, and make life worth living.

(d) *The fear of the Lord.* The sayings in the final group cover much the same ground as the last but one, but they have shifted into a higher gear. In them it is the fear of the Lord which is "a fountain of life" (14:27; cf. 13:14), while the path to death is walked by those who despise God (14:2). Notice that these sayings are not tacked on at the end of Proverbs as a kind of afterthought or as an optional extra for the religiously minded, but are scattered throughout chapters 10–31, as though to remind the reader every now and again of the lessons taught in chapters 1–9 concerning where true wisdom for living is to be found, and wherein it consists.

Three of these earlier lessons on fearing the Lord are particularly reinforced here: (1) *It is the best education in wisdom.* The fear of the Lord is "instruction" which makes a man truly wise (15:33; cf. 16:20). Not only is it the foundation of all true wisdom (see the comment on 1:7); it is also its goal (see the comment on 2:1–5). So man's quest for wisdom bears its ripest fruit when he comes to "understand the fear of the Lord and find the knowledge of God" (2:5); (2) *It bears fruit in righteousness.* In chapter 2:6–15 the "sound wisdom" which God gives is a guide and a guard against evil men and their perverse ways.

That thought is picked up in 14:2 (cf. 16:6). It is with this moral outworking of the fear of the Lord that Proverbs is most concerned. So in the thought of the wise, fearing the Lord goes hand in hand with turning away from evil (see 8:13; 16:6; cf. Job 1:1; 28:28); (3) *It is the best security in life.* The man who fears and trusts in the Lord walks safely and securely along the path to life, and will neither slip on the banana skins life throws at his feet, nor suffer the calamity which will overtake those who despise God (see the comment on 2:20–22; 3:5–8, 21–26). Concerning 23:17–18, see the comment on 3:31–35.

III. WAYS OF MAN AND THE WAYS OF GOD

OBSERVATIONS ON NATURE AND SOCIETY

Proverbs

30:15 The leech has two daughters;
  "Give, give," they cry.
 Three things are never satisfied;
  four never say, "Enough":
30:16 Sheol, the barren womb,
  the earth ever thirsty for water,
  and the fire which never says, "Enough."
30:18 Three things are too wonderful for me;
  four I do not understand:
30:19 the way of an eagle in the sky,
  the way of a serpent on a rock,
 the way of a ship on the high seas,
  and the way of a man with a maiden.
30:21 Under three things the earth trembles;
  under four it cannot bear up:
30:22 a slave when he becomes king,
  and a fool when he is filled with food;
30:23 an unloved woman when she gets a husband,
  and a maid when she succeeds her mistress.
30:24 Four things on earth are small,
  but they are exceedingly wise:

30:25 the ants are a people not strong,
    yet they provide their food in the summer;
30:26 the badgers are a people not mighty,
    yet they make their homes in the rocks;
30:27 the locusts have no king,
    yet all of them march in rank;
30:28 the lizard you can take in your hands,
    yet it is in kings' palaces.
30:29 Three things are stately in their tread;
    four are stately in their stride:
30:30 the lion which is mightiest among beasts
    and does not turn back before any;
30:31 the strutting cock, the he-goat,
    and a king striding before his people.

(i)

The observations on nature and society brought together in this chapter take the form of numerical sayings. We had an example of the graded number pattern ("three . . . four") in 6:16 ("six . . . seven"), and other examples of it can be found elsewhere (see Job 5:19; 33:14; Amos 1:3, 6, 9 *etc*). We noticed in connection with 6:16 that the same pattern is also found in Ugaritic literature. Indeed, it was a standard literary convention in wide use throughout the ancient Near East. It was particularly useful to the wisdom teachers, for it provided them with a ready-made form for cataloguing their observations in a way which helped their pupils to memorize them.

On the basis of these sayings it has been thought that rudimentary instruction in zoology and the general sciences was given in the wisdom schools. But while deep wonder at and keen observation of the natural world lies behind them, their primary interest is not so much nature as human society. The sages interest in nature is primarily for the light it can shed on human life and behaviour and for the lessons it can teach. The sayings, however, never press their lesson, but leave it to the reader to ponder and tease out.

(ii)

(a) *Four insatiable things* (vv. 15*b*–16). Neither Sheol's appetite for human victims (see the comment on 1:12), nor a barren woman's appetite for children, nor a parched land's appetite for water, nor a fire's appetite for fuel is ever satisfied. In 27:20 human greed and covetousness were likened to the insatiability of Sheol. So perhaps here too we have a comment on greed. But while that seems to be the thought in the saying about the leech (v. 15*a*), the next one points to the "barren womb" as its point of interest or comparison between nature and human life. Perhaps then it is a comment on the passionate but unfulfilled desire of a barren woman for children—for which Sheol, the earth, and fire, serve as word-pictures.

(b) *Four marvellous things* (vv. 18–19). What the "way" of the soaring eagle, the gliding snake, and a ship on the high seas have in common—which makes them a mystery to be marvelled at—is itself a bit of a mystery. Is it the mystery of how they propel themselves? Is it that they leave no trace behind them? Is it their easy mastery of difficult environments? Or is it the grace and beauty of their motion which captures the writer's imagination? Perhaps it is that their ways are inaccessible to men. The eagle soars high in the sky, the snake slithers in and out of the deep and hidden nooks and crannies in the rocks, while this ship makes its passage through the high or open sea and not through the familiar coastal waters. Notice that with the fourth and final marvellous thing we again move from the natural to the human realm. It is even less evident what the "way" of a man with a woman has in common with the others. Possibly nothing is intended beyond that it too is incomprehensible. Here "way" evidently refers to the mysterious, magnetic power of attraction between the sexes which finds fulfilment in sexual intercourse.

(c) *Four unbearable things* (vv. 21–23). Here we have four people who were at some disadvantage in society, but upon whom fortune has smiled kindly: the slave becomes a king; the fool has a full stomach (*ie* is successful); the unattractive and querulous spinster has bagged a husband; and the maidservant has won the affection of her mistress's husband and has taken her place in the household. Each instance is described exaggeratedly and humorously as an earth-shattering event. The sense may be that these are all upstarts who have overturned the status quo. Alternatively, it may be an observation that people who experience a dramatic change in fortune for the better often become quite unbearable to live with.

(d) *Four small things* (vv. 24–28). The general theme of this saying is "small, but wise"—or as we might say, 'brains over brawn'. The first line of each verse underscores the 'smallness' of the creatures, and the second line their wisdom. Ants are commended for foresight and industry (cf. 6:6–8), badgers for enterprise and skilful engineering, locusts for discipline and orderliness (cf. Joel 2:4–9), and the lizard for adeptness at 'getting places'. The saying points to the lesson that wisdom and not strength is the key to success, and that "one talent" used wisely can go a long way.

(e) *Four stately things* (vv. 29–31). These verses evidently compare the majestic bearing of a king at the head of a procession with the proud gait of the lion, the barnyard cock and the he-goat. The identification of the second animal as a cock is not certain. This identification rests on the *Septuagint* version (see RSV ftn.). The Hebrew is literally "girt of loins", evidently a nickname like 'strider'. Other suggestions are that it is a greyhound (AV), or the warhorse (NEB ftn.). The last part of this verse is "unintelligible" (NEB ftn.), and some commentators have thought that a fourth animal and not a king is meant. If we accept the RSV's guess at its meaning, the saying is expressing the fittingness of a king's regal bearing—unless it is a gentle gibe at his pomp and circumstance, in which case he would have fully approved of our modern royal 'walkabouts'.

WISE WAYS WITH WORDS—I

Proverbs

> 18:21 Death and life are in the power of the tongue,
> and those who love it will eat its fruits.
> 18:20 From the fruit of his mouth a man is satisfied;
> he is satisfied by the yield of his lips.

12:14 From the fruit of his words a man is satisfied with good,
and the work of a man's hand comes back to him.
18:4 The words of a man's mouth are deep waters;
the fountain of wisdom is a gushing stream.
20:15 There is gold, and abundance of costly stones;
but the lips of knowledge are a precious jewel.

13:3 He who guards his mouth preserves his life;
he who opens wide his lips comes to ruin.
21:23 He who keeps his mouth and his tongue
keeps himself out of trouble.
10:19 When words are many, transgression is not lacking,
but he who restrains his lips is prudent.
29:20 Do you see a man who is hasty in his words?
There is more hope for a fool than for him.
12:18 There is one whose rash words are like sword thrusts,
but the tongue of the wise brings healing.
18:13 If one gives answer before he hears,
it is his folly and shame.
24:26 He who gives a right answer
kisses the lips.

The power of the tongue for good or ill is underlined in 18:21. It may deal in death and destruction or in life and healing. We have already heard much about these contrasting ways with the tongue, but especially about its deadly ways. The proverbs we shall be looking at in this and the next section correct the imbalance by highlighting some of its happier and healthier ways—ways which are fruitful for the speaker and his hearers alike.

Like James after them (see Jas. 3:1–12), the sages were much more impressed by the tongue's power to wound and maim than to bring health and healing. So besides warning about its dangers, they spend most time stressing the need to carefully guard the tongue not only from wicked, but also from thoughtless and garrulous, speech (13:3; 21:23). Short of silence when it is time to be silent, three things mark the man with a guarded tongue:

(a) *He is a man of few words* (10:19). The person who likes the sound of his own voice too much is batting on a sticky wicket. The percentages work against him. Even though he has the best will in the world and means no harm, sooner or later he will say something wrong and hurtful which he would like to recall, but cannot.

(b) *He thinks before he speaks* (29:20; 12:18). "Hasty" is a bad word in Proverbs: a hasty temper (14:29), hasty promises (20:25), hasty judgments (25:7b–8), hasty decisions (21:5), hasty actions (19:2), haste in acquiring wealth (13:11), and here now hasty words, all alike fall under the sages' condemnation. Once again, the person who is in a hurry to open his mouth may do so with the best of intentions. But at best his words are unhelpful and ruffle rather than soothe a difficult situation or strained relationship, while at worst they can be as wounding as a razor-sharp sword. The *Instruction of Amenemopet* also gives the good advice to think before we speak:

> Another good deed in the heart of the god
> Is to pause before speaking.

(c) *He listens before he speaks* (18:13). This saying condemns that common failing of being a good talker and a poor listener. In particular, it has in mind being so eager to put forward our own point of view in a discussion that we never listen to the other fellow's opinion or give him a chance to express it. The net result is that we have a discussion with our own opinions, and undermine any wisdom in them by our stupidity.

WISE WAYS WITH WORDS—II

Proverbs

> 25:11 A word fitly spoken
>   is like apples of gold in a setting of silver.
> 15:23 To make an apt answer is a joy to a man,
>   and a word in season, how good it is!

12:25 Anxiety in a man's heart weighs him down,
      but a good word makes him glad.
16:24 Pleasant words are like a honeycomb,
      sweetness to the soul and health to the body.
15:4 A gentle tongue is a tree of life,
      but perverseness in it breaks the spirit.
16:21 The wise of heart is called a man of discernment,
      and pleasant speech increases persuasiveness.
16:23 The mind of the wise makes his speech judicious,
      and adds persuasiveness to his lips.
27:2 Let another praise you, and not your own mouth;
      a stranger, and not your own lips.
25:27 It is not good to eat much honey,
      so be sparing of complimentary words.
25:12 Like a gold ring or an ornament of gold
      is a wise reprover to a listening ear.
28:23 He who rebukes a man will afterward find more favour
      than he who flatters with his tongue.
27:5 Better is open rebuke
      than hidden love.
10:10 He who winks the eye causes trouble,
      but he who boldly reproves makes peace.

In these proverbs, four wise and winsome ways with words now receive the sages' commendation:

(a) *Fitting words* (25:11; 15:23; 12:25). These are words which are fitting (1) in their expression, and (2) in their timing. The proverbs of the wise provide good examples of their ideal of fitness in expression. They are brief and to the point, nicely polished and balanced, and decoratively restrained. A word fitly spoken says much and says it well. That is something we would all be the better for aiming at, not least the teachers among us. If we value our thoughts, we will be careful about how we express them in words. It is fitting expression which is meant in the saying, "Fine speech is not becoming to a fool" (17:7). We noted earlier, however, that even a fool can sometimes come out with fine words; it is his bad sense of timing which gives him away (cf. 26:7, 9). A fitly spoken word is therefore also a word in season. Out of season it is ineffective and counter-productive. The need to suit word to time and occasion is nicely illustrated by comparing the good word of 12:25 with the out of tune song of 25:20. The kind of artistic design envisaged in 25:11 is unclear, although the point being made is clear enough: well-expressed and well-timed words are like golden apples in a silver setting—things of great artistry, beauty and value.

(b) *Pleasant words* (16:24; 15:4; 16:21; 16:23). In 16:24 we have honeyed words at their best; words which are not only sweet, but also healthy for the speaker and his hearers (contrast 5:3). The word "gentle" in 15:4 conveys the same idea. The Hebrew has "a healing tongue". In this verse the healing tongue which promotes life and vitality ("tree of life") is contrasted with the evil tongue of the mischief-maker, while in 12:18 it was contrasted with the sword thrusts of the rash tongue. Even more familiar to our lips and ears are the ordinary, everyday curt and unkind words of the irritable and impatient tongue. This world of ours would be a brighter and better place to live in for the price of a few more kindly words and cheery smiles. "Persuasiveness" (16:21; 16:23) is ambiguous. The Hebrew could mean either that (as in 7:21), or it could mean "learning" (as in 1:5). So these proverbs may be a reminder that no arguments are won by harsh words, or that harsh words ill-serve the wise to teach and commend their wisdom to others (see NIV).

(c) *Complimentary words* (27:2; 25:27). "A man is judged by his praise", says 27:21 (see the topic, *A Good Name*); but not if his own mouth is doing the praising, says 27:2. No-one likes the person who blows his own trumpet. It is usually a sure sign that no-one else can find the slightest reason to blow it for him. A German proverb makes the point sharply: *Eigen-Lob stinkt, Freundes Lob hinkt, Fremdes Lob klingt*—"self-praise stinks, friends' praise limps, strangers' praise rings".

The next proverb (25:27) begins by reminding us that we can have too much of a good thing (cf. 25:16), and then—at least according to the RSV—applies the principle to paying compliments; compliments likewise are healthy in moderation, unhealthy in excess. The person paying the compliments must exercise restraint or else he might be found a flatterer and his compliments become snares (cf. 29:5). The Hebrew text here is difficult, however. It actually reads, "searching out their honour is honour". The RSV has taken a lead from the *Septuagint* and altered the text. The New International Version follows the Hebrew, but has to insert a "not" ("nor is it honourable to seek one's own glory", cf. AV), whilst the New English Bible gets sense from the Hebrew as it stands by assuming a word play between "honour" and "weight" ("and the quest for honour is burdensome"—cf. the comment on 3:16).

(d) *Reproving words* (25:12; 28:23; 27:5; 10:10). If the sages qualified their approval of complimentary words, they have no such reservation about the value of reproving words, whether those of parent, teacher or friend. Matched to a listening ear, the words of a *wise* reprover are like a gold ring (25:12—probably an "earring", NEB); words which will enhance and adorn the hearer's character and conduct (cf. 1:9; 3:22; 4:9). Of course, while the sting of rebuke is still sharp and fresh, the hearer might take some convincing that it is the reprover and not the flatterer who hands out the gold earrings (28:23). The operative word in this saying is therefore "afterward" (cf. Heb. 12.11). The wise reprover need expect no thanks at the time.

In 27:5 we might have expected a contrast between open rebuke and hidden resentment. The meaning of the second line is not clear. At a stretch, it may mean the misguided love which turns a blind eye to the faults of another for the best of motives, but which in the end does nobody any favours. If the "wink[er]" in 10:10 is the man who turns a blind eye for the sake of preserving the peace (cf. NEB) and not the mischief-maker of 6:13, then this saying makes much the same point.

SADNESS AND GLADNESS OF HEART

Proverbs

> 17:22 A cheerful heart is a good medicine,
>   but a downcast spirit dries up the bones.

15:13 A glad heart makes a cheerful countenance,
         but by sorrow of heart the spirit is broken.
18:14 A man's spirit will endure sickness;
         but a broken spirit who can bear?
15:15 All the days of the afflicted are evil,
         but a cheerful heart has a continual feast.
25:25 Like cold water to a thirsty soul,
         so is good news from a far country.
15:30 The light of the eyes rejoices the heart,
         and good news refreshes the bones.
13:17 A bad messenger plunges men into trouble,
         but a faithful envoy brings healing.
25:13 Like the cold of snow in the time of harvest
         is a faithful messenger to those who send him,
         he refreshes the spirit of his masters.
13:12 Hope deferred makes the heart sick,
         but a desire fulfilled is a tree of life.
14:10 The heart knows its own bitterness,
         and no stranger shares its joy.
14:13 Even in laughter the heart is sad,
         and the end of joy is grief.
25:20 He who sings songs to a heavy heart
         is like one who takes off a garment on a cold day,
         and like vinegar on a wound.

These proverbs offer some reflections on the theme of joy and
sorrow.

(a) In the first two (17:22; 15:13) we have a perceptive
comment on the connection between happiness and health.
Israel's sages might not have used the term 'psychosomatic',
but the idea was familiar enough to them. The contrast drawn
here is not between the joy and sorrow which we all feel at
certain times, but between set dispositions towards life. The
person with a "glad heart" is that remarkably cheerful individual who has a positive and optimistic outlook on life, who always
seems to find something to be happy about, and whose smile is
infectious. Such a disposition pays dividends in a healthy body
and a healthy complexion (cf. 3:8; 14:30). At the other extreme,
the person with a "sorrowful heart" is that morose or anxiety-

laden individual who is always down in the dumps, who always finds something to complain or fret about, and who dampens the atmosphere around him like the proverbial wet blanket. This disposition pays its dividend in bad health. It debilitates the body, clouds the eyes and leaves its etchings on the face.

(b) You may perhaps recall the lines of the ditty:

It's the same the whole world over,
It's the poor wot gets the blame,
It's the rich wot gets the pleasure,
Ain't it all a blooming shame.

Many other people besides the composer of these lines also tend to confuse happiness with pleasure, and have the wrong idea that happiness depends on material things. The proverbs at 18:14 and 15:15 are concerned to point out that happiness in life does not depend on personal circumstances and material conditions. On the contrary, where circumstances like ill-health or physical disability (18:14) and conditions like poverty and want (15:15— "the afflicted" are the downtrodden poor) work against us, the inward happiness of a cheerful heart can give us the courage and the strength to endure and to overcome them. When conditions become difficult and life becomes hard it is the inner disposition of an individual, his morale and spiritual strength which really matter; for that will make the difference between swimming on top of life's waves and billows, or sinking beneath them without trace.

This kind of deep-seated joy which brings health to the body and strength to the spirit does not come naturally or very easily to most of us. It is a fruit (cf. Gal. 5:22) which needs to be carefully cultivated. Notice the secret of its growth in Philippians 4:11–13.

(c) The sayings about good news in 25:25 and 15:30 become more pointed if we remember that before the days of the pony express, let alone modern telecommunications, news travelled agonizingly slowly. The picture we have of Eli sitting by the side of the road anxiously waiting for news and looking out for the messenger (1 Sam. 4:13) must have been a common sight. The expression, "the light of the eyes" (15:30) may perhaps refer to the happy look and infectious smile of a cheerful friend; or, in view of the next line, to the sparkle in the eyes of the messenger as against the downcast eyes of a bearer of bad news. The joy and refreshment that good news brings is nicely illustrated for us in Genesis 45:25–28. When Jacob hears that his son Joseph is alive and well, his "spirit . . . revived"—the good news brought him back to life again. Remember that letter we have always been meaning to write . . . ! As an aside, 13:17 and 25:13 observe that there are good and bad messengers as well as messages.

(d) The sayings in 14:10 and 14:13 catch the sage in a pensive mood, brooding over the enigmas of joy and sorrow in human experience. In 14:10 he reflects on the privacy of these emotions. While we can share our joy or sorrow with others (cf. Rom. 12:15), there is always a depth to it which is known only to ourselves. An old English proverb makes much the same point: "No-one knows where the shoe pinches so well as he that wears it". In 14:13 he goes a step further. Here he reflects that no human joy is ever unalloyed. Even our happiest, most joyous moments are tinctured by sadness; and sorrow follows hard on the heels of joy. This rather pessimistic thought need not always hold true, of course. But there will be at least some who will recognize the truth in it. If we may draw from these reflections a reminder of the need to be sensitive to the feelings of others, the tuneless song in 25:20 admirably makes the point (see the comment on 12:25, *Wise Ways with Words—II*).

PRAYER, SACRIFICE AND VOWS

Proverbs

20:25 It is a snare for a man to say rashly, "It is holy,"
       and to reflect only after making his vows.
15:8 The sacrifice of the wicked is an abomination to the Lord,
       but the prayer of the upright is his delight.
21:27 The sacrifice of the wicked is an abomination;

how much more when he brings it with evil intent.
15:29 The Lord is far from the wicked,
    but he hears the prayer of the righteous.
28:9 If one turns away his ear from hearing the law,
    even his prayer is an abomination.
21:3 To do righteousness and justice
    is more acceptable to the Lord than sacrifice.
16:6 By loyalty and faithfulness iniquity is atoned for,
    and by the fear of the Lord a man avoids evil.
28:13 He who conceals his transgressions will not prosper,
    but he who confesses and forsakes them will obtain mercy.

These are among the very few proverbs which touch on aspects of Israel's worship (see 3:9–10).

(a) Vows is the subject of 20:25, although in fact the proverb serves as a case in point of the folly of rash speaking, which is so deprecated by the sages. Once taken, the person who made the vow was bound by it: "it [the thing vowed] is holy"—that is, it has become the property of God. So to vow and not to fulfil his vow, was a very serious matter (Num. 30:2; Deut. 23:21–23), while to vow rashly and to fulfil it could be a very costly matter (cf. Judg. 11:30–40). The advice of the wise was: "it is better that you should not vow than that you should vow and not pay" (Ecc. 5:5; cf. Deut. 23:21–22).

(b) The point that 15:8 is making is not that prayer is spiritually superior to sacrifice. The two are not being set against each other. Prayer and sacrifice were always closely linked and belonged together in Israel's worship. We have to read the Book of Psalms alongside the Book of Leviticus to get a full picture of Israel's religious services. Rather, the point is that sacrifice has no merit in itself, but is only meaningful and acceptable to God when offered in sincerity of heart. The next three sayings (21:27; 15:29; 28:9) press home the point. The "evil intent" which compounds the offensiveness of the sacrifice in 21:27 is best known to the wicked man. Evidently he feels he has more scope for his activities by pretending to be very religious. He has modern counterparts in those who are in the business of religion for the money they can squeeze from the pockets of the religiously gullible. The lesson is drawn in 21:3: righteousness and justice is more acceptable to God than sacrifice. What matters most to God is not our fine-sounding hymns and well-phrased prayers, our cherished doctrines and forms of service, but the kind of people we are and the kind of lives we live. How we live and behave in our daily lives outside the church determines the value God places on what we do inside the church. This is a lesson which was repeatedly driven home by the prophets in the strongest possible terms (see Isa. 1:11–17; Jer. 7:21–26; Hos. 6:6; Amos 5:21–27; Mic. 6:6–8; cf. 1 Sam. 15:22; Pss. 40:6–8; 50:8–15).

(c) The last two proverbs are more closely related in theme to 21:3 than at first sight they might appear. The word "atoned" (16:6) belongs to the technical language of the offering of sacrifices for sin (Lev. 4:20, 26 *etc;* 16:1–34). But here it is not sacrifices but man's "loyalty and faithfulness" (see the comment on 3:3) which is said to make atonement for sin. The sage is not suggesting that we can dispense with "by grace through faith"—which is just as great an Old as a New Testament principle. Rather, he is giving a needed reminder here, and in 28:13, that God's grace cannot be picked up casually and that faith without works is dead. The path to God's mercy and forgiveness in the Old as well as in the New Testament is the three-fold path of (1) confession of sin (cf. Pss. 32:3–5; 51:1–17; 1 John 1:8–10), (2) repentance—not merely saying "sorry", but *turning* the back on sin and the face towards God (cf. Jer. 3:11–14; Hos. 6:1–3; Matt. 3:2; 2 Cor. 7:10), and (3) amendment of life (cf. Isa. 1:16–20; Mic. 6:6–8; Jas. 2:14–16). It is the broken and contrite heart which is the acceptable sacrifice to God and which he will never despise (Ps. 51:17).

WEIGHED IN THE BALANCES

Proverbs

15:3 The eyes of the Lord are in every place,
    keeping watch on the evil and the good.

22:12 The eyes of the Lord keep watch over knowledge,
    but he overthrows the words of the faithless.

15:11 Sheol and Abaddon lie open before the Lord,
    how much more the hearts of men!

17:3 The crucible is for silver, and the furnace is for gold,
    and the Lord tries hearts.

21:2 Every way of a man is right in his own eyes,
    but the Lord weighs the heart.

16:2 All the ways of a man are pure in his own eyes,
    but the Lord weighs the spirit.

30:12 There are those who are pure in their own eyes
    but are not cleansed of their filth.

20:9 Who can say, "I have made my heart clean;
    I am pure from my sin"?

20:11 Even a child makes himself known by his acts,
    whether what he does is pure and right.

20:27 The spirit of man is the lamp of the Lord,
    searching all his innermost parts.

24:10 If you faint in the day of adversity,
    your strength is small.

24:11 Rescue those who are being taken away to death;
    hold back those who are stumbling to the slaughter.

24:12 If you say, "Behold, we did not know this,"
    does not he who weighs the heart perceive it?
    Does not he who keeps watch over your soul know it,
    and will he not requite man according to his work?

(i)

In 15:3 and 22:12 we meet again (see 5:21) the thought of the all-seeing eyes of God, keenly observant and far-ranging, probing and penetrating. Nothing escapes God's searching scrutiny. No small act of goodness is too trivial, no peccadillo too commonplace, to catch his eye and earn his blessing or his condemnation (15:3). In his capacity as the ever-watchful God, God is the guardian and the champion of truth and the enemy of falsehood (22:12). Assuming a different meaning for "knowledge", the New English Bible produces much the same thought, but now in terms of the lawcourt—"The Lord keeps watch over every claim at law, and overturns the scoundrel's case".

The penetration of God's eyes is the theme of 15:11. Sheol, as we have seen (see the comment on 1:12; on its synonym "Abaddon", see the comment on 27:20, *The Greedy*), was located by the Hebrews in the heart of the earth, inaccessible to the eyes and beyond the ken of the living; a land shrouded in darkness and obscurity, mystery and secrecy. So, says this proverb, if the dark, mysterious depths of Sheol are "naked" before God (cf. Job 26:6), how much more transparent is the human heart. Here, as in the other proverbs in this section, "heart" stands for the inner aspirations, secret desires and motives which are the source and spring of a person's actions. It is these things—things which are inaccessible to others and, as other sayings will go on to point out, partly to ourselves—which lie open, exposed to the scrutiny of God, and which form the basis of God's assessment and judgment.

Two metaphorical expressions are used to describe God's assessment of the heart. *First,* God "tries" the heart (17:3). Much as an assayer tests the genuineness and purity of silver or gold in a crucible, God "tests" the heart to determine the genuineness and purity of men, stripped bare of their pretensions, appearances and professions. *Second,* God "weighs" the heart (21:2; cf. 16:2). There may be a distant echo here of the conception in Egyptian religion that the heart of the deceased was weighed against "truth and right" (*maat,* see the comment on 3:16) on the judgment balances of the supreme god Re. There is no thought in these proverbs, however, of judgment after death. Here "weighs" has much the same meaning as "tries", and has to do with God's assessment and judgment of men here and now.

(ii)

We turn now from the eyes of God to the eyes of man. The difference is nicely put in 1 Sam. 16:7: "The Lord sees not as man sees; man looks on the outward appearance, but the Lord looks on the heart". It is little wonder then that the assessment of men is so often at variance with the assessment of God—not least when it comes to self-assessment (21:2; 16:2). These two sayings are not a comment on the hypocritical, self-righteous person, who is so proud of his rectitude that he has eyes only for the faults in others (cf. Matt. 23:25–26; Luke 18:10–14). Those are the kind of people envisaged in 30:12, seen in the company to which they really belong (see 30:11–14). Rather, they are a comment on: (1) *the poor standards men weigh themselves against*—"it's just not cricket!" and the like. It is of interest to note here that instead of "the Lord weighs the heart/spirit", the New English Bible translates, "the Lord fixes a standard for the heart/spirit of man", which the Hebrew could also mean. In any case, the notion of weighing involves the thought of weighing up against a standard. That standard must be God's, and not our own; (2) *man's amazing facility for self-deception:* "The heart is deceitful above all things, and desperately corrupt; who can understand it?" (Jer. 17:9). This passage in Jeremiah immediately goes on to say that God searches the mind and tests the heart to requite every man according to his ways (v. 10). Other passages remind us, however, that God's testing is a refining process which is designed not simply to reveal what kind of people we really are, but to make us better people (see Ps. 139:23; Isa. 1:25; Mal. 3:2–3; 1 Pet. 1.7). The lesson was well-learned by the Psalmist:

Search me, O God, and know my heart!
  Try me and know my thoughts!
And see if there be any wicked way in me,
  and lead me in the way everlasting!

(Ps. 139:23–24)

The saying in 20:27 does not fit in too well with this. It suggests that a man's conscience is as searching and as illuminating of impurity of heart as the eyes of God—unless its sense is that God's searching lamp (and man's willingness to be searched) is life-giving "breath" (the literal meaning of the word; cf. Gen. 2:7) to a man.

The theme of God's weighing the heart is illustrated by a concrete example in 24:10–12. What exactly the circumstances alluded to in verses 10–11 are, is not absolutely clear. Probably it speaks about those who turn a blind eye to the oppression of the poor and do nothing to help them. Their excuse is either that they could do nothing about it (v. 10) or that they did not know what was happening (v. 12). But "he who weighs the heart" perceives only the callous indifference to their plight, and will accept no excuses.

MAN'S PLANS AND GOD'S PURPOSE

Proverbs

21:5 The plans of the diligent lead surely to abundance,
　　　　but every one who is hasty comes only to want.
15:22 Without counsel plans go wrong,
　　　　but with many advisers they succeed.
11:14 Where there is no guidance, a people falls;
　　　　but in an abundance of counsellors there is safety.
20:18 Plans are established by counsel;
　　　　by wise guidance wage war.
21:22 A wise man scales the city of the mighty
　　　　and brings down the stronghold in which they trust.
24:5 A wise man is mightier than a strong man,
　　　　and a man of knowledge than he who has strength;
24:6 for by wise guidance you can wage your war,
　　　　and in abundance of counsellors there is victory.
24:27 Prepare your work outside,
　　　　get everything ready for you in the field;
　　　　and after that build your house.

16:1 The plans of the mind belong to man,
　　　　but the answer of the tongue is from the Lord.
16:9 A man's mind plans his way,
　　　　but the Lord directs his steps.
19:21 Many are the plans in the mind of a man,
　　　　but it is the purpose of the Lord that will be established.
20:24 A man's steps are ordered by the Lord;
　　　　how then can man understand his way?
21:30 No wisdom, no understanding, no counsel,
　　　　can avail against the Lord.

21:31 The horse is made ready for the day of battle,
    but the victory belongs to the Lord.
16:3 Commit your work to the Lord,
    and your plans will be established.
27:1 Do not boast about tomorrow,
    for you do not know what a day may bring forth.

(i)

Two closely related thoughts run through the first group of proverbs: the need to plan, and the need to consult. The general principles are set forth in the first two sayings. The key to any successful venture is careful and diligent planning; hasty, ill-considered courses of action generally prove to be fruitless (21:5). Equally unproductive, however, are plans formulated without the widest possible consultation (15:22). Two heads are always better than one, and three are better still. The thought that there can be too many cooks is not entertained! These principles are then applied to three areas of life where careful planning and wide consultation are essential:

(a) *In the affairs of state* (11:14). This maxim reflects again the close connection between wisdom and statecraft, which we noticed in relation to 8:15–16 and the proverbs dealing with the king and his courtiers, among the most important of whom were the king's counsellors (cf. 2 Sam. 16:5–17:23). The word "guidance" is literally "steering", as of steering a ship. The ship's captain in Jonah 1:6 is 'the chief steerer'. So this is a proverb meant for those at the helm of the ship of state, underlining that to steer it through stormy waters to a safe haven requires well-thought out policies which put the interests of the people first and which are the result of the deliberations of many minds.

(b) *In the conduct of war* (20:18; 21:22; 24:5–6). While the strength and courage of the soldiers are indispensible, wars are seldom won by these alone. It is the wisdom of the strategy implemented and the tactics employed which wins the day. Here again it is the wise general who will engage in wide consultations before drawing up his plan of campaign, so as to ensure that all the angles have been covered and that, as far as possible, all contingencies have been allowed for.

Although few of us are likely to be government ministers or generals, two lessons can be drawn from these sayings which are applicable to us all. The *first* is to think a thing through carefully before acting upon it; and the more important the decision to be made, the more thought we ought to take. The *second* is to seek advice. None of us is so wise that we can get through life without taking advice from others; but some of us give it a jolly good try!

(c) *In building a house* (24:27). This saying takes a different tack on the topic, and touches on an aspect of planning that is worth noticing. This is a piece of advice to the young farmer who is planning either to build a house or to marry a wife and raise a family. The Hebrew idiom could mean either (see Ruth 4:11 for the latter). Both would, of course, often go together. The advice is that initially he should make sure that his fields are in good shape and are fully productive. Otherwise he might find himself in the position of being unable to finish the house or to provide adequately for his wife and children. Counting the cost and ensuring it can be met is a part of wise and careful planning.

(ii)

The wise, therefore, robustly assert the value of planning and consultation in the conduct of human affairs. To neglect them is to court disaster, whether in government, on the battlefield, or in any other human venture. But, as Burns puts it:

The best laid schemes o' mice an' men
  Gang aft a-gley.

Men no more than mice are the masters when it comes to implementing their plans. More penetrating are the words of Shakespeare's Hamlet:

There's a divinity that shapes our ends,
  Rough-hew them how we will.

That is the counterbalancing note sounded in the second group of proverbs: "Man proposes, but God disposes". Men may have their plans, their grand schemes, even their dreams; but when it comes to translating them into action, God always has the final word: "it is the purpose of the Lord that will be established" (19:21), and no human counsel, however wise and discerning, can thwart it (21:30).

The thought that God controls and overrules the actions of men and nations according to his own will and purposes is fundamental to the faith of the Old Testament:

> The Lord brings the counsel of the nations to naught;
>   he frustrates the plans of the peoples.
> The counsel of the Lord stands for ever,
>   the thoughts of his heart to all generations.
> (Ps. 33:10–11; cf. Isa. 44:24–28; Dan. 4:34–35)

Indeed, the story the Old Testament tells is in large measure the story of God's movement in history, working out his purposes in judgment and salvation. This theme can be viewed on a large canvas in Exodus 1–15 and Isaiah 40–55; on a smaller canvas in passages like Genesis 45:4–8 and Numbers 22–24. But it finds its most telling expression in the words of Peter on the day of Pentecost: "This Jesus, delivered up according to the definite plan and foreknowledge of God, you crucified and killed by the hands of lawless men" (Acts 2:23; cf. 4:27–28).

Why then should we pray, "Thy will be done on earth as it is in heaven", when there seems so little doubt that God's will *will* be done? Part of the answer lies in the fact that to pray these words expresses a willingness on our part for our lives and our plans to be shaped according to God's will. It is important to notice that these proverbs do not pronounce a divine veto on the wisdom and value of our planning and taking counsel together. As 21:31 implies, it is always well to make ready the horse for the day of battle, even though it is stupid to rely on the horse and chariot for victory, for it is God alone who can carry the day (cf. Pss. 20:7; 33:16–19; Isa. 31:1–5). Rather God's veto is reserved for those plans of ours which do not accord with his will and do not serve his purpose. The lesson therefore is not on the futility of planning, but the need to consult with God when making our plans: "Commit your work to the Lord and your plans will be established" (16:3; cf. 3:5–6). If our plans are to be fruitful and not frustrated, then they must be wedded to God's purpose. The divinity that shapes our ends must help to shape our plans.

But there is another, more fundamental reason why we should commit our work to God, beyond seeing our plans come to fruition. A man only deludes himself if he thinks that he is in control of his steps through life and can make his way safely without coming to grief; for he is unable to chart a wise course through life without God's help and guidance (20:24). The sure and steady steps along the path of life are "ordered by the Lord". The counsel of God not only stands and has the final say in human affairs; it also has the very best say for those who trust in him.

Most of the sayings in the Book of Proverbs have what was called in the Introduction a *secular* character. They assume that in all sorts of situations a man can choose the wise course of action and avoid the foolish; and that is true now as it was then. But there is a deeper dimension to life, and the proverbs we have been looking at show that Israel's sages did not neglect it. We can in the last resort only live wise lives if we give first place not to our own wisdom but to the divine wisdom, and strive with God's help to make the two wisdoms one. The fear of the Lord is the beginning of wisdom, and it is its end too.

THE WORDS OF AGUR

Proverbs

30:1   The words of Agur son of Jakeh of Massa.

        The man says to Ithiel,
          to Ithiel and Ucal:
30:2   Surely I am too stupid to be a man.
        I have not the understanding of a man.
30:3   I have not learned wisdom,
        nor have I knowledge of the Holy One.

30:4　Who has ascended to heaven and come down?
　　　Who has gathered the wind in his fists?
　　　Who has wrapped up the waters in a garment?
　　　Who has established all the ends of the earth?
　　　What is his name, and what is his son's name?
　　　Surely you know!

30:5　Every word of God proves true;
　　　he is a shield to those who take refuge in him.
30:6　Do not add to his words,
　　　lest he rebuke you, and you be found a liar.

Agur was evidently a non-Israelite sage who hailed from the same tribe or region in North Arabia as Lemuel (31:1; but see the comment there on "Massa", *What King Lemuel's Mother Taught Him*). The second part of verse 1 poses problems. If the RSV is correct, Ithiel and Ucal were presumably two of Agur's pupils. But both names can be otherwise read. So, for example, the New English Bible translates, "I am weary, O God, I am weary and worn out" (cf. NIV ftn.). By slightly different orderings of the text, however, various other translations have been offered by commentators. The truth is that we do not know what the line means and can only guess.

(i)

Two viewpoints are expressed concerning man's knowledge of God, the one sceptical and the other reassuring:

(a) *God's hiddenness* (vv. 2–4). Here Agur expresses his exasperation with those who profess to know all that there is to be known about God and to whom the ways of God with men are patently obvious. With gentle irony he says that compared with such learned folks he is as stupid as a dumb animal (v. 2), for the knowledge of God which they so confidently claim, has eluded his best efforts to find it (v. 3). Doubtless they have learned about God at the feet of someone who has paid him a visit and got the full measure of God and his activities! (v. 4a). Perhaps then they would be kind enough to tell him his name so that he too can study under him and share their knowledge? (v.

4*b*). These are not the words of an atheist or an agnostic—at least, not in the sense of someone who has an open mind on the question of whether there is a God or not. (In verse 4 there is tacit recognition of God's existence, and that he is the creator of the world.) Neither are they the words of the scoffer debunking religious faith. Rather they are the words of a man who has discovered the limits of human wisdom and who is burdened by a sense of the hiddenness of God. Behind the gentle sarcasm he shows humility, recognizing the mystery which surrounds God. But it is a mystery which cannot be penetrated and which hides God from man.

(b) *God's revelation* (vv. 5–6). The reassurance given in these verses is that God has made himself known to man through his "word", a sure and certain word. The word rendered "proves true" is the word used for the refining of metals (cf. Ps. 12:6), and so the thought could be either that God's word is "unalloyed" (JB) or that it has "stood the test" (NEB). In either case, the point is that it is thoroughly reliable and trustworthy. In the present context, the reference is probably to the written word, to the Hebrew scriptures. The warning not to add to God's words echoes Deuteronomy 4:2; 12:32 (cf. Rev. 22:18–19).

(ii)

Coming hard on the heels of verses 2–4, these words sound rather as if Agur is being given a firm rap on the knuckles for his scepticism; or that he now has had better thoughts, and has come to recognize that what his human wisdom has failed to unlock, God's revelation had already opened. But are the two viewpoints meant to be so diametrically opposed to one another? They are at any rate simply laid side by side. And while it is clear that verses 2–4 by themselves would lead to despair, it is not at all clear that verses 5–6 are intended to silence the voice heard in them altogether.

At our distance from the text, it would be very easy to caricature these two viewpoints and play them off against one another. We could do this in either of two ways—depending on our predilections: either (1) the intellectual integrity of the wise man, who is conscious of the mystery of God's management of the world and the perplexing problems of human existence, *against* a complacent orthodoxy which thinks it can read God's mind like a book and which has an easy answer and chapter and verse for everything; or (2) the faith of the pious man, who trusts God at his word, *against* the doubtings of the sceptic who loses himself in a sea of human speculation and makes shipwreck of faith. But that will hardly do.

The Agur of verses 2–4 finds a kindred spirit in Job. Both share the same deep sense of the power and might of God; the same awareness of the hiddenness of God and the inscrutability of his ways, and the same impatience with the know-alls who think they can speak God's mind. In the denouement (Job, chs. 38–42), the "answer" Job receives is somewhat along the lines that God and his ways are indeed beyond human comprehension. He has created and he sustains the world in wisdom, although his wisdom is impenetrable to man. Job must therefore learn to have more trust in God and in the wisdom of his providence. This means too that he has to learn to live with his own ignorance, his perplexities and even his doubts. So here in Job, at the very moment of revelation, when God (for the first time) *speaks* to Job from the "whirlwind" (38:1), he remains "hidden" and his ways remain inscrutable. God conceals himself even as he reveals himself (contrast Isa. 45:15 with 45:19). If then we need verses 5–6 to remind us that God has spoken a sure word and we need never erect an altar to "the unknown God", no less do we need verses 2–4 to remind us that now we see "in a mirror dimly" and know only in part (1 Cor. 13:12). For only then will faith abide with perplexity, and humility with faith.

FURTHER READING

Blenkinsopp, Joseph. *Wisdom and Law in the Old Testament: The Ordering of Life in Israel and Early Judaism*. New York: Oxford University Press, 1983.

Crenshaw, James L. *Old Testament Wisdom: An Introduction*. Atlanta: John Knox Press, 1981.

Jones, Edgar D. *Proverbs and Ecclesiastes: Introduction and Commentary*. Torch Bible Commentaries. New York: Macmillan Co., 1962.

Kidner, F. Derek. *Proverbs*. Tyndale Old Testament Commentaries. Chicago: Inter-Varsity Press, 1964.

McKane, William. *Proverbs*. Old Testament Library. Philadelphia: Westminster Press, 1970.

Scott, R. B. Y., ed. *Proverbs and Ecclesiastes*. Anchor Bible. Garden City, N.Y.: Doubleday & Co., 1965.

von Rad, Gerhard. *Wisdom in Israel*. Nashville: Abingdon Press, 1973.

Whybray, R.N. *The Book of Proverbs*. New English Bible Commentaries, Old Testament. New York: Cambridge University Press, 1972.

APPENDIX: BRIEF COMMENTS ON PROVERBS NOT INCLUDED IN PART TWO

> 12:9 Better is a man of humble standing who works for himself
>   than one who plays the great man but lacks bread.

A gibe at social pretentions. At the end of the first line the
Hebrew reads "who has a [*ie* one] servant" (so NEB, NIV). The
RSV follows the *Septuagint*.

> 13:7 One man pretends to be rich, yet has nothing;
>   another pretends to be poor, yet has great wealth.

This saying not only makes the observation that appearances
can be deceptive, but also that there is no accounting for the way
people act. The New English Bible footnote gives an alternative
translation which strikes a deeper note: "One man grows rich
though he has nothing; another may grow poor though he has
great wealth" (see Luke 12:15).

> 14:4 Where there are no oxen, there is no grain;
>   but abundant crops come by the strength of the ox.

The precise sense of this saying is obscured by the difficult
Hebrew at the end of the first line, and the modern English
versions go different ways to make sense of it. The Hebrew
probably means "there is a trough of grain". However, the
general point seems clear enough. The wise farmer knows the
value of investing in oxen. Money spent in buying them and
time spent in looking after them are time and money well spent.
As a lesson on being productive, there is a word of wisdom in it
for more than the farmer.

> 14:28 In a multitude of people is the glory of a king,
>   but without people a prince is ruined.

This saying observes that a king's prestige is relative to the
number of subjects at his command. The second line suggests

that the lesson to be drawn is—to put it in more general terms—
that a leader must earn the loyalty of those he leads or he will
end up no leader at all.

> 16:19 It is better to be of a lowly spirit with the poor
> than to divide the spoil with the strong.

A contrast is drawn between humility and pride ("the strong" is
literally "the proud"), and between the poor and the rich. The
rich "divide the spoil". This refers to their sharing out the
proceeds of their crimes (cf. 1:13–14); and, reading between the
lines, it is the poor they have robbed. Although it neither
equates humility with poverty nor pride with wealth, it does
suggest that the proud will never stoop to help the poor and
oppressed: the humble will.

> 17:11 An evil man seeks only rebellion,
> and a cruel messenger will be sent against him.

The setting for this proverb is probably the royal court. It is a
warning to courtiers that they need expect no mercy from the
king if they plot rebellion against him. The "cruel messenger" is
a reference to the king's executioner, or perhaps to death (see
16:14).

> 19:2 It is not good for a man to be without knowledge,
> and he who makes haste with his feet misses his way.

One man picks his steps with forethought and care, and
achieves what he set out to do; another man is in much too great
a hurry to stop and think, and gets nowhere fast.

> 19:10 It is not fitting for a fool to live in luxury,
> much less for a slave to rule over princes.

This is one of several sayings which show the sages' keen eye for
incongruities (cf. 11:22; 17:7; 26:1) and their strong dislike of
social upstarts (cf. 30:21–23).

> 20:5 The purpose in a man's mind is like deep water,
> but a man of understanding will draw it out.

"Purpose" is better translated "strategies". The saying seems to make the point that, however profound a man's strategies are, they are worthless unless translated into action.

21:26 All day long the wicked covets,
> but the righteous gives and does not hold back.

In the first line the RSV follows the *Septuagint* (see ftn.). The New English Bible retains the Hebrew and makes the verse a continuation of the saying about the sluggard in verse 25. In either case, the verse places a high premium on generosity. In later Judaism the word "righteousness" also came to mean "almsgiving". This was not meant to suggest that giving alms won merit before God, but to stress that it was a sacred duty.

25:16 If you have found honey, eat only enough for you,
> lest you be sated with it and vomit it.

This saying stresses the virtue of moderation. Even healthy things (see 24:13) can quickly become harmful through over-indulgence.

26:2 Like a sparrow in its flitting, like a swallow in its flying,
> a curse that is causeless does not alight.

Behind this saying lies the ancient thought that, once spoken, a curse (or a blessing) assumed an identity of its own with the power to bring about what was expressed in it. The law made provision for the pronouncing of curses, especially in cases where the guilty party might escape detection: the curse would find him out (see Deut. 27:15–26). The saying makes the qualification that a malicious curse aimed at an innocent victim will fly harmlessly past its mark.

27:7 He who is sated loathes honey,
> but to one who is hungry everything bitter is sweet.

As a comment on food, the meaning is clear. As a comment on life its meaning is not so clear. Perhaps it contrasts success with ambition, observing that the one can dampen, and the other sharpen, a person's perception and enjoyment of life.

28:2 When a land transgresses
  it has many rulers;
  but with men of understanding and knowledge
   its stability will long continue.

As the RSV translates this verse, it is a contrast between political instability and stability. The Hebrew, however, is very obscure, especially in the second half of the verse. The New English Bible follows the *Septuagint* and renders: "It is the fault of a violent man that quarrels start, but they are settled by a man of discernment".

28:17 If a man is burdened with the blood of another,
  let him be a fugitive until death;
  let no one help him.

The RSV may be along the right lines in taking this as a warning against helping a murderer on the run, but the Hebrew text is almost meaningless. The New English Bible hazards, "A man charged with bloodshed will jump into a well to escape arrest".

29:18 Where there is no prophecy the people cast off restraint,
  but blessed is he who keeps the law.

The first line says that lawlessness results when prophecy ceases, and the second commends obedience to the law of God. The saying perhaps has the situation of the Jewish community after the return from exile in mind, when the great prophets belonged to the past and increasing emphasis was being given to keeping the law.

29:26 Many seek the favour of a ruler,
  but from the Lord a man gets justice.

"Favour" is literally "face" (NEB, "audience"). The proverb reflects further on the topic of the king's administration of justice. It tempers the idealism of the just king (see the topic, *The Measure of a King—I*, p.211) with the realism that kings are only human, and it encourages faith in God.

AN INDEX TO CHAPTERS 10-31